# PRO BONO

# THE 18 YEAR DEFENSE OF CARIL ANN FUGATE

Jeff McArthur

Bandwagon Books
Burbank, CA

Published by
BANDWAGON BOOKS
1331 N. Cordova St, #M
Burbank, CA  91505
www.bandwagononline.com

# CONTENTS

# PROLOGUE

It is a story that has gripped the entire state of Nebraska for decades, and entered into the collective unconscious of the whole country. Stephen King became a horror writer because of it. Bruce Springsteen made an entire album about it. Countless movies found their inspiration from it, launching the careers of filmmakers like Terrence Malick and Peter Jackson. It has been talked about and debated on the internet, in documentaries and in books for more than fifty years. It has been referred to in songs and poems, and has, unfortunately, been the source of several copycat crimes.

I grew up surrounded by the story, but I took it for granted; it was just something with which my grandfather was involved. From my vantage point as a child, he wasn't the hero that some people said he was, nor was he the villain that others claimed him to be. He was just the guy who taught me to slurp spaghetti; the amusing grandpa that liked to get me wound up, much to the chagrin of my grandmother.

But in 1958, he had been thrust into the center of one of the most controversial events in legal history, the trial of the century; a 14-year-old girl named Caril Ann Fugate was accused of helping her 19-year-old boyfriend, Charles Starkweather, on a murder spree that paralyzed the nation. For two weeks the two teenagers disappeared from public view, and in their wake, ten people died.

When it was all over, Starkweather and Fugate were returned to Lincoln to face trial. The people of Nebraska wanted revenge not only for the crimes committed and the lives lost; but because the murders had ushered in a new era of fear. Before, residents in many parts of the country were unafraid to leave their doors unlocked at night. There was a certain sense of safety and security that was lost, and these murders played a large role in that loss of innocence.

The teenagers had broken into homes and killed the residents wherever they found them, even in their own bedrooms. If this could happen in middle America, it could happen anywhere. Charles Starkweather, a boy who resembled James Dean, was rebellious, swaggering, and arrogant. The media described Caril Fugate as his stone-faced, heartless accomplice who had killed her own family.

John McArthur, my grandfather, was assigned to represent Caril as her attorney, and even though he received dozens of death threats from frightened local residents, he carried out the responsibility with dignity. He believed passionately in the Constitution, and he believed with a firm conviction that everyone, even those who were guilty of terrible crimes, deserved an attorney.

John learned, however, that the story was far more complicated than what the newspapers were reporting. The media had sensationalized Starkweather and Fugate as the new Bonnie and Clyde, and painted Fugate as a hardened killer, but John found a mousy, frightened little girl who did not even understand she was being charged with murder. Fugate thought the questions that the police had asked her were to convict Charlie, and she had spoken freely to them without knowing she should ask for an attorney. She claimed to have been Charlie's captive, not his accomplice. She hadn't been allowed to read any newspapers, so she didn't know that public opinion was strongly against her.

My grandfather had to tell Caril that she would stand trial for murder, and, at the young age of 14, she could receive the death penalty. Her only hope at staying alive and out of prison was to change the public's opinion of her.

The case was still being argued many years later when I was born, but I didn't realize its importance until high school when I heard people saying things about the case that were not true. I had met Ms. Fugate on many occasions, and had heard the stories of what happened dozens of times, and it simply didn't match what people were saying.

I wondered if perhaps my view of the case had been too heavily biased because I had grown up in the family of Caril's attorneys, so I researched the entire case independently, going to the Nebraska State Historical Society, examining the court records, reading documents and comparing notes. I was surprised by what I discovered. What people were passing on as truth was based on the stories of Charles Starkweather, an unquestionably psychotic lunatic who merely wanted to take as many people down with him as he could. The stories were perpetuated by a police force that was embarrassed at having not caught Starkweather earlier, and a media who saw the new Bonnie and Clyde as better for selling newspapers than the more complicated truth.

After decades of seeing rumors spread and lies presented as facts, I feel compelled to set the record straight, which is a major part of the reason why I wrote this book. But most of all, this is a book about my grandfather, a man who saw an injustice and fought against it for two decades, in the face of how unpopular it made him, even despite the death threats against himself and his family. I have the utmost respect for my grandfather's search for the truth, which puts a burden on me to be equally truthful. Though I admittedly come from a biased family connection, I have written this book with a great deal of care for veracity based on the facts of the case. It is for this reason that, near the beginning of this book, I do not narrate what happened during the murder spree. Even though Caril has told exactly the same story of what happened for more than fifty years, and even though I personally believe it, I am only using what can be verified by public records to express matters of the case itself. As for information about my grandfather and his family, I am using knowledge from the people who knew him throughout this dramatic period.

Other people play important roles in the story as well, such as Ninette Beaver, one of the first female television reporters in the country, Merril Reller, who worked with my grandfather in the early years, and my own father, James McArthur, who worked with him in later years, and has always believed passionately in Caril's innocence. To tell their stories, I have used a combination of public records, their own explanations, and interviews with other people who knew them.

As for Caril, she remains somewhat of a mystery to me. No one will ever know for certain what happened during those two fateful weeks in 1958, and no one can ever truly be sure what was happening in Caril's mind and heart. But while she may never be able to prove her innocence, she has more than proven her desire to be believed. It has never been enough to her that she be released from prison. She stayed in prison without seeking parole for years longer than she needed so she could receive a new trial to prove her innocence to the world.

Since Fugate has been out of prison, she has done everything she can to prove that she did not go along with Starkweather willingly. She has taken a lie detector test, truth serum, and even gone under hypnosis to see if she had repressed memories of her actions.

The world still sees her as guilty; perhaps it always will. The story has passed into legendary status. References continue to describe her as a murderess, and they continue to base their stories on Starkweather's testimony.

But the truth is far more interesting.

*"I wanted you to see what real courage is, instead of getting the idea that courage is a man with a gun in his hand. It's when you know you're licked before you begin but you begin anyway and you see it through no matter what... The one thing that doesn't abide by majority rule is a person's conscience."*
*-Adicus Finch, 'To Kill a Mockingbird' (by Harper Lee)*

*In memory of my grandfather John McArthur*

*whose integrity inspired his family and is the basis of this book.*

# Chapter One
## Service

John McArthur only went to church when Christmas fell on a Saturday. His wife was Seventh-day Adventist, which meant that their family worshipped the Sabbath from Sundown Friday night to sundown Saturday night. Every week she dressed up their children and took them to church while John stayed at home and, during the fall, watched the Nebraska Cornhuskers football game. He supported her beliefs while he practiced his own type of spirituality. When a pastor confronted him about this stay-at-home religiosity by saying, "I haven't seen you in church lately," John responded by saying very simply, "That's because I haven't been there."

But he remained true to his tradition of attending church when Christmas was on the Sabbath. His son Frank would never forget sitting next to him on one of those occasions, watching as the pastor called the names of people who had done good deeds that year. They approached the podium where they received a plaque that certified their positive public service.

Frank was confused when he glanced over at his father and saw a disgusted look on his face. His dad had always been a moral man, sometimes even outspoken when standing up for his principles. When Joseph McCarthy had led a campaign of fear and paranoia against "Communist agitators," John called it for what it was, a group of bullies damaging people's lives for their own political gain. Many criticized John for his views, but he stuck to his guns, regardless of what it might do to his reputation and career. And in the end, like with so many issues, time showed that he was right. But John never rubbed it in. He simply carried himself with a silent dignity, and went on with his business. Why he should be angry at the church for giving out awards for people doing good deeds was beyond Frank.

At last Frank heard his father mutter under his breath the reason he was so turned off by this display, "I thought that's what we were *supposed* to do." Frank understood immediately. His father never received awards for what he did, and he never asked for them. He probably would have refused if one was offered. He believed that serving the public good was a reward unto itself, and anything beyond that damaged the credibility of the courtesy.

He saw the purpose of his work as an attorney to be to help those in need. He provided his services for little or no cost, taking only what he needed to raise his family and giving anything extra back to the public. Sometimes he took trade goods, such as livestock from farmers, or other such gifts, in exchange for legal advice. Despite all this, he never boasted of his work.

Frank would later describe his father in one simple word... Service.

*　　*　　*

In the Bible there are two disciples named James and John, known as the Sons of Thunder. They were so named because of their loud antics and occasional misbehavior. The same could be said about young James and John Jr. McArthur of Lincoln, Nebraska because of the excitement and sometimes trouble they would cause when left to their own devices.

Throughout their youths in the 1940s, the two got themselves into all sorts of trouble. They locked one another in closets, shot each other with Roman candles, and explored the expansive city storm sewers, which they dubbed "Underground Lincoln." They bought useless items at a nearby auction and took them home, despite the fact that they didn't fit into any room. Once, when they were in a barn with their younger sister, they tried raising her to the balcony with a rope and almost hanged her. Another time, when they were asked to clean the gutters of their house, John Jr, the oldest, had a plan to make the job faster. They poured lighter fluid onto the leaves inside the gutter. When the can was empty, they struck a match and threw it onto the trail. A mighty blast erupted, throwing the boys onto their backs. The boom was audible throughout the neighborhood, and it was probably only because the house was made of brick that it did not burn to the ground. The brothers would catch hell-fire from their mother, and would have to paint the gutters again, but the chore was completed in record time.

John Jr. was named after his father, who was away on a ship in the Pacific working as a signal man during World War II when John Jr. and James were babies. Their mother had her hands full during those years raising four children, John Jr., James, and their older brother Frank, and older sister Sue, on her own. It was almost longer when John was caught trying to smuggle a man out of China while the Communists were taking over the government. Luckily, the charges against John were dropped, and he was able to return to his family and his job as an attorney. But both John Jr. and James had gone without their father during the first few years of their lives, which perhaps partially accounted for their reckless behavior.

James' first name was actually Arthur, but he didn't enjoy the alliteration of Arthur J. McArthur; and so he went by his middle name, which had been passed down through the family since the Civil War. The last person to possess this name in the family had been John Sr.'s oldest brother, Andrew James McArthur, who had left the family and vanished when John was a young boy. Since the name had disappeared along with him, John decided to pass it along to his third son.

It was a Saturday in the middle of February, 1958 when James came home from church to find the phone ringing. He was 16, and had outgrown a lot of the recklessness of his past. He had also gone to great effort to overcome a childhood stutter, which often made it difficult for him to communicate. It was especially frustrating for him since he had a father who was well known for public speaking. James had spent the previous year away from home at boarding school where he gained the self-confidence that helped him overcome the speech impediment that had so plagued him. He returned with a sense of maturity, beyond his years.

He picked up the phone and answered, "Hello?"

"Is John McArthur there?" came a stranger's voice. James knew that the man meant his father, not his brother. John Sr. often got calls from people regarding his law practice at home. James could usually tell by the sound of their voices whether they were his clients, or people who didn't like his clients. It was obvious from the tone of the man's voice that this was one of the latter.

"No, he's not here right now," James answered.

"Well, tell him we've got a necktie party waiting for him here in Bennet," the voice said, and the line went dead.

James had never heard a death threat before, so it took a moment to register. When it finally did, he understood what case his father must have taken on; that of a 14-year-old girl who had been captured by police and charged with assisting in the murders of almost a dozen people.

She had been in the company of a young man named Charlie Starkweather. For two days, the state was gripped with fear as bodies began to appear in and around the towns of Lincoln and nearby Bennet. The two had been captured in Wyoming, and the outraged public was screaming for their heads.

It was later discovered that Charlie was responsible for another death a month and a half earlier, and the public fury was at a boiling point. They wanted vengeance, and they wanted the media and the prosecutors to show them who to lay their anger upon. This new Bonnie and Clyde was the answer to their blood lust, and photographs that the newspapers printed of the smiling couple in happier days was just what was needed to blow the top off the kettle.

John returned home a few hours after the phone call and confirmed what James suspected; he had been called in to defend Caril Fugate, the girl who had been with Starkweather during the murders. No one in the family criticized his decision to take the case. No one feared the public reprisal. This was John's job. Whatever the girl had, or had not done, it was his responsibility to represent her as best he could so she could receive a fair trial.

The phone calls kept coming throughout the day. John fielded some of them, his wife Ruby answered others. At last John walked to the phone and took it off the hook; and so it remained the rest of the evening.

# Chapter Two
## The Murders

It was a cold Monday evening at the KMTV newsroom in Omaha, Nebraska and the reports that typically fed their telecasts were as flat and frigid as the snow-covered plains outside. There had been no extreme weather, no upcoming events, and nothing affecting the farming community, which were the usual news items in this typically bucolic part of the country. With the holidays over, it was going to be more of the same until spring thawed the stillness of the news.

The reporters often filled the time learning how to use the motion picture cameras they had only recently received. The cameras were a necessity for television news, which was typically not regarded with the same prestige as the well-established print media. If the local station hoped to compete with the newspapers, it would have to give the public what still photographs and typed words could not. But with no news stories in motion, nothing could be filmed.

The slow Monday ended and the executives went home. The few remaining technicians and reporters scrabbled together whatever they could to fill news stories that night. In the meantime, the station gave way to the Huntley-Brinkley report out of New York and Washington. It was a slow news day for them as well. The local Unitarian congregation was kicking off a fund drive to build a new church, the national debt was nearing $280 billion, and their lead in for the evening was "World's Greatest Cartoons."

Mark Gautier, alone in a dark control room upstairs from the bright lights of the studio, turned the volume of the television up to tune out the buzzing of the machines behind him. They were supposed to bring in information, but now they were only causing a useless racket.

Then he noticed a lot of chatter coming from the police radio on the shelves above the TV. It was unusual to hear much more than an occasional smattering of reports referring to domestic disputes and traffic problems coming from the box. What he heard now caused Mark to get to his feet and grab a pencil. He wrote what he heard:

*"Be on the lookout for a 1949 black Ford. Nebraska license number 2-15628. Radiator grille missing. No hubcaps. Believed to be driven by Charles Starkweather, a white male, nineteen years old, 5 feet 5 inches tall, 140 pounds, dark red hair, green eyes. Believed to be wearing blue jeans and black leather jacket. Wanted by Lincoln police for questioning in homicide. Officers were warned to approach with caution. Starkweather was believed to be armed and presumed dangerous.*

*"Starkweather is believed to be accompanied by Caril Fugate, fourteen years old, female, white, 5 feet 1 inch tall, 105 pounds, dark brown hair, blue eyes, sometimes wears glasses. Usually wears hair in ponytail, appears to be about eighteen years old. Believed wearing blue jeans and blouse or sweater. May be wearing medium-blue parka."*

It was 5:43 pm, January 27, 1958.

*       *       *

John McArthur heard the news report on the radio in his office the next day. He was a news junky, often listening to what was happening while at work, only to come home to watch a more in depth recap of the day's events on television. This time it was the opposite way around. There had been sketchy information about a triple homicide the night before, and now they had further information about it on the radio. A 14-year-old girl and her 19-year-old boyfriend had disappeared, her family was discovered murdered, the parents' bodies left in a chicken shack behind their home, and a baby's body was in the outhouse; its head had been crushed by a rifle.

The sheer audacity of the murders was shocking enough to catch anyone's attention and everyone turned on their radios and televisions to learn what was happening.

John didn't have to turn far to reach his radio. Only a short swivel brought his legs into contact with a wall, or filing cabinet, or some other piece of furniture. Though John was a thin man, even his gaunt frame barely fit through the narrow passage into his office. If a drawer was open, he had to duck under or climb over it. If his partner Merril Reller wanted inside the office, it became a back and forth dance for one to enter and the other to leave. A chair rested outside the doorway because when clients came to visit they had to sit outside the office looking in.

The report on the radio was interrupted by a break in the case. The police had surrounded a farmhouse near Bennet, approximately 20 miles east of Lincoln, where Charlie was believed to be holed up. His car was parked in front, and no one answered a call to come out, not even the farmer who owned the property. A small army of police officials slowly moved in on the home, guns drawn.

*    *    *

Blackie Roberts and Dick Trembath, two of the reporters for KMTV, stood in the still, gelid air beside their car at the Meyer farm outside of Bennet. They had rushed from Omaha, more than sixty miles away, to film the capture of the two fugitives for KMTV. Before them, the police formed a wide perimeter around the house, and waited for the dispersal of tear gas before moving in.

Scattered among the men in uniform were farmers with shotguns, eager to see the young murderer captured or killed. They knew that August Meyer, the man who owned the farm, would never willingly aid a killer, even though Charlie had been a friend of August for years.

August, who was seventy, had allowed Charlie to hunt on his farm from time to time. He had seen Caril whenever Charlie brought her with him, but he barely knew her. Now no one could discern what was going on inside; if the two were preparing an ambush, or if they would surrender as soon as it got hot.

"How come all the local people?" Blackie asked one of the sheriff's men. "Did you form a posse?"

"No, that's something else," came the reply. "They were just in the area and came over to help."

"What else is going on?"

"A couple of teen-agers from Bennet were reported missing last night and the neighbors have been out looking for them."

A patrol car engine roared to life. It was the signal. "Let's move out!" someone shouted. "Spread out and stay low!"

The police car moved forward, and the men in uniform surged ahead. When the car rumbled into place in front of the house, it stopped. The men got out of the car and took cover behind the doors.

A loudspeaker squealed to life. "This is the police! We know you're in there! We'll give you five minutes to come out of there with your hands in the air!" They were met by silence, and police answered with the loud cocking of their guns.

A half dozen troopers ran as they spread out across the front lawn keeping low, carrying their stubby, wide barreled guns. Half way to the house they dove to the ground. A white flash trailed from one of the men, and a moment later a window crashed. A thin trail of smoke slowly began to snake its way out of the hole as the farmhouse filled with tear gas.

The troopers charged the home from every direction. The front door was kicked open, and as the smoke poured out, they rushed in, guns at the ready.

One man called out from the back of the house. It was not what they expected, not a shout at Charlie to drop his weapon, or a signal to tell the others where he was, but a genuine scream of disgust.

The man who had called out was at the doorway of a small, white shed attached to the back of the house. Inside was the body of August Meyer. There was no sign of struggle, no visible bullet wound. The only evidence of his death was a thin layer of blood peeking out from under him.

Blackie Roberts, who had followed the police inside, now shot a whole roll of film for the news. This was certainly a change from their usual photographs of placid pastures and town meetings. He just had to get past the crowd of police huddling around the house.

August's brother was among the officers outside. One of the policemen who had seen the body confirmed what they had found. "Oh my god," was all he could say.

Dick Trembath, also outside, walked down the lane to take photographs of Starkweather's car, which was stuck in the mud just down the street. There was nothing unusual about it, except that Charlie had collected tires in the backseat.

As Dick was returning to the Meyer place, he was approached by a farmer who asked where he could find a policeman. There were plenty available, which Dick pointed out, and he asked the perplexed man what was happening. The man waved him off and continued toward an officer. Dick stood close enough to hear, but not so close to scare them away.

The man's name was Everette Broening. The night before he had heard a car accelerate at high speed around 10 pm. The next morning, after hearing about the missing teenagers, he had found a pile of school books along the side of the road a few miles up. All Dick heard him tell the officer after that was, "They're in the storm cellar."

*     *     *

The police stood on the pale, frozen ground surrounding the cement entrance of the storm cellar a couple miles from the Meyer residence. One civilian stepped up to the entrance, looked down inside, then covered his mouth and turned quickly away, his shoulders heaving.

Dick tried to make his way to the doorway to get a photograph. He was stopped by a trooper a foot taller than him. "Come on, I've got a job to do," Dick said.

"You don't want any pictures of what's down there," the man told him gravely.

The two teenagers who had been reported missing the night before, Robert Jensen and Carol King, lay at the bottom of the cellar. The girl was naked, her body lying zig zagged across the floor, her breasts and groin fully exposed, her face as contorted as her body. Her blue jeans were bunched at her feet around her white bobby socks. One arm, still attached to the sleeve of her jacket, was wrapped around her back, while the other arm reached down to her knee as if making one last attempt at modesty. Her small hand rested in the fold of her leg. A blood stain led out of her buttocks and trailed down her thigh where she had been raped, and then stabbed. Her body was on top of her boyfriend, Robert. A pool of their mixed blood ran down the floor away from them.

Lancaster County Attorney Elmer Scheele soon filed first-degree murder charges against Charlie Starkweather. After what they had seen of the King girl, there was reason to believe Fugate was probably dead as well, and they expected to find her body dumped along the side of the road.

Neighbors were warned, posses were formed, and farmers from across the area converged on the narrow, unpaved main street of Bennet, a town of 490 people 18 miles southeast of the capital city of Lincoln, where the primary police headquarters was set up. The search centered around a line of police headlights and moved out from there into the dark, vast reaches of the nearby farmland. The heavily armed men stretched out into the night, some almost shooting one another as they spotted shapes in the dark. One officer was fired at when he tried to approach a farmhouse to warn the residents about Starkweather. It appeared they already knew, so he continued on to the next house.

Back at the KMTV newsroom, Ninette Beaver, a junior reporter, speculated that Charlie could have gone to the closest major town, Lincoln. "I doubt that," Mark Gautier told her as he got his jacket to leave. "If he's not holed up somewhere around Bennet, he's probably made it out of the state by now."

"Good lord, I hope so," Ninette said. Her sister Joanne lived in Lincoln, and if Starkweather was going there, who knew what would happen. She waited for Mark to leave, then quickly called Joanne.

\*     \*     \*

County Attorney Elmer Scheele had to duck his head slightly as he entered the magniloquent home of C. Lauer and Clara Ward. He was often the tallest man in any room. Though thin and introverted, his presence was imposing, and his gaze through his black, horn rimmed glasses was focused and intimidating.

The murder spree had gone from bad to worse. Only one day earlier Scheele and the Nebraska police had thought they had Charlie pinned down in a farmhouse, only to find its owner dead inside the house. And then they had found two teenagers brutally murdered, their bodies left locked in a storm cellar near a school. Never in the history of Nebraska had there been such a chain of killings, and now it had moved from the scattered small communities of the rural farmland into the more densely populated city of Lincoln. And even more disturbing, it had come to the upscale neighborhood near the country club.

Lincoln was a conglomeration of many small communities that had grown together over the decades. The resulting contrast in wealth and class was visible as one passed from the less developed north side of "O" Street to the more affluent south side of town, where the houses were larger, and the vast yards stretched out greener. For this type of bloodshed to enter any part of Lincoln was shocking enough. For it to enter the home of such a prominent figurehead was downright unthinkable.

Yet there was Mr. Ward, a well respected businessman, president of Capitol Steel Works, and a friend of the most influential people in the state, just inside of his front door, dead from a shot at point blank range with a shotgun. The last person to see him alive, in fact, was his close friend, Nebraska Governor Victor Anderson. Lauer Ward's wife Clara was found dead upstairs, a knife sticking out of her back, and their maid, Lillian Fencl, was found with her hands and feet bound, a gag in her mouth, and a knife embedded in her torso.

Scheele was a professional at hiding his feelings, but outrage was beginning to boil over as the pressure was building. Charlie had eluded every road block and patrol that was out to stop him, and now he had to be stopped before panic spread. Something else disturbed him; a smell overwhelming the second floor of the house. It was more than the stench of death, which Elmer was used to. When he followed it to its source, where the odor was strongest, he found the body of Mrs. Ward, bound and gagged and lying dead between the two beds.

Then he identified the aroma. It was perfume. Someone had tried to cover the smell of death by pouring it all over the room.

Mrs. Ward's drawers and closets had been ransacked. Women's clothes were scattered all over the place, as if someone had been shopping and had left the discarded apparel behind. Among them was Carol King's jacket. Elmer was incensed. Up to this point he had been expecting to find Caril Fugate's body in a ditch somewhere. But now it was clear. She was alive. And she was traveling as Charlie's companion.

Outside, Merle Karnopp, the county sheriff, was talking to reporters. "Well, since discovering the last three bodies, which makes a total of nine that we know of so far, Mayor Martin and I have made an appeal for all adjoining counties, including Omaha, to send all available help they can to Lincoln. It is our opinion that the car is still in this vicinity. We know he has been for the last three days, and we want to cover Lincoln block to block."

*       *       *

James McArthur was a junior in high school at Union College Academy, a small Seventh-day Adventist school of about eighty to a hundred students that was squeezed into the fourth floor of the Union College Administration Building. The lower grades had not been allowed to recess because of fear that Starkweather was in the vicinity. Now that Charlie was known to be in Lincoln, the school immediately sent all of the students home.

Lines of cars driven by armed parents appeared at Lincoln's schools. At Lincoln High School, one student was almost lynched when his bright red hair caused him to be mistaken for the murdering teenager. Inside homes, children were told a key word that, if the parents spoke it, would mean that they were to run and hide.

At Whittier Jr. High School, students raided Caril Fugate's locker and kept her possessions as souvenirs. Few had ever paid any attention to this tiny, reticent girl, but now dozens of students grappled over who would walk away with her belongings now that she was an infamous fugitive. Many who had ignored her before now made claims to have known her well, and claimed that she had always been a trouble maker.

James and his little sister Linda piled into John's truck and they headed home through the madness. Along the way they witnessed stores closing, people getting into their homes and bolting the doors, some boarding their windows. Lincoln had been a town where few ever bothered to lock their doors, but now the entire city was digging in as if under siege. Police from Omaha and the surrounding communities converged on the capital city. Even the National Guard was called in by Governor Anderson after he learned that his good friend had been murdered. Soldiers piled out of their armored vehicles and marched in formation through the empty streets of downtown.

A posse was called for at the courthouse, and so many people showed up that some had to be turned away. Those who left mostly went to gun stores, which sold out within an hour. Small groups of private citizens spread into Lincoln neighborhoods to search for Starkweather and almost shot each other. Armed civilians subjected individuals who drove cars similar to the one Charlie was now driving to repeated searches.

Reports of Starkweather sightings rolled in from places as near as the county courthouse in Lincoln to as far as the western end of Kansas.

In one small Kansas town, police were rushed to the airport for reasons they could not be told. Some thought they were being sent to capture Starkweather, and they pulled their guns to be ready. When the airplane landed, they found that it was President Eisenhower, who was flying in to Kansas City for the funeral of his brother Arthur, but had been diverted to the smaller airport due to bad weather.

The sightings the police took most seriously were those of the Ward car with a single teenage occupant. This led many to believe Starkweather was now alone, and a new search began for the body of Caril Fugate.

One reporter for the local newspaper, the Lincoln Journal, appeared at the office while he was supposed to be shadowing police officers. When asked why he was there, he said, "Just look at me!" He was red headed and had a freckled face. Worse yet, he drove a

Packard, just like the one Starkweather was reportedly driving. "I'm double parked and I'm not going out there," he said.

John Jr. drove his brother James and sister Linda home from school as fast as he could. Once there, James turned on the news to watch the chaos. The rest of his other brothers and sisters trickled home rapidly after that, all of them sent home from school, and their mother, Ruby, didn't allow anyone to go outside the rest of the day while she waited anxiously for her husband to come home. John returned late in the afternoon and joined James at the television, watching the historic chaos.

KFOR, a Lincoln radio station, reported that Starkweather had been seen at Capitol Steel Works, the company where Lauer Ward had been the president, but it was an incorrect report by the Associated Press who had misinterpreted the events of the day. It was easy to do. New information was coming in so quickly it was hard to know what was fact and what was gossip. The news team had to not only keep track of new stories, but also corrections to previous ones. It was especially difficult for a continuity writer such as Joanne Young to keep track of the most recent information. She was juggling correcting copy with answering the flood of calls from reporters all over the world who wanted to know more about what was happening.

KFOR was pre-empting every show they had, and using the radio not only for information to the public, but also to give police as much information as was coming to them. This wasn't the usual job for the press, but this incident was different, more terrifying. Their evening radio announcer, Bob Asky, had come in the night before after having visited the Fugate house where he saw the three bodies of Caril's family. All he could say was "it was really bad." The next morning, when the Wards were found dead in their own home and chaos gripped the city, the president of the radio station arrived at work with a gun, and ordered the doors locked.

Joanne had a personal connection to the danger. The husband of a good friend of hers, Robert Colvert, had been murdered the month before, and Charlie had been a lead suspect; and now her cousin, Chuck Green, a stocky, red headed teenager, was somewhere out there in the city, a target for citizens mad with fear. A police car pulled him over, and to make sure they knew he wasn't Starkweather, he jumped out of the car and announced, "It's not me!"

Newspapers, long the reliable source of information for the people of Nebraska, could not keep up with what was happening. Bodies were appearing three at a time in a seemingly random pattern. No one knew where or when Starkweather would strike next. Lincoln had two papers, one in the morning, the Star, and one in the evening, the Journal, and each had to keep adjusting and updating their headlines as new stories developed.

Police, meanwhile, were trying to decide what leads to follow. A series of reports arrived throughout the day that a couple matching the descriptions of Caril and Charlie were spotted driving northwest along Highway 60 through the Sandhills of Nebraska towards Wyoming. Though these reports were numerous, the police disregarded them, and set up roadblocks south of Lincoln to prevent the couple from escaping into Kansas.

Ninette Beaver was one of the people bringing some semblance of order to the chaos in the KMTV newsroom. Although she was in the relative safety of Omaha, 50 miles removed from the action, her sister Joanne was in the middle of it.

Joanne had described over the phone what was happening in Lincoln to Ninette. She had been stopped by a man with a shotgun on her way to teaching dance class. She thought it was Starkweather as he leaned down and checked out her car. When it was over she rushed home and locked the doors. Ninette got goose bumps as her sister told her the story.

Ninette and the others in the KMTV office tried to keep up with the quickly changing information. There were reports that Charlie was alone, reports that Caril was with him, and reports that Caril was dead. As the news came across the wire, Ninette delivered it to her boss, Floyd Kalber, and others who then reported it on the air. Ninette was only supposed to be at KMTV on a temporary basis, and now she was in the middle of a major event. A full blown panic had caught the attention of an entire nation. Soon, even news stations in Europe began covering the story.

At 2:30 p.m. on January 29th, Ninette took a call from Blackie Roberts, one of their reporters chasing the story, still in the field after no sleep for two days. He told her that Elmer Scheele's office was filing first-degree murder charges against both Charlie *and* Caril.

"He's charging the girl, too?" Ninette asked.

"That's it," Blackie told her.

"Hang on, the bell's ringing," Ninette told him, and she turned to the Teletype machine. Floyd jumped out of his chair and joined her.

DOUGLAS, WYO., JAN. 29 (AP) – CHARLES STARKWEATHER, 19, RUNTY NEBRASKA GUNMAN SOUGHT IN NINE SLAYINGS, WAS CAPTURED TODAY IN THE BADLANDS NEAR THIS WYOMING COWTOWN.

Everyone began moving. The story had moved to Wyoming, and they couldn't be the only station without footage.

Then the Teletype machine interrupted them again:

A TENTH MURDER VICTIM WAS FOUND NOT FAR FROM WHERE STARKWEATHER WAS CAPTURED. THE DEAD MAN WAS MERLE COLLISON, 37-YEAR-OLD GREAT FALLS, MONT., SHOE SALESMAN.

WITH STARKWEATHER WAS CARIL FUGATE, THE 14-YEAR-OLD GIRL WHO FLED WITH HIM FROM LINCOLN, NEB., WHERE POLICE SAID HE KILLED NINE PEOPLE. INCLUDED AMONG THE VICTIMS WERE CARIL'S PARENTS.

THE TWO TEENAGERS WERE RUN TO EARTH IN RUGGED COUNTRY WHERE OLD WEST GUNMEN OFTEN HOLED UP.

THE GIRL WAS ALMOST HYSTERICAL AND RAN FLEEING TO DEPUTY SHERIFF BILL ROMER CRYING OUT HER FEAR STARKWEATHER WOULD KILL HER. SHE WAS IN A STATE OF SHOCK SHORTLY AFTERWARD.

ROMER SAID SHE SCREAMED TO HIM:

"HE'S COMING TO KILL ME. HE'S CRAZY. HE JUST KILLED A MAN."

# Chapter Three
## Caril

January 29 was a Wednesday, but the days had run together so much that it was hard for Caril to keep track. It was also hard to keep up with where she and Charlie were; somewhere in western Nebraska perhaps; or maybe they had crossed into Wyoming. She had just seen Charlie kill a man who was sleeping in his car. The car they were in, the Packard they had stolen from the rich man's house, was having problems, and it was too easily recognized. Charlie wanted to switch vehicles, and this was how he always got the next one; he killed for it.

Now she sat in the back seat of this new car, the body of the man who had driven it slumped in the front passenger seat, his head blown open, and eight more bullet holes spread over his body. It was as if Charlie couldn't get enough of shooting someone even after they were dead.

Caril had always been afraid of guns. Once, when Charlie took her out hunting at the farm of his friend, August Meyer, she had lifted the gun with difficulty, shakily pointing it at the bottles Charlie was using as targets. She took a shot, then gave it back. Now, over the past week, she had had her fill of gunfire as Charlie seemed to shoot everyone they encountered.

She didn't dare run; where could she go? The badlands surrounding them stretched on forever. And it was cold... bitterly cold everywhere they went, especially at night. Even if she did somehow get away, Charlie had told her that his friends were holding her family hostage, and if she left him, he would find the nearest phone, call his friends, and tell them to kill her family. This was too much. She couldn't continue watching him kill innocent people. She cried openly while he tried in vain to release the emergency brake.

She saw a motorist pulling up behind them. A man got out of the car and approached Charlie. He thought that Charlie owned the car, and was perhaps stranded. Charlie got out of the car and pointed his rifle at the man. Caril expected the loud bang to follow, but instead Charlie said, "Raise your hands. Help me release the emergency brake or I'll kill you."

Joseph Sprinkle was tall, stronger than Charlie, a former navy officer who had just been discharged a month before; but none of that would matter if Charlie shot him. He looked into the car and saw Caril, as well as the dead man on the floor.

Joseph knew that Charlie would kill him anyway, but he had no choice at the moment but to help, so he leaned into the car and began working at the emergency brake. Caril watched him, tears in her eyes, certain that Charlie would shoot him in the back at any moment. He was leaning up behind Joseph, watching him work, the gun held carelessly.

This was Joseph's only chance. He spun around and grabbed the rifle, pointing the barrel away from him, trying to pull it out of Charlie's grasp. Charlie kept hold of it with one hand while he hit Joseph with the other.

Caril, meanwhile, saw a patrol car stopped behind a truck that had halted nearby when the fight broke out. The office inside clearly didn't see what was happening past the truck. Caril leapt from the car and ran for the officer.

At last Joseph got the rifle out of Charlie's hands. Outmatched, and seeing Caril running away, Charlie ran for the Packard.

Caril screamed and waved her arms as she ran towards the officer. Deputy Sheriff Bill Romer finally saw her and let her in the passenger door. She was shrieking, tears pouring down her face.

Caril was crying hysterically and Officer Romer couldn't understand what she was saying. He at last distinguished something about a murder, and heard her say the word that sent a chill down his spine, "Starkweather." She pointed past the truck in front of them, and he looked around it to see the two men in the road. One of them had bright red hair and was running for the Packard, and Romer realized the identity of the girl in his car.

As Romer watched, the boy with the red hair leapt into the Packard and raced away. Romer didn't follow. Instead, he picked up his radio. Robert Ainslie, Chief of Police in Douglas, Wyoming, heard the report over the receiver. Sheriff Earl Heflin was in the passenger seat next to him. Starkweather was driving in their direction, so Ainslie swerved his car into the middle of the highway to block Charlie's escape. Charlie raced toward Ainslie and Heflin without slowing then swung his car around them. Ainslie pushed his glasses on tight, put the car into gear and took chase. By the time they reached Douglas, the speedometer had reached 115 miles per hour.

Residents scattered as the two cars sped down Main Street. The sheriff was firing at the Packard's tires, but stopped when they entered traffic and Starkweather had to slow to get around the locals. Seeing his opportunity to catch up with the murderer, Ainslie rammed Charlie's car. His front bumper hooked onto Charlie's back bumper, but Charlie saw an opening in the traffic and sped away.

Outside of town the chase resumed at high speed. Sheriff Heflin took two shots. One hit the back bumper and the other passed through the rear window of the car. Charlie stopped suddenly. He opened his door and stumbled out, clutching at the side of his head. Blood was oozing out and he was crying.

Heflin told him to get on the ground. Charlie, still clutching his ear, ignored Heflin, continued forward, stumbling away from his car. Hefflin fired between Charlie's legs and Charlie dropped like a rock onto his chest. When Heflin and Ainslie reached Charlie, they found that a piece of broken glass from the back window had nicked off part of his ear. It had caused some bleeding, but that was all.

When Caril heard the news of Charlie's capture over the police radio, she relaxed as if a giant weight was lifted off her shoulders. She had been crying and rambling incoherently while the chase was in progress. Romer had tried to comfort her, tried to understand what she was saying, but she had been hysterical, and unable to form a thought into words.

Caril was unstrung, shivering and in tears, but she calmed down after she knew Charlie was in custody. Then she asked a question that both confused Deputy Romer and disturbed him. "Where are my parents? I'm afraid something might have happened to them." She also asked for her sister. She wanted to make certain they were all okay.

Romer didn't know how to answer that. Her mother, step-father and half-sister were dead, and it was generally believed she had assisted in their murders. He didn't answer; that wasn't his job. He took her to the jail in Casper where they arrived about the same time as Charlie. She wanted to avoid him, and the closer she got, the more she fidgeted.

By the time Caril was introduced to the sheriff's wife, Hazel Heflin, Caril had again reached a point of hysteria. She was asking for her parents, wanting to know where they were, if they were safe. She asked about her baby sister; technically her half-sister, but Caril always referred to her as her baby sister. Mrs. Heflin didn't know how to answer; neither did her husband, or any of the other men of the department. The more they dodged her questions, the more agitated Caril became, and at last they sedated her.

Caril was taken to the state hospital because she was 14, too young to be placed in a jail. As she was examined by psychiatrists and doctors, Mr. and Mrs. Heflin became increasingly convinced that she had been a hostage of, rather than a partner to, Charlie. When they found a note inside her jacket pocket which read, 'Help. Police. Don't ignore.' they became even more certain that she had not been part of his murder spree.

No one told Caril she would face criminal charges, nor did she believe there was any reason that she would. She continued to ask about her family, and everyone still avoided telling her they were dead. Caril told Mrs. Heflin several times how excited she would be to see them again. No one had the heart to tell her what had happened, and so it was left for someone else to be the bearer of the bad news.

Elmer Scheele arrived to take both Charlie and Caril back to Lincoln to stand trial for murder. He did not immediately inform Caril of this fact. He had learned to be shrewd while working for the FBI during the high tide of J. Edgar Hoover's reign. A top notch student,

Scheele had joined the bureau directly out of school, moving to Washington, DC where he served with distinction. He returned to Nebraska when he was offered a job in the county attorney's office. There, he had worked his way up to chief deputy, and was elected county attorney himself in 1954.

He was known for his extreme focus, concentrating on one case at a time rather than spreading himself out like many other attorneys did. He spoke little and chose his words carefully. When others in his office came to him with a problem, he usually asked them what they thought, and most times when they answered he said, "That's why I hired you."

He was a strong disciplinarian, expecting a lot from those who worked under him, and from his family. When his son was picked up for alcohol possession, Scheele let him stay in jail overnight so he would learn his lesson.

Despite his solidity, his co-workers were very loyal, but few felt close to him. He was distant, talking very little about personal matters and rarely getting to know much about the personal lives of his co-workers. He went home for lunch every day, and often left the details of running the office to the assistant DA, Dale Fahrnbruch. Like most in his profession, he was a heavy smoker, and did not know the results of the habit until it was too late in life.

The most unusual aspect of his office was a noose which hung close to his desk. What would seem like a sick joke was actually a necessary tool for his neck and back. It was a hoist used to stretch his neck. When he used it, which was most days, he stuck his head through as though he was going to hang himself, then pulled upward on the rope to straighten out his body.

Now in Wyoming and far away from his office, Scheele sat and talked to Caril in his blunt, yet amiable demeanor. He was so genial that Caril believed he was on her side. She knew he was there to make Charlie accountable for what he had done, and he explained that charges could be brought against her if she didn't cooperate. She did all she could to tell him every detail. She did not understand that what she was telling him and the other officials he brought would be used against her in a trial where she could receive the death penalty. Scheele merely asked her in his soft, benevolent voice what had happened. As she spoke, the court reporter, Audrey Wheeler, took her statement.

With Scheele were Edwin Coats, psychiatrist at the Casper hospital, Eugene Masters, assistant police chief, and Dale Fahrnbruch, the assistant district attorney from Nebraska. Caril had no attorney present on her behalf.

Elmer Scheele told Caril that she could return to Lincoln willingly, or she would be forced to by a court order. He never explained that she had the right to fight extradition, nor did he even tell her why she was being taken back to Lincoln. As far as Caril understood, she was being offered a ride back home where she would be reunited with her family. Caril's understanding was that she could either go with the Nebraska police to help press charges against Charlie, or she could be forced to do the same thing. She told them she would go willingly. It was placed into the record that Caril was not going to fight extradition. Caril, meanwhile, did not even know what the word meant.

Caril was driven to Gering, Nebraska near the Wyoming border and placed in the prison to await transfer to the custody of the Lincoln police department. Caril continued to believe that she was in police custody because she was a minor, and she required adult supervision until she was reunited with her mother and step-father. Mrs. Warick, the wife of the Scottsbluff County sheriff, who did not know the information had been kept from Caril, simply blurted out that they were dead while she was with Caril. When Caril became extremely distraught and begged for more information, Mrs. Warick said nothing else.

Caril was always handed over to the wife of the sheriff whose custody she was under, so when Sheriff Karnopp from Lancaster County arrived, Caril was placed under the custody of his wife, Gertrude. A stern disciplinary woman, Gertrude Karnopp had already determined Caril was guilty. But this belief was tested when Caril's first question to her was, "Are my folks dead?"

Taken aback, Gertrude didn't answer. Then Caril persisted, "Who killed them?"

"Don't you know, Caril?" Gertrude said.

Caril told her about hearing of their murders for the first time not long before Gertrude had arrived. When Gertrude confirmed the story, she gave Caril tissues to hold back the tears that were now streaming down the little girl's cheeks. She cried for a long time while Mrs. Karnopp watched. When Caril was all out of tears, she began twisting the tissues into the shapes of tiny dolls.

*　　*　　*

John McArthur was led down the wide, sterile hallway of the mental health facility to Caril's room. When Caril was brought back to Nebraska, she had neither the means to hire a lawyer herself, nor did she have parents who could do it for her. Caril's biological father was alive, but on the day she was brought back from Wyoming he had been arrested himself for participating in a bar fight. The presiding judge, Harry Spencer, had assigned a lawyer to her. Spencer had chosen McArthur presumably because he knew that John would neither shrink from the responsibility, nor take advantage of it for his own gain. Many other lawyers would refuse the job out of fear of the public's reaction, or accept because the notoriety of the case would help them promote their own practice.

His new client was being held in the mental health facility because she was too young to be put in a jail, and there was nowhere else to detain her. Juvenile hall had not yet been created.

The state, for that matter the whole country, had never experienced a capital case that involved a minor, and no one knew how to handle the issue of Caril's representation. At first the Nebraska State Bar Association assigned an attorney named William Blue to appear on her behalf for her arraignment, then they assigned Edwin Belsheim, the head of Wesleyan University's law school, to represent her until an official, practicing attorney could be appointed. Belsheim's first course of action was to file for the case to be moved to juvenile court. Even though it was natural to handle such cases there, the State denied it, claiming that this was simply too serious of a charge to handle in juvenile court.

In Federal law, every person had a right to an attorney upon arrest, but in the state of Nebraska, no such right existed until the accused reached their preliminary hearing. Six days after Caril was taken into custody, Judge Spencer finally ruled that "In the interests of justice, considering the age of the applicant and the circumstances surrounding the alleged offense, I find that her request should be granted and counsel appointed. I hereby appoint John McArthur as counsel for Caril Ann Fugate."

John knew the case would be difficult on his family, but his wife Ruby had stood by him through thick and thin. She knew what she had signed up for when she married him, and she understood that his decisions sometimes made their family unpopular. This time, however, he had not been able to call home after being assigned the case to warn Ruby before death threats reached the house. His son James took the first call, and Ruby fielded most of the rest. Had the television or radio been on, they would have heard the news, but it was Saturday, the Sabbath for them. As such, they did not have luxuries of any kind from sunset Friday night to sunset Saturday night. The television was not to be turned on all that day, except for a few select shows with which John would not be parted.

John had no opinion on the case before him. Elmer Scheele, the county attorney, who was a close friend of his, had filed charges of first-degree murder against the girl, and it seemed clear from the news reports that Caril had gone along at least somewhat willingly on a terrible murder spree. She had had several opportunities to get away, but at the same time, she was only fourteen years old. John decided to leave judgment to the jury. He would hear her side of the story, and interpret it to the court as best he could, even if it seemed hopeless.

John's first impression of Caril was how small she was. She stood less than five feet in height, and her build was tiny and frail. Though she was fourteen years old, she looked more like she might be twelve, or younger. Her hair was in a pony tail, and she wore the very plain clothes the hospital had provided her. She was fidgeting with some tissue dolls she had made.

"Hello Caril. I'm John," he told her. John was a consummate gentleman; formal, yet warm to everyone he met. She greeted him with a smile and introduced herself. He sat down and asked her about what she liked to do during the long days. She told him how she busied herself with whatever she could find, and showed him the dolls she made.  Once the pleasantries were done, he began talking about what had happened.  She spoke freely about what Charlie had done, about how frightened she had been of him, and how dangerous he was.

When he told her that he was there to work on her case, Caril didn't seem to understand why.  She thought she had been helping the police to prosecute Charlie.  John had read in the newspapers a detailed description of Charlie and Caril's arrival in Lincoln.  Caril sat in the backseat of the sheriff's car smiling at reporters.  She was acting the way a rescued girl would, not the way a captured killer would.  The sheriff's wife had rolled up the window and not allowed Caril to speak with reporters.

Now it was clear why.  The reporters might have told her just how serious this was, and Caril would have been less forthcoming with her answers to the county attorney, who was using her own testimony as evidence against her.  By keeping her in the dark, Elmer Scheele had managed to get Caril to make incriminating statements.  With her family dead, no one could stand up for the girl except John.

But damage had already been done.  The newspapers had already painted Charlie and Caril as the new Bonnie and Clyde.  She was always named as Charlie's girlfriend.  No one mentioned the fact that Caril had broken up with Charlie the Sunday before the murders.  The image of two young lovers on a rampage was more captivating, and that's the image the media presented to the public before Caril could ever speak to a lawyer, before she even knew that anyone thought she was guilty.

John was dumbfounded.  He had known Elmer Scheele for a long time.  They had been friends, even though they were rivals.  But this went beyond the common maneuvers of attorneys to find the best angle for their clients.  Scheele had used deceit to push a small girl closer to the electric chair.  He had not considered reasons or alternatives, and he had used methods which, though common for the time, were highly unethical.

John looked at that girl now.  There was certainly strength inside her, though anxiety took control of her face once she knew that her life was once again on the line.  She told John that the most important thing to her was that people know she was not guilty of murdering anyone.  Going to prison or even dying was less important to her than the public understanding that she would never commit such horrible acts. John asked her if she was ready to give her statement to him, and she said she was. So he told her to tell her side of the story.

*     *     *

Caril claimed that she had been at school the entire Tuesday, January 21st, when her family was murdered. So far, the story checked out. Her attendance was perfect that day, and the prosecution could not refute the dozens, or even hundreds of witnesses who would have seen her, as well as the attendance records, which John had examined. Meanwhile, no gunfire was reported by the Bartelett neighbors after school hours and the police investigators agreed that the murders took place before Caril returned home, so clearly she had not been at her house when her family was murdered.

Caril walked to her house after school with a friend, then, she said, she walked inside to find it empty except for Charlie. He told her that his friends were holding her family hostage, and if she didn't do exactly what he said, he would call his friends and have her family killed. She didn't believe him at first. Charlie had liked to play make-believe games like cowboys and Indians. Caril hated how childish he was, and thought he was playing games again. Charlie insisted that it was real, that he and his friends planned to rob a bank, and Caril was going to help them. When her parents didn't come home that day, Caril felt that she had no choice but to believe Charlie.

During the six days they were in the house alone together, Caril asked everyone who came to the door to leave because the family was sick with the flu. Visitors had included her sister, her brother-in-law, Charlie's brother, four police officers, and her grandmother. She had left a note on the door which read, "Stay a way. Every body is sick with the flue. Miss Bartlett". The last part, 'Miss Bartlett, was underlined twice. She had hoped this would be a clue that things were not right because Caril went by her original name, Fugate. Bartlett was her step-father's name, which her mother used, making her Mrs. Bartlett. The only Miss Bartlett was her two-year-old step sister.

When Caril's older sister Barbara arrived at the house, Caril told her to go away, then leaned out and whispered that their mother was in trouble and would get hurt if she didn't leave. Caril then followed Barbara to the car and told her again that their mother was in danger and she needed to stay away until Monday. When her grandmother visited, Caril peeked out the window to talk to her. As she told her grandmother to go away because everyone was sick, she placed her hand in front of her mouth and pointed to the side at the door where, she claimed, Charlie was hiding with a gun ready to shoot anyone who entered the house.

Charlie became frightened after Caril's grandmother threatened to return with the police. He said that he didn't want to get caught before he and his friends could commit the bank robbery. So Charlie and Caril got in his car and he drove southeast out of Lincoln to the home of his friend August Meyer, who might be able to hide them. Charlie's car got stuck as they turned into Meyer's driveway, so Charlie and Caril walked up to the house and asked August if they could borrow some horses to help get their car out of the mud.

They were walking with Mr. Meyer toward the horse stables when Charlie suddenly raised his gun and shot the old man in the back without warning. This was the moment, Caril said, that she realized how serious everything was. She had never seen anyone killed before, and now Charlie had shot his close friend right in front of her. Charlie then beat August's dog to death with the same rifle, hitting it so hard that the gun broke. He gave the damaged gun to Caril to carry while he took August's rifle. Caril, stunned, just stood there holding the gun.

They managed to get the car out themselves, then returned to Lincoln to have the car serviced and to get some food. They met up with several people that Caril could have told about what Charlie had done, including the garage attendants and people at the restaurant, but she didn't. She claimed that, after seeing what Charlie had done to his friend, she was too scared to tell anyone what was happening. She was afraid that if she said anything, Charlie might kill the people she talked to, that if she tried to escape and failed, she could be killed; and even if her escape was successful, her family would be murdered by his friends. She did, however, write a note, asking for someone to rescue her, which was found in her jacket pocket in Wyoming after they were captured.

After they had their car serviced, Caril and Charlie returned to the Bennet area. They found themselves stuck in the mud again, this time on the road approaching August's farm. Another farmer named Genuchi happened along during this time. Again, Caril could have said something, but Charlie was right there, and she was too frightened to even try giving a sign. After Charlie shot August right in front of her, everything seemed impossible to Caril, and she believed Charlie would kill anyone, even her. Charlie, Caril, and the farmer tried to dislodge the car, but when they were unsuccessful, Genuchi continued on, and Caril felt she had saved his life by not saying anything.

Charlie and Caril began to walk toward a nearby storm cellar Charlie knew about where they could stay for the night. They were walking along a bend in the road when Robert Jensen and Carol King stopped and asked if they needed a ride. They were two kids who saw fellow teenagers stuck on a cold, country road and only wanted to help. Charlie and Caril got into the car and Robert drove toward Bennet.

When they arrived in Bennet, Charlie pointed his gun at Robert and Carol and told Caril to take Robert's wallet. Caril hesitated, and Robert told her to do it so Charlie wouldn't kill anyone. Then Charlie told Robert to drive to the storm cellar near August's farm he and Caril had been walking toward. Charlie said he only wanted their car and he would leave them in the cellar until someone came along and found them. When they arrived, Charlie told Robert and Carol to get out. Robert was more cooperative, but Carol King didn't trust him, and wouldn't leave the car. Charlie then told Caril Fugate to point her gun at King. When Fugate refused, Charlie yelled at her and threatened to kill her, so she pointed the gun at the girl.

Fugate watched Charlie disappear into the storm cellar with both Robert Jensen and Carol King. She shook in the cold air, but not because of the freezing temperature. She was scared, and she was afraid of what was coming.

Two gunshots rang out, and only Charlie emerged, holding Carol King's jacket. He gave the jacket to Caril and got back into the car. They didn't go far before Charlie drove the car directly into a ditch.

He told Caril that if she helped him get the car out, he would take her home to her family. She did, and they headed into Lincoln. Caril told John that at this point she noticed some school books on the seat next to her. She knew that Charlie might not ever let her go, so the best thing she could do was to throw the books out the window so the police would have a trail. After tossing them, she explained to Charlie that she didn't want to be reminded of school.

Charlie drove to Caril's house, but the police were all around it. Caril didn't know they had found the bodies of her family. Charlie drove past the police cruisers and parked a block away. He and Caril slept in the car until sunrise.

Charlie had told Caril that her family was being kept in a house on Woodsdale Boulevard, a meandering, curved road covered with trees just north of Lincoln's country club. He knew the neighborhood from his garbage collecting days. He drove her to that area, but instead of taking her to the house, he stopped a block earlier on 24th Street. He chose a house at random; the third one from the end of the block at Van Dorn Street. It was a white, two story, upper-middle class home with a long driveway where Charlie's car could disappear in the back under an enclave of trees. Tall windows gazed out on a long lawn that during summer months was a lush green, but now was crusted over with a pale layer of ice.

Caril remained in the car while Charlie gained entry into the house, then emerged and ordered her to come inside.

Faux wood paneling covered the spacious walls of the crisp, tidy rooms. Empty chairs sat on top of clean, flat carpets that stretched across wide floors without a speck of dirt on them. Upon entering the house, Caril met the woman responsible for this cleanliness, Lillian Fencl, the maid. She was deaf, and was taking orders from Charlie as he wrote them on pieces of paper. Mrs. Ward, the lady of the house, was also there, and was cooperating fully with him. It was almost domestic the way everyone was being so calm about the situation. Exhausted from the past couple days, and with no imminent danger, Caril found a couch, lay down and took a nap. When she woke up she saw only the maid in the house, then she saw Mr. Ward's car pulling into the driveway. She told Charlie, and Charlie met the man at the door. Mr. Ward tried to take the gun from Charlie, and the two wrestled over it until Charlie shot him just inside the front door.

Charlie then grabbed the maid and took her upstairs, ordering Caril to follow. He tied the maid up to the bed, then stabbed her multiple times, Caril crying as she watched. As the woman bled to death, Charlie took Caril back downstairs and they left.

Caril claimed that after leaving the Wards' she asked Charlie several times to leave her somewhere in Lincoln and she would find her way home. Charlie refused, telling Caril that she'd tell the police what happened and how to catch him. Instead, he drove west with the intent of driving to Washington where one of Charlie's brothers lived. They headed out of town, passing the police station on the way, and got onto the highway heading west. After that, their only stops were for gas until they reached Wyoming the next day.

*     *     *

Joint services for Carol King and Robert Jensen were held at the Bennet Community Church. The building overflowed with mourners of every age. All businesses in the small town were closed, even gas stations. Schools were dismissed, and all students were allowed to attend the ceremony.

The two teenagers had been popular, their parents beloved in the community. Robert's father ran the general store where everyone purchased their goods. Both kids had overcome a lot recently. Robert Jensen was suffering from polio, but did not let it show, nor had he felt sorry for himself. Carol King had had her own difficulties, having lost her father the month before. Now her mother had endured two funerals in less than thirty days.

People were angry, and they wanted vengeance.

John McArthur was all too aware of this as he returned to his office after meeting with Caril. He had known this case would be big, but he didn't realize until he talked with the girl just how multifaceted it would become. Often, John would go to his partner, Merril Reller, to talk over a case and get another perspective. For this case, he would need all the advice he could get.

Reller had inherited wealth and invested it wisely. Despite his affluence, he was a hard working attorney who threw himself into his career. Whenever he got involved in anything, he went in one hundred percent. Whenever he took time off, it was to travel, and he took frequent hunting trips in various parts of the world. He hung the trophy heads proudly on his walls.

Talkative and passionate, Reller was in many ways the opposite of John. Merril came from wealth and the city, John from a farm in the quiescent Sand Hills of western Nebraska. Merril expressed his feelings openly; John was more reserved, and it was hard to read what he was feeling. Merril was the one who typically became more emotionally invested, and the one who clients felt they could turn to about their feelings. John was more factual, and the one everybody counted on to solve problems.

Merril admired and respected John for the same reason most people did, because of his quiet wisdom. The two men stood up for each other in hard times. When McArthur voiced unpopular ideals, Reller echoed him. McArthur, in turn, used his substantial skills at law to support his friend. Once, when a judge came down hard on Reller for a legal issue he knew the judge was wrong about, John took the case all the way to the Supreme Court. When the judgment was reversed, the judge, stunned by what McArthur had brought out, accused Reller of "hiding the law from him."

Now John needed every bit of Reller's support and expertise. After interviewing Caril, he had to wait a few days to speak with Reller while Reller returned from one of his regular Safaris.

After John told him the whole story, Merril asked him the obvious question, why didn't she just run away?

John knew that would be the hardest part to explain, but he had seen her. He saw how frightened she was, how easily susceptible she could be to orders. There was no question in his mind she was very scared, and had been under Charlie's control. Even when he was out of the room, she could not mentally escape. Besides, nine grown people had died trying to confront or run away from him during that week; how could a tiny girl?

The trick was going to be to explain this to the jury.

# Chapter Four
## The State of Nebraska v. Charles Raymond Starkweather

"I always wanted to be a criminal, just not this big of one," Charlie said on his way back to Lincoln from Wyoming when one of the officers had asked why he killed so many people. He had not fought extradition back to Nebraska, though he could have. Since he murdered a man in Wyoming, he could be tried in either state. Ironically, killing this eleventh victim almost saved his life because even though Wyoming had the death penalty, the governor commuted every death sentence in his state. "I want to go back to Nebraska," Charlie said, "because Wyoming has a gas chamber and I don't like the smell of gas. I suppose they'll have the chair ready for me."

Charlie was being returned by squad car because he had a fear of flying. Most of the officers who drove him were surprised at his easy-going demeanor. Scheele had said to him when they first met, "My name is Elmer Scheele, and I am going to do my damnedest to put you in the electric chair." Charlie had only smiled back at him in return, like Elmer was an old friend who had just paid him a compliment. Scheele was not easily intimidated, but that unsettling smile was one of the only things to ever catch him off guard.

Charlie told the officers he was riding with that he "wasn't mad at anyone," but "just wanted to be somebody." Then he casually told them about another murder he had committed, one they had known about, but remained unsolved. On December 1st Charlie had killed Robert Colvert, a 21-year-old gas station attendant who had recently been discharged from the navy. Colvert wasn't even supposed to be on duty that night, but was covering for a friend. Police had received several tips right after the murder that Charlie had been the killer, but they had not followed up on them. "If you had caught me then, none of this would have happened," Charlie taunted.

They were ill-equipped for such a massacre, and Charlie did his best to remind them of this fact whenever he could. They had missed him at several turns. He had driven past them at the Bartlett home. He had stopped at a red light next to a squad car while driving the Packard, but they hadn't noticed because they were searching for Robert Jensen's vehicle, and he had changed his hair color with shoe polish. The school books Caril had thrown onto the street when they were heading toward Lincoln should have told the police which direction they were moving. Even though the police found the books west of where the teenagers had been killed, they had assumed he would never return to Lincoln, and went east into the country in search for him.

At only 19 years of age, Charlie had eluded the police for two months, and was at last brought down only because Caril had run to an officer who had not yet noticed them.

The newspapers began to pick up on this, running stories about how dissatisfied many of the townspeople were with law enforcement's inability to catch Charlie. Walter W. White, who published the Lincoln Star, sent a public telegram to Sheriff Earl Heflin of Wyoming, saying, "I humbly offer to you and your men my sincere thanks for doing a job at which our police force proved inadequate. Our community owes you a real debt of gratitude."

The public also began questioning why the police had not caught Charlie earlier. They couldn't understand why it had taken them so long, especially when it became known that Charlie had driven past the police several times during the spree. Even on his way to Wyoming, a truck driver from Broken Bow had called in a description of him and the car he was driving, but the police did not follow the lead, holding fast to the belief that he was still in Lincoln.

Outrage increased when the populace learned of the first murder of the Crest gas station attendant in December and the tips that should have pointed at Charlie. If they had captured him for that murder/robbery, he would not have gone on the murder spree. A number of people had pointed Charlie out as a suspect. Robert McClung, one of the gas station attendants who had previously worked the same shift as the attendant, told the police that Charlie often slept in his car outside the gas station during the same hours when the murder took place. Charlie often slept in his car on nights when he was homeless because he had been locked out of his apartment. Had the police checked, they would have found that on December 1st, Charlie had been locked out for not paying his rent. But the next day he paid his rent in full. McClung even knew Charlie personally, and woke him up some mornings so Charlie could get to work on time. McClung described Charlie and his car to the police, but the police never investigated further. They even left a parking citation on the same car McClung had described during the murder spree in January, but still, no further investigation was made.

The authorities were also approached by Mrs. John Kamp, the owner of the Clothing Resale and Gift Shop. She reported that Charlie had bought $9.55 worth of used apparel, paying all of it in change. She had been suspicious not only because of the large amount he had paid in coins, but because the news had recently reported that $10 in change had been stolen from the gas station at the time of the murder. She described him in detail to the police, but again, they never looked into it. Several other people who knew Charlie, and knew how little money he had, had reported to the police that he had seemed to have a lot more money than he usually had and that he seemed to have gotten it out of the blue. He had even told one of his friends that he had "lots of things to do" with the money he had taken from the gas station.

Charlie's own recounting of the events described suspicious behavior that others had reported to the police, such as the fact that he had painted his car and changed the tires the day after the murder. He had even left the shotgun in a shallow creek near the murder scene several days before returning and fishing it out.

As stories such as these emerged in the aftermath of the killing spree, citizens were outraged. Merle Karnopp, the county sheriff in charge of the investigation, (ironically born on the exact same day and year as John McArthur,) and others in the police department countered by saying in a statement that the public was to blame for "failing to cooperate."

This enraged the public even more, being blamed by the police for what the police should have been doing. Police Chief Joseph T. Carroll tried to cover up at least in part for the officers who made the initial investigation by explaining that when they initially investigated the Bartlett home, they had not missed anything. "Blood was everywhere," he explained. This had the opposite effect than he was wanting, as the public now asked that if blood had been everywhere, why had the officers not done something about it rather than sending the relatives away.

Carroll tried to dig out of the hole he was digging by explaining, "Even the relatives were apparently satisfied with our investigation," If he had been throwing kindling on the fire before, the police chief now had thrown gasoline on it. Having spoken for the relatives without ever having spoken *with* them, the relatives of both Charlie and Caril now spoke out about what had truly happened.

As they recounted the story, they had gone to the police many times while Charlie and Caril were at the Bartlett house. They had first become suspicious when Barbara, Caril's sister, and her husband Robert Von Busch had gone to the Bartlett home for a visit. Robert was an old friend of Charlie's, his former boss, and the couple lived in the same apartment building as Charlie. Despite the drizzling rain and the fact that they had their baby with them, Caril did not let them inside. They insisted, and Caril told them that everyone was sick with the flu.

When Barbara said she would go in alone, Caril leaned forward to her and said, "If you know what's best you'll go away so Mother don't get hurt." Frightened, Barbara and Robert got back into the cab they had come in, but just before they pulled away, Caril ran out to them. "I'm sorry I was so cranky," Caril said, "but I had to be that way."

"Why?" Barbara asked.

"I can't tell you.  Just go home and don't come back till after Monday.  If you do, things will happen.  Mom will get hurt."  Before Barbara could ask another question, Caril ran into the house.

After going home, Robert went to see Charlie's brother Rodney, who had not heard from Charlie in a while, and they returned to the Bartlett house that evening.  After knocking several times, Caril finally answered and told them to go away, but Bob insisted that he had to pay her mother back for something.  When he tried to force his way in, Caril begged, "Please don't try to get in.  Mom's life will be in your hands if you do!"

It was at that time that Bob and Rodney first went to the police.  The department dispatched two officers to go to the house, Donald Kahler and Frank Soukup.  As Bob and Rodney looked on, the officers approached the house and Caril told them that everyone was sick, and the doctor had ordered that they not see anyone.  The officers did not ask for the doctor's name, nor was any investigation made.  Instead, they asked why her brother-in-law would want to call the police.

"We don't get along too good," she said.

After the officers left, Robert and Rodney went to the station to ask what had been said.  The officers told them, and Robert knew something was wrong.  Explaining that he and Caril got along great, he insisted that something must be wrong in order for her to lie about their relationship.  He insisted they go back, but the officers refused.  So Bob did what Kahler and Soukup had not bothered to do, he called the Bartletts' doctor.  The doctor had not seen them recently, and had no idea they were sick.  When later questioned about this particular matter, the police chief blamed Caril, saying that she did too good a job of convincing the police not to investigate further.

When Bob returned home, Barbara told him that Charlie Starkweather had called him twice, once to tell him that he had left a .22 rifle at Griggs' garage and that he was stranded at Tate's service station.  The other call was to tell him that he had taken groceries to the Bartletts, that they were all sick with the flu, and that everyone should stay away.  Bob called Rodney again, and they went to the garage.  The couple who ran it, Mr. and Mrs. Griggs, said that Charlie had returned the gun, but that the butt plate was missing.  Rodney drove out to Tate's Service station only to find Charlie had not been there.

The next morning, Charlie's sister Laveta approached the Bartlett house. Caril met her at the screen door, paused a moment, looked behind her, then whispered to Laveta, "Some guy is back there with Chuck. He has a Tommy gun. I think they're going to rob a bank." Laveta took the information back to her father, who then called the police. The police ignored him.

The next morning, Caril's grandmother, sixty-two-year-old Pansy Street, approached the house. When Caril gave her the same story about being sick, she refused to believe it, and began calling into the house for her daughter and her baby granddaughter to answer. Caril, meanwhile, stepped back away from the door, covering her mouth, which at first looked to Pansy like she was crying, but then it looked as though she was pointing to the corner as she said, "Go home, Grandma... Mommy's life is in danger if you don't." Pansy could see through what was happening. "You've got Chuck in there with you, and don't try to tell me you don't!" she insisted. With that, she gave up and returned to her cab, going directly to the police.

They were slow to react, and only finally sent two officers back to the house with Mrs. Street when Charlie's own father called them and said he believed Charlie was at the Bartlett home. When they reached the house, they knocked several times. No one answered. The officers wanted to leave, but Mrs. Street insisted that they break in.

She was so insistent that one of the officers at last climbed in a window and let the others in. They did a quick walk-through of the house, and inside they found rope lying in a chair, and the barrel of a sawed off shotgun resting on the TV.

Declaring that nothing was out of place and that the house looked normal, the officers left. Pansy wasn't satisfied. They had not yet checked the outside buildings, such as the chicken shed and the outhouse. Inside the house, the bed sheets and other furniture were too neat to have just been filled with sick people. Despite her insistence that something was still amiss and they should continue to investigate, they called it off and took her home. On the ride back, they told her that she should stop sticking her nose into her children's affairs, and that they probably didn't want her around.  The officers implied that she might be senile, then left her off at her house.

Bob Von Busch returned to the police insisting that they return to the premises and do a more thorough search.  He was told that the Bartletts were "probably gone on vacation."  The police then told him they were tired of him, and that he should "stop bothering them."

"It sure seems crazy that sick people would go on vacation leaving a 14-year-old girl behind," Robert said.  He and Rodney then decided to take matters into their own hands and returned to the premises to search for themselves.  They found the bodies, wrapped in blankets, in the chicken coop behind the house.  Two-year-old Betty Jean was found later in the outhouse.  Robert contacted the police again, telling them about the bodies.  "Now will you come take a look?" he said.

Even Guy Starkweather, Charlie's father, was after the police to catch his son.  "The police had a duty to perform," he said.  "They aren't carrying those pistols for nothing."

Newspapers were reporting each day about leads the police could have followed but didn't.  Many people were horrified at the incompetence.

Then suddenly, and inexplicably, the Lincoln Journal turned around 180 degrees, burying all of their stories that implicated the police in their inadequacies and running a story that read "Performance of Lawmen Supported" which stated how much the City Council stood behind the police's handling of the events, and downplayed the issues brought up by other citizens.  But the people still were not satisfied, and the City Council eventually held a special session covering the police work.  An investigation was held, but no actual policy changes took effect, and no one on the police force was ever disciplined for their lack of action.

\*　　　\*　　　\*

Arriving back in Lincoln, it was as though Charlie was a celebrity.  Everyone wanted to know about this young man who had evaded police and killed so many people.  Reporters crowded the car Charlie was in and their bulbs flashed like lightning around him.

Hoards pushed forward, trying to get a look. What they saw resembled a real life celebrity. He was almost the spitting image of James Dean, but with bright red hair. Black and white photographs were extremely similar to the famous actor, but the handcuffs on Charlie gave him away. He even smoked his cigarettes like Dean, carelessly hanging it out one side of his mouth while he looked at the camera with an indifferent cockiness.

The difference came out when he walked or talked. His feet turned in and his legs rounded out in a bowlegged fashion. He stuttered when he spoke, and had difficulty communicating. He may have looked handsome, but he was anything but charming. His stare, however, could burn right through a man.

Once, on a stairway, a reporter from Iowa made a rude comment about Charlie to get him to look his way. Charlie jumped the man and choked him until he was yanked off. The next day while Charlie was being moved, he was forced to go to the man and apologize. "I'm sorry," Charlie said. The man sighed with relief. Then Charlie grabbed him quickly and brought the man's face next to his. "Next time, I'll kill ya," he said quickly with a wry smile before he was dragged away.

Everything was now a joke to Charlie. He knew his life was over. It had been over before the murders, as far as he was concerned. His eyesight was going bad, and a few months earlier he had been told by a doctor that he would be blind within a year. Not long after, he had been kicked out of his parents' home when he had allowed Caril to drive his father's car and she damaged it. He was fired from his job as a garbage collector, and within a few weeks was evicted from his apartment for lack of payment. He told his landlady that he would get the money and pay her. Caril broke up with Charlie that same day, and three days later he began his murder spree.

But now that he had killed eleven people, he had more attention and respect than he could have ever hoped for. He would go down, but he would go down famous, and he would drag down others with him. At the moment, however, he wouldn't drag down Caril. As soon as he was caught, he told officers, "The girl had no part in it. Don't get rough with her."

Reporters were often at Charlie's cell, and he paced around like a caged tiger, sitting occasionally to write letters, and sometimes in a diary. He had a talent for drawing and he often drew sketches, mostly of old west scenes.

Since he couldn't afford to pay for an attorney, the state assigned C. Gaughan to represent him. Charlie immediately didn't like Gaughan. He thought the man weak, a wimp who wanted to save Charlie's soul, as well as his body, and was willing to degrade himself to do it.

But Charlie liked Scheele, the man who would do his best to put him in the electric chair. He admired the man's strength, the directness in his eyes. He didn't care that this man wanted him dead. Every time Scheele was around, Charlie looked full of energy, as though his best friend had come to visit him.

Scheele could not accept the fact that Charlie was declaring Caril's innocence. Charlie had thus far made four statements, all of them contradicting one another. The first two accounts were letters he had written during the killing spree when he thought Caril and he were going to be killed before the end.

The first letter was written in his handwriting, but switched points of view, as if Charlie couldn't decide if he wanted the letter to be from himself or from Caril:

*This is for the cops or law-men who fines us. Caril and i are writing this so that you and every body will know what has happem. On tue.day 7 days befor you have seen the bodys of my non, dad and baby sister, there dead because of me and Chuck,Chuck came down that tue.day happy and full of jokes but when he came in nom said for him to get out and never come back, Chuck look at her" and said why" at that my dad got mad and begin to hit him and was pushing him all over the room, then Chuck got mad and there was no stoping him, and he had his gun whit him cause him and my dad was going hunting, well Chuck pill it and the (drawing of a bullet) come out and my dad drop to the foor, at this my mon was so mad the she had a (drawing of a knife) and was going to cut him she Knot the gun from Chucks hands, Chuck just stood there saying he was sorry he didn't want to do it. i got Chucks gun and stop my mon from killing Chuck.*

*Betty Jean was about 10 steps fron her, he let it go it stop some where would not stop Chuck had the (drawing of a knife) so he was about ten steps from her, he let it go it stop some where by her head. me and Chuck just look at them for about 4 hrs. then we wrapped them and pull them out in the house in back. my sisters and everyone eles we not belived this but it's the true and i say it by god then me and Chuck live with each other and Monday the day the bodys were found, we were going to kill ourselves, but Bob VonBruck and every body would not stay a way and hate my older sister and bob for what they are they all ways wanted me to stop going with Chuck show that some kid bob Kwen could go with me. Chuck and i are sorry for what we did, but now were going to the end. i feel sorry for Bar. to have a ask like bob. i and Caril are sorry for what has happen. cause i have hurt every body cause of it and so has caril, but i'm saying one thing every body that came out there was luckie there not dead even Caril's sister. Chuck S. Caril F.*

Both names were signed in Charlie's handwriting.

The second letter was a note to Charlie's parents written from his Wyoming cell:

*Dear Mon and Dad. i'm a way I hate to write this or maybe you will not read it, but if you will i would like to have you read it, it would help me a lot.*

*i'm sorry for what I did in a lot of ways cause i know i hurt everybody, and you and mon did all you could to rise me up right and you all ways help me when i got in bab with something But this time i would like you not to do any thing to help me out. i hope you will under stand, i Know my sister and brothers even nom, that this well take a long time befor people stop looking at them in a funny way. so it would make me happy if everbody well go on just like anything didn't happen. the cops up here have been more then nice to me but these dam reporters, the next one that comes in here he is going to get a glass of water.*

*But dad i'm not real sorry for what i did cause for the first time me and Caril have more fun, she help me a lot, but if she comes back*

*don't hate her she had not a thing to do with the Killing all we wanted*
*to do is get out of town. tell every body to take care.        Chuck*
*P.S. tell Bob VonBruck to thing of somebody besides him he help to*
*cause this.*

His third statement was one he had written out while in the
Wyoming jail. He stated that he had gone to the Bartlett's to go
hunting with Caril's father. Mrs. Bartlett told him that no one wanted
him there anymore, and told him to leave. Charlie said something
about Caril's sister, which started a fight between the two. The father
came in with a hammer and threatened Charlie with it, at which time
Charlie went into another room and loaded his brother's rifle. Mr.
Bartlett then ran at him with the hammer and Charlie shot him. Then
Mrs. Bartlett ran at him with a knife and he shot her. The baby was
screaming, so Charlie hit her, but he didn't remember how many
times.
　　　Caril came home at 4:00 and he told her that her parents were
gone. He wrote that he'd found Mrs. Bartlett's shotgun, and then
dropped off his brother's rifle at a friend's place. When Caril's
grandmother came to the door and threatened to go to the police,
Charlie became scared, and left, taking Caril with him.
　　　He did not describe the murder of his friend August Meyer, and
said only of Robert Jensen and Carol King that he didn't want to shoot
them. He then claimed that Caril was listening to a report on the radio
about her parents' death when he returned to the car. He explained
that at the Wards, he had broken in and convinced both Mrs. Ward and
the maid, Lillian Fencl, to be civil and no one would get hurt. After
Caril fell asleep, Charlie allowed Mrs. Ward to go upstairs for
something. When she didn't come back down for a long time, he went
up to see what was happening. She tried to shoot him with a .22 pistol
but missed. When she tried to run, he threw a knife into her back, then
drug her over to the bed. When Mr. Ward came home, he attacked
Charlie and tried to get the gun from him, but Charlie won and he shot
the man. Charlie never explained how Mrs. Fencl, the maid, was
killed.
　　　Charlie told the police that after leaving the Wards', he and
Caril then made a run for Washington, but he wanted to change cars in

Wyoming.  He stopped and tried to steal the salesman's Buick.  But the man tried to wrestle the gun from him, so Charlie killed him.

The fourth statement was some writing on the prison wall in Gering, Nebraska.  It read:

*by the time any body will read this i will be dead for all the killings*
*then they cannot give caril the chair to.*
*from Lincoln Nebraska they got us Jan. 29, 1958.*
*1958 kill 11 persons   (Charlie kill 9) all men*
*(Caril kill 2) all girls*

He had also drawn a heart with Charlie and Caril's name inside it, and more writing in pencil: "they have so many cops and people watching us leave I can't add all of them of."  His math was the most unusual part as there had been six male and five female victims.

Scheele brought Charlie into his office for an official statement on the record.  It was going to be easy to convict Charlie; he was even helping them accomplish that goal.  But Scheele was hoping for some kind of information that would incriminate Caril, the harder of the two to convict.  Scheele was convinced of her guilt, and he wanted anything that gave evidence to that, even if it was from the mouth of a madman.  But Charlie's story this time ran pretty much parallel to Caril's version of events:

He told Scheele he had arrived at Caril's home long before her, had killed her family, had hidden them in the chicken coop and abandoned outhouse.  When she got home, he told her that his friends were holding them hostage at the home of an elderly lady and she had to do everything he said or he'd call his friends and have them all killed.  He, too, recounted how each person came to visit.  She was made to send them away or he would call his friends.  After a couple days the two of them left.

This time he explained that they were going to hide at August's farm, but their car got stuck, so they went and warmed up in the storm cellar before they walked up to August's farm to borrow horses to get the car out.  He claimed that August had gone into the house for his coat, but had come back out with a gun and shot at Charlie, who then killed August in self-defense. Caril was around the corner and did not see it.

After that he said that they cleaned up the mess, then drove into Lincoln to fix up the car and get some food. On the way back, Caril didn't want to return to the house, so they started for the storm cellar and got stuck again. That's when Robert Jensen and Carol King came along. Charlie described them giving him and Caril a ride into Bennet, then back out to the storm cellar. He told Scheele how he had told Caril to take Robert's wallet, then point a gun at Carol King to make her get out of the car.

"Did Caril have the four-ten in her hands at all times that you were in the car with this young boy and young girl?" Scheele asked.

"Yes," Charlie answered.

"So then you got out of the car and Caril got out of the car?" Scheele continued.

"No. Caril stayed in the car." Charlie then explained that he was sending Robert and Carol into the storm cellar when Robert suddenly turned and lunged at him, and Charlie shot him, then shot Carol King.

The next part of the story matched Caril's pretty much exactly. She helped him get out of the mud in exchange for him taking her home. When they got there, police were all around, so they went elsewhere and slept in the car.

At the Ward's house, Mrs. Ward and the maid were very polite, and gave Charlie anything he wanted. They went on with their business as if Charlie and Caril were invited guests. Mrs. Ward even made coffee for Caril, and waffles for Charlie. Eventually, she asked to go upstairs for something, and when she didn't come back down, Charlie went upstairs, where she shot at him with her .22 and missed, and he threw a knife into her back. He then said that he ran downstairs, woke up Caril, giving her an unloaded revolver and told her to watch the maid, then ran back upstairs to Mrs. Ward "to give her a band aid."

He described the fight with Mr. Ward in greater detail, how they fell into the basement where he wrestled him into submission. Then Charlie led him up the stairs, but when the man tried to make a run for it, Charlie shot him next to the front door. Mrs. Fencl, the maid, was deaf, so she had not heard what happened. Charlie told Scheele that Caril helped him tie her to the bed upstairs, then they left without killing her. The rest of the statement was the same, claiming that they were on their way to Washington when they were stopped in Wyoming.

Then Scheele went for the information he was really wanting. "Had Caril Fugate ever made any attempt to get away?"

"No… she never did… she had all the chance she wanted to."

At that, Scheele concluded the interview. He wrapped it up with the usual formalities. Regarding the transcript, he said, "You understand that it can be used against you in court, I have told you that when we started?"

"Yes," Charlie answered.

"And after the reporter gets it typed up will you read it over and sign it?"

"Yes."

"Have I made any threats or promises to you this evening at all?"

"You're darned right."

"What did I say?"

"Nothing."

"Did I promise you anything?"

"No."

"Did I threaten you with anything?"

"Not yet."

"What?"

"No."

*　　　*　　　*

John McArthur tried to move Caril's trial to juvenile court because of her age, but the crimes were so heinous, and so widely publicized that Judge Spencer would not allow the case to be moved out of adult court. James, who was learning more and more about his father's profession, asked him how the judge could do that. John told him that, though courts had rules of what they were supposed to do, they were merely guidelines that individual judges could overrule in what they considered to be extraordinary circumstances. Furthermore, state courts were not bound by the same rules that federal courts were. All rights guaranteed in the Constitution applied only on a federal level, and state courts could ignore them if they wished. Although John didn't agree with the court's decision, it was at least giving him grounds for an appeal.

*     *     *

While McArthur tried to move Caril's case to juvenile court, Clement Gaughan, Charlie's attorney, was trying to have Charlie labeled clinically insane. The insanity plea was the only not guilty plea Charlie could hope for, but there was one thing Charlie hated being called more than anything, and that was insane. As he later told a psychiatrist who tried to diagnose him, "Nobody remembers a crazy man." His hatred for his own attorney grew, and he verbally lashed out, insisting he wasn't out of his mind. He claimed that every murder he had committed was in self defense.

Scheele latched on to that anger. Caril had been claiming that Charlie was insane all along. When she was first taken into custody and asked why she had broken up with him a few days before the murders, she had said very bluntly, "Because he's crazy." Elmer Scheele and Dale Fahrnbruch, the Chief Deputy who would take the official statement from Charlie, went immediately to Charlie's cell and informed him that Caril was telling everyone that he was insane. Fire was suddenly lit into Charlie's eyes. He paced around even more furiously as Scheele fanned the flames. He told Charlie what Caril was saying about him; that he was a lunatic, he wasn't very bright, and that she had been afraid of him even before the murders began, that she had left him because she didn't want to be anywhere near him.

Suddenly, Charlie's story changed. "I want to tell you the truth now," he said. "I'm not gonna cover for her no more!"

In his new version of the story, Charlie arrived with his brother's rifle to go hunting with Mr. Bartlett, but this time, when Mrs. Bartlett told him to leave, she hit him a couple times, and Charlie left. He drove around the block a few times, then returned. This time Mr.

Bartlett kicked him, then threw him out the front door. Charlie decided he was going to kill him, so he phoned Watson Brothers Trucking where Mr. Bartlett worked as a night watchman and told them Marion Bartlett wouldn't be in to work for a few days.

Around 3 pm, he returned to the Bartlett's, but no one answered, so he headed toward Caril's school to pick her up. On the way, his car broke down and he parked it in front of a friend's house. He then walked back to the Bartlett home and sat down on their back porch. Soon he heard Caril come home and begin arguing with her mother. Charlie went in and Caril's mother began accusing Charlie of getting Caril pregnant. Caril ran from the room, and soon Mr. Bartlett entered the fray, this time with fists. The fight between he and Charlie moved into another room until Bartlett ran to his tool shed and Charlie ran to the bedroom. He loaded his gun as Mr. Bartlett ran at him with a hammer, and Charlie shot him. According to Charlie, Caril looked in curiously, but said nothing as Charlie stepped out into the living room. Mrs. Bartlett then grabbed a knife and came at Charlie.

At this point, Charlie claimed, Caril grabbed the gun from him and pointed it at her mother saying she'd blow her to hell. Her mother knocked her down, and Charlie told Scheele he grabbed the gun from Caril, spun like an action hero, and shot Mrs. Bartlett just in time. Mrs. Bartlett didn't fall back, however. She continued past Charlie and Caril, staggering as she went, until she reached the baby's crib. She wouldn't fall, so Charlie hit her twice with the butt of his gun until she finally came down. The baby was crying, so Charlie hit her with the gun. She continued to cry, and Caril yelled at her, telling her to shut up.

"And what happened then?" Dale Fahrnbruch asked.

"Well, Caril said that the old man was moving around... I picked up the knife that the old lady had... and started to walk in there, in the bedroom... and the little girl kept yelling, and I told her to shut up, and I started to walk again, and just turned around and threw the hunting knife at her... they said it hit her in the throat, but I thought it hit her in the chest." Charlie then went on to describe how he stabbed Mr. Bartlett several times because he was still moving around, then he went into the kitchen for a glass of water. All the while, he claimed that Caril was just standing there. She asked what they were going to do with the bodies. He asked her what she wanted to do with them, and she walked into the living room and watched TV. Charlie cleaned up the bodies, rinsing off the body of the little girl in the sink because "it was easier to wash up the blood." Then he went to the store, bought some Pepsi, some potato chips, returned, and they watched TV and played gin rummy while the bodies remained in the house with them.

Charlie went on to tell them that the next day when a friend came by to walk to school with Caril, they didn't answer the door. Instead, they discussed what they would do if they got caught. "We was trying to make up a story, and it didn't work too well... I thought if we got caught we'd make up like she was hostage, you know, and we'd start messing around and make it look like it." He then explained that he and Caril put rope around her arms to leave a mark so it would look as though she'd been tied up. When people came to the door, Charlie said he didn't know who was there because Caril had gone to talk to all of them. He denied having been around the corner with a gun pointed at her.

He continued to implicate Caril for far more than he had before, contradicting many of his earlier statements. He claimed that when their car got stuck at the Meyer farm, Caril suggested they go "blast the shit" out of August Meyer for not shoveling his lane. When they went to the house, August argued with him, then went inside to get a shovel, but when he came out, he returned with a gun, so Charlie shot him. Caril was unmoved by the murder, he said.

He then repeated that Caril remained in the car while he shot the two teenagers in the storm cellar. But this time he added how he had come back to get a flashlight from the car, then returned to the storm cellar and watched Robert squirm until he died.

"And then what happened?" Fahrnbruch asked.

"Temptation."

"What did you do?"

"Well, I pulled her jeans down, but I didn't screw her."

"What did you do to her?"

"Nothing."

"Charlie, you told the officers different, haven't you?"

"I didn't screw her... I couldn't get to the point... it was colder than hell... I left her lay there and left." Charlie claimed that when he walked away her body was still on the ground outside the storm cellar. He never explained how her body got into the cellar and down the stairs where the police later found it.

He told Fahrnbruch that when he returned to the car and got stuck in the ditch again Caril got very angry.

"Did Caril leave the car then?" Fahrnbruch asked him.

"A couple times, yes... she was pissed off anyway... she just called me a dirty bastard and all sorts of things."

"Why did she tell you that?... Did you do something in that cave that she might have seen?"

"Well, she might have come up to that cave and thought, but I wasn't."

"As a matter of fact you asked her for sexual relations?"

"Yes, but I never got them."

"What did she say?"

"I already had mine for the night... she probably walked up there and seen me down there... she could have guessed."

"What could she have guessed?"

"What I was doing."

"What did you do?"

"I didn't do nothing."

He changed his story again, this time explaining that he and Caril went back to the storm cellar, took Carol King's body to the basement, closed it up, then got the car out of the ditch using blankets under the wheels to give them traction. He claimed that Caril yelled at him as they drove back to Lincoln, and that he wanted to turn himself in to the police, but Caril wouldn't let him. Instead, they went to the Ward's house, and he admitted to killing Mr. and Mrs. Ward, but that he had not touched the maid. He also claimed that he had only stabbed Mrs. Ward once.

The questions moved on to the murder of the salesman, Collison, in Wyoming. He told Fahrnbruch that Collison had agreed to give him his car, then began wrestling for the gun. He said that Caril brought him his other gun, and he shot Collison.

"Now, Charlie," Fahrnbruch began, "you've previously told us about Caril's activities, and now you have changed your story as to exactly what she's done during all this time. What is the reason that you changed your story?"

"Well, I don't know."

"Are you now telling the truth relative to Caril's activities?"

"Yes."

"Have you told us about everything that you know about what she did?"

"Well, there might be a lot of things, but I can't remember them all at one time."

"And those other things about her in these previous statements are untrue, some of them?"

"They ain't nothing in them other statements that are untrue… I just didn't tell you anything about her."

"What was the reason for not wanting to tell?"

"Because I thought she could get away with it easier."

\*       \*       \*

Charlie's trial was swift. It took the prosecution only three days to present its case. Charlie didn't deny killing anyone. In fact, he was proud of it, admitted so to the press, and claimed it was all in self defense. The only hope his court appointed attorneys had was to convince the jury that Charlie was insane, and belonged in an institution instead of the electric chair. They had a pretty good case for it. Charlie had been smashed in the head when he was very young, and again in his teen-age years. This last accident had caused him constant headaches. He had been held back in the third grade and did even worse the second time, being sent on only because he was getting bigger than the other children. He was made fun of ruthlessly at school not only because he was older than everyone else in his grade, but also because of his bow-legs, and the funny way he would pronounce the letters "R" and "W." His red hair was the object of the most ridicule; it was so bright it typically outshined anything in a room. He was often called "Big Red" or "Little Red," both of which he hated.

Even though an insanity plea was his only hope for life, Charlie looked at his attorneys with resentment. During his attorney's opening statement, his face turned red, he grasped the side of the table and bit his lip as Gaughan declared that Charlie had a "diseased and defective mind," and that he was "maladjusted" and "abnormal." He said Charlie's IQ, which was 86, showed him to be only "a point or two above an idiot."While they questioned Edwin R. Coats, a psychiatrist who had tested him, Charlie didn't listen, but instead read a book on psychiatry. Even Charlie's family resented him being called insane. They told the press they didn't believe there was anything wrong with his head, and they wanted a psychiatric evaluation of their own to prove it. They said this was enough of a tragedy and claiming that he was mentally handicapped would only make it more of one, even if the alternative meant his death.

Charlie sat at the table often with a smile on his face. This was the most attention he had ever received in his life, and it was worth cutting that life short for these few days of infamy. His attorneys sat next to him, and the prosecution team sat across from him at the same table, which was forward and a little to the side of the judge, whose own podium was dramatically large and imposing.

When Charlie's attorneys questioned him on the witness stand, he looked annoyed and bored, but when Scheele spoke, Charlie straightened up, excited. He admired the man, and enjoyed listening to him.

Clement Gaughan, the lead attorney, struggled as his own client and his client's family opposed the only chance they had to save Charlie's life. Charlie's mother was always in court, and was often complaining at the way Gaughan and his partner were handling her son's case. So at last Clement changed tactics by calling her to the witness stand. He asked her how she felt about his handling of her son's case, and she admitted that she did not like that they were trying to "defend" Charlie by calling him insane.

"You do not feel there is anything mentally wrong with Charlie; is that right?" Gaughan asked her.

"Not at the present time," she responded.

Gaughan then went on to ask her many of the same questions he had been asking other witnesses, about Charlie's headaches and the accident that had caused them. He asked her directly if she believed Charlie was insane. "I refuse to answer!" she declared defensively. "I'm his mother. You have no right to ask a mother something like that."

Gaughan then turned the direction of the conversation, and the entire defense strategy. "Mrs. Starkweather, in order to be fair with you and in order to be fair with everybody else, is there anything, while you are sitting on that witness chair, that you can think of that you want to tell the jury?"

"Yes sir," she said. "It was right after Charles started going with Miss Fugate. Before that, he was the best of friends with his brother. They were together constantly, no arguing or anything. But soon after he started going with Caril, it seemed like his family was pushed behind and his whole life centered around her. That's the way it seemed to me. He wanted to be with her. She seemed to have a hold on him."

"You think he was a different boy after that?"

"Yes, sir."

The blame now shifted to Caril. She became the mastermind behind it all who had manipulated Charlie away from his family, and had led him to a life of crime and murder. It was even eluded to that Caril was to blame for Charlie's head injury. She was the perfect scapegoat, the only answer to a proper defense of Charlie without calling him insane.

Charlie's father, Guy Starkweather, had refused to take the witness stand until subpoenaed. When he was at last on the stand, Gaughan first asked him about some of the eccentricities of Charlie, continuing to bring out aspects of his insanity. Guy admitted that when he took Charlie out hunting, Charlie would continue to shoot an animal long after it was dead. He took a certain glee in not only killing things, but mangling the corpses. But he also said that Charlie had told him he wanted to give himself up to the police after Robert and Carol had been killed, but Caril wouldn't let him, and Charlie was afraid to not do what she said because she was holding a gun.

Gaughan at last called Charlie to the stand. Spectators rose to see him until a look from the judge sat them back down. Charlie was pleased to see so many people interested in him. His pleasure deflated when he looked down from the witness stand to his own attorney.

"Charlie, you have been accused of a lot of alleged acts concerning the death of a considerable number of people. Why did you kill these people, Charlie?"

"The ones *I* killed?"

"Yes."

"I thought I was killing them in self-defense."

"You killed them all in self-defense?"

"The ones *I* killed, yes."

"Charlie, in your confession pertaining to the Jensen case, right after you left the cave out there, I think your confession said that you were mad at Caril about something. I don't think those were the exact words, but you were mad at her. What were you mad at her about, Charlie?"

"What she did."

"And what did she do there?"

"Shot Carol King." The crowd stirred with emotion. Though this was yet another alteration from his previous statements, few seemed to care, and the attention began to shift from Charlie to Caril.

As Elmer Scheele began cross-examining him, Charlie smiled and relaxed, more delighted to speak with his nemeses than his ally. The trial now took on a strange tenor not only because the defendant got along so well with the prosecutor who was trying to end his life, but also in that the prosecutor was making the same case as the defense attorney, shifting the blame from Charlie to Caril. Rather than questioning Charlie's changing statements, Scheele helped Charlie clarify why he had changed his story by asking, "Now, the reason that you told me to begin with that you shot Carol King was because you were trying to protect Caril Fugate; is that right?"

"Yes, sir."

Scheele asked no more questions. He asked nothing more about the murders, about Charlie's thirst for killing, nothing about what he had done to Carol King, nothing to prove he was sane and therefore eligible for the death penalty. The case against Charlie was a slam dunk, so Scheele was using the last half of this hearing to build a case, and public sentiment, against Caril Fugate.

Gaughan then continued to focus the attention on her. He produced a letter Charlie had written to Elmer Scheele after his interview with Fahrnbruch. This would be his eighth confession, which again offered a contradictory account of his crimes and Caril's role in them. In the letter he told Scheele he didn't mind being convicted of what he had done, but he'd be damned if he would be sentenced for something he hadn't done.

Charlie wrote that when he shot Robert Jensen, his body fell back into the storm cellar. Carol King stood motionless at the top of the stairs. She continued to stand there while Charlie strolled back to the car where Caril Fugate was still sitting in the front seat. She remained there while Charlie reloaded the .22 rifle, took a flashlight and went down into the cellar to see if Robert Jensen was dead. Suddenly, Charlie became frightened and ran up the stairs. As he passed Carol King he told her to get into the basement with the body of her boyfriend. According to Charlie, he ran all the way to the car, jumped in, and, still frightened, drove the car into a ditch. Then he and Caril Fugate returned to the cellar and ordered Carol King to come out.

Charlie wrote that he gave Caril Fugate his .22 to point at Carol King while he went back to the car and jacked it up to get them out of the ditch. While he was working at the tire, he heard a shot. He ran back concerned about what had happened and saw Carol King lying dead. Fugate told him that King had tried to run, so she had shot her. Fugate coldly returned to the car and sat down while Charlie lifted the dead girl's body and took it down to the storm cellar. In this account, he did not explain why Carol's clothes were removed from her body, how she had been stabbed, or whether she had been raped.

Charlie's statement went on to claim that in Wyoming, he had shot Collison several times, but he still had a lot of life left in him. Charlie asked Caril to bring him his gun, but Caril decided to shoot the man herself. Collison said something about having a wife and kids, but Caril said, "That's too bad," and continued to riddle his body with holes. Charlie concluded by implying Caril had done even more, and wrote, "caril fugate was the trigger happy person i ever seen," a quote later repeated by many who believed Caril to be guilty as "the most trigger happy person I ever saw."

Now it became clear why the prosecution had charged Charlie Starkweather with Robert Jensen's murder and not Carol King's. Though he had killed as many as eleven people, they were charging him with only one for a faster trial. It could be easily proven that he had robbed and stolen Robert's car, and that he had killed him for it. But the murder of Carol King, even though she had been brutally raped, would fall on the shoulders of Caril Fugate.

John McArthur sat in the courtroom taking studious notes on his yellow legal pad. He was a creature of habit and he always wrote on the same size of note paper with the same grade of dull pencil. As the spectators around him reacted with animated fascination, he sat stoically watching the proceedings. His eyes would narrow on the witness's face, his head bobbed occasionally as though, while he was thinking to himself, he was really talking, and reacting to his own conclusions.

He studied the prosecution team; his old friend Elmer Scheele who was leading them. John knew what Elmer was doing. He had seen about every trick there was. Once an attorney decided he was going to win, he did everything he could to achieve his goal, no matter the cost to others. John had a healthy respect for the police, sheriffs, and district attorneys who did their jobs with dignity, but he had no respect for those who abused their power, and he took pleasure in bringing them down in court. But this was harder, more personal. Elmer was a friend, and the target of his vengeance was a girl who had had testimony drawn from her before she even knew charges would be levied against her. Now they were implying accusations of her during Charlie's trial, giving her no chance to defend herself. There were no objections from either side, as both had an interest in laying blame on Caril.

John took notes, watched, and waited.

The defense took a little longer to present their case than the prosecution had. Gaughan had to change tactics mid-stream, but once he sufficiently planted the seed that Caril had been the mastermind behind the murders, and Charlie merely her puppet, he was well on his way.

At one point during the questioning a gunshot boomed from another part of the courthouse. Everyone jumped with fear. There was a near panic. Some thought for a moment Charlie had escaped, but he was sitting at the defense table. Others thought someone was coming to rescue him.

Police officers rushed downstairs toward the source of the sound. They found one officer standing at an evidence locker, a look on his face as afraid as they were. He had been moving some of the evidence around and had dropped the shotgun. No one had unloaded it, and the gun had gone off.

The day of closing arguments, crowds waited in line to get a seat. The courtroom was packed. People even waited outside to hear the results. James McArthur, John's son, was allowed to leave school for the day to watch. On his way in through the back stairs he stopped short. Charlie was being brought in wearing shackles on his hands and feet. He could not enter the court bound, so the police stopped him and removed his chains. As they did this, Charlie looked up at James. His icy stare bore through the teenager and gave him chills he never forgot. Such a glance had power, control. James retreated from it and went into the court through a different entrance.

James had a beautiful blond girl with him. Now that his father was in the middle of the trial of the century, James and his siblings had become the center of attention, which was sometimes a curse, and sometimes a blessing. They received death threats on the phone and mean looks at school, but they also became popular curiosities to their classmates and other members of the community. James now gained the attention of Dick Trembath of KMTV who was sitting a few seats down from him in the press section. Since James had taken an interest in his father's work, he was often near the action and met many of the members of the press. But Dick had never met him, and he mistook James for a young reporter. He was quickly corrected by a friend who told Dick he was the son of Caril's lawyer. Dick introduced himself and told James, "Your daddy's really going to have a tough job, Jim. You'll see. Elmer Scheele's very good."

If Dick had been expecting an indifferent and immature teenager, he was soon proven otherwise by Jim's bright enthusiasm. "My dad likes tough jobs," he said with pride.

The closing arguments played out like a battle, with the secondary attorneys skirmishing first to feel out the competition, leaving the primary lawyers to clash with a climactic barrage. Dale Fahrnbruch began, presenting the facts of the case that proved Charles Starkweather had robbed Robert Jensen of his billfold, killed him, then taken his car. William Matschullat, Charlie's second attorney, then rose for the defense. He was also factual, stating that Charles was not mentally capable of telling right from wrong, which was the definition of "not guilty by reason of insanity." This was still their ultimate goal, despite the seeds of doubt they had planted in the jury's heads about Caril's role as ring leader of the murders, and despite Charlie and his family's objections.

After a recess, the main event began. Clement Gaughan presented the emotional side of his case. Some would say he overdid it, but it quickly became evident why he had been so passionate about defending Charlie Starkweather. He spoke about his own childhood and how Charlie reminded him of those struggles he had faced. "I hated everybody and everything," he said, "and I could lick anybody – that society treated me as it treated Charles Starkweather. But the good Lord gave me, possibly, a little better parents." He stood before the jury and orated in a grand, impassioned voice, raising his hands as he gave his confession, "But for the grace of God, I could be sitting there in his place right now!" he said with tears in his eyes. "Do not believe," he continued, "that when the prosecution argues that not guilty by reason of insanity means that some day Charles Starkweather will go free. Not even an act of Congress could ever make that happen. Our society, which spawned this young man, has iron clad, uncompromising rules to ensure the proper punishment of the criminally insane."

Gaughan's religious views made him a strict opponent of the death penalty. He admonished the jury, telling them, "The Bible commandment which says 'Thou shalt not kill' applies just as much to you as to Starkweather." He then gave a description of what would happen if they disobeyed this commandment, "Now, if you decide that revenge must triumph over reason, that two wrongs do make a right, I will ask each of you to come with me when I bring my client to the death house. There, with his trousers cut to his knees, and his arms stripped bear, you will see him strapped in that chair. And watch, as the switch is pulled, we will all stand back in horror as the electricity surges, the smoke comes from his head, and his lifeless body falls forward."

Everyone was listening attentively. Though most had made up their minds about Charlie's guilt and how to punish him, few could claim that they were not moved by Gaughan's passion. Then he turned their attention to Caril Fugate: "If you want the life of this boy, Caril Fugate deserves the same punishment." He did not explain why this was relevant to the case, but it seemed to be an attempt to divert the public's anger at a different target.

Gaughan concluded in bold, dramatic fashion, raising his arms before the jury and stating, "In the name of mercy, and the great commandment, thou shalt not kill, I ask you for the life of Charles Starkweather!" When he was finished, even Charlie was moved. Instead of watching his attorney with annoyance, he seemed close to tears as he stared at this man who had done everything he could to save his life. Gaughan fell back in his chair, having expended every length of energy on the red headed boy who sat beside him.

After that, the court needed another recess, so they left and returned in an hour. Elmer Scheele then stood up and stepped before the jury. He straightened his tall, thin frame and looked at the members of the jury with his gentle, firm eyes behind the horn-rimmed glasses. "That was," he said, "one of the most emotional appeals I have ever heard." He told them that he could be emotional, too, recounting his own experiences. "I could describe how I felt when I had to go to Robert Colvert's home in December and talk to his widow, the pregnant wife of a dead young man… I could describe the sight I saw in the small abandoned outdoor toilet and chicken house behind the Bartlett home… the August Meyer farm and what I found there… the storm cellar and what I saw there." He held up the graphic photograph of the bodies of Robert Jensen and Carol King. It was so horrific it made the jury wince.

"I could take you to the Ward home to tell you what I saw there, and how the relatives felt when they identified the bodies. But I don't want to put you through that. It took me weeks to get those things out of my mind."

Remembering all of this, Elmer Scheele took a deep breath, then let it all out. It was not a performance; it was his own, quiet, dignified way of dealing with such an abhorrent chain of events. "Now let's get our feet back on the ground," he continued. "It is time to face up to our responsibilities." He talked about Starkweather's confessions. He made sure that Caril was mentioned within them, but the blame was still on Charlie. The defense had tried to point out how contradictory they were as proof that he wasn't in his right mind, but Scheele insisted that they were "remarkably parallel except for the early portions when he was first trying to protect Caril Fugate."

Scheele insisted they not let him get away on the insanity plea. "Charlie knows the difference between right and wrong and knows the nature and quality of his acts." He pointed out that the psychiatrists had refused to say that Starkweather was suffering from paranoia. "His own parents will tell you he acted perfectly normal," he said. "The defense tried to hoodwink you into grasping at the straw of insanity… It's ridiculous to place the blame on society and ask you to do something about it."

He told them in his four years as county attorney, he had never asked for the death penalty, "but it is one of the duties I have had to face up to since I took my oath of office… After what this man has inflicted on innocent people and their loved ones, is he a man who can ever be released on society again?"

Finally, just as Gaughan had asked for the life of Charles Starkweather, Elmer Scheele ended by asking for the death penalty.

The jury spent the rest of the day and half of the next day deliberating until, at 2:14 pm, they rang the bell. The court was filled and the verdict was read. Guilty. The death penalty. Charlie took the news with indifference. No one was really surprised. As his parents walked out of the courthouse, his father said to one of the reporters, "The Lord giveth, and the Lord taketh away."

# Chapter Five
## A Quiet Man

John McArthur meandered along the path that tangled through the thin, stiff trees of the woods that surrounded his house on Pioneer Street along the outskirts of Lincoln, his German shepherd Duke at his side. He was deep in thought. This was the restful place where he could go to think, where he could get the blood flowing as he moved among the brushing leaves and whispering grass. He had always wanted to live on a farm, like the homes of his youth among the Sand Hills of western Nebraska where the wide open prairies that Willa Cather had written about stretched out to meet an infinite sky.

They had lived on two farms. The first, a brick and mortar ramshackle called Hardscrabble that lived up to its name, had been destroyed in a tornado that killed his brother Frank. The next, Whitelodge, a more respectable homestead under the shade of an alcove of trees. It was a serene countryside where John could sit under a lone tree and read, his favorite way to occupy himself, which he did most days, or watch the animals with his sister Winnie.

In high school, John found his love for deliberation in debate club and an enjoyment in language through the Latin club. He was the lead in the high school play his junior year, and when other students turned to him as a leader, John formed the fraternity Delta Handa Polka.

During this time, John taught at a nearby grade school, giving every penny he earned to his parents to help take care of the family.

He was close to his mother, Mabel, who had traveled across the prairie in a covered wagon and seen Nebraska grow around her.

She was the third wife of the widowed town doctor, Andrew James McArthur. He was a prominent member of the community, a hard worker, and the inspiration for John's love of books. Andrew was fond of saying, "A book worth reading is a book worth owning," and took the statement so seriously that he sometimes put the purchase of a book before the necessities of the family.

Andrew and Mabel ran the local print shop together, the Northpark Printery, which printed the newspaper they produced together, and other periodicals. They had no car to distribute their paper; their only means of transportation was a blind horse, to which they occasionally attached a buggy if they needed to carry anyone, such as a patient. For house calls they had a telephone, but it rarely got used since they were one of the first in the county to get one.

Andrew was famous for his integrity. People would talk years later of the time he turned away the Ku Klux Klan while he was treating a black man. John never forgot how his father risked his own life to stand up for what was right, which became the reason he grew up to study law.

When John graduated high school in 1928 at the age of 18, he received a $25 scholarship for the University of Nebraska in Lincoln. He packed up his Model T Ford, which he had recently bought, (the blind horse might not have found its way,) and prepared to leave. His mother gave him five dollars to start his new life, and bade him farewell.

John used the money efficiently, until he got a job at a mortuary where he lived and worked while he made his way through college.

One of his closest friends was an ex-Nebraska football player named Corby Holbert. Loud and bombastic, Corby was the opposite of John, which seemed to be why John liked him so much. With lifetime season tickets to the football games, a possession worth gold in Nebraska, Corby often took his friend and made as much noise as he could while John sat quietly and chuckled at his antics. At the Orange Bowl, Corby talked his way into the locker room and introduced John to all the players, despite the fact that Corby didn't know any of them.

Once, in court, Corby, excited that he would be doing the same job as his friend, called himself to the witness stand and asked himself questions, ending only when he asked the judge for a five minute recess so he could consult with his client.

In 1930, Corby introduced John to Ruby Schaefer, a woman who did not really like Corby, but talked to him with a polite indignation which Corby did not pick up on.

Ruby was a farm woman from the prairies of Kansas who was ambitious and tough. Whether doing twelve-hour shifts as an in-house nurse, or going to disaster areas with the Red Cross, Ruby was a leader, and one could always see the members of the teams she worked with turning to her.

John was attracted to her instantly. He wrote later why she had taken his heart so quickly: "We had listened to the same kind of meadowlark in summer, and the same kind of coyote howl in winter. We were used to the same kind of dust storms, rain storms, wind storms, and snow storms. We had everything in common, from freckles to frostbite."

Between Ruby's work at the hospital and John's law school studies, the couple had very little time together, but they stole opportunities to see each other when they could. They were married in 1934 on a hot summer day. It was a simple affair in front of a justice of the peace. They had no family or friends present, and John had to pick a stranger off the street to serve as witness. Afterward, their honeymoon was at an ice cream shop where they shared the largest malt available.

Their biggest difficulty was figuring out where to live. Ruby loved to socialize and wanted to live in the city while John wanted to live on a farm the way his parents had. They tried it John's way, living on an acreage outside of town where they could raise pigs, horses, and other animals. John loved this sort of life, but he was no farmer. He struggled with maintenance. Physical chores were not his talent. Cerebral and bookish, he could handle theory far more than he could work with tools, so he had to do other work to make ends meet.

As the children grew up, they enjoyed the spacious room of the farm, much the way John had enjoyed it. John Jr. and James, both very young, got into trouble disturbing the neighbor's cows. One climbed on the animal and held on for dear life while the other twisted the tail like a crank to send it racing off across the pasture.

But his little utopia could not last. Ruby pointed out the many failures, and the massive chores John simply could not keep up with while running a law business. One day, when John was placing a door on a barn, he hammered the wood on the frame several times, and the entire rest of the barn crashed to the ground. All that remained standing was the doorway he had been hammering into place. "Okay, that's it!" he conceded to his wife. "We're moving to Lincoln!" And so they moved into a small house in the suburbs close to downtown.

At first, John supplemented their income with a restaurant he named The Hotel d'Hamburger. His hands smelled of onions so badly when he came home that he had to tuck them under the pillows to be able to sleep.

The hamburger shop did not work out, and so, in 1935, John began his law practice. He started by running for county attorney, placing up signs with his high school photograph around town. He didn't want to win; he in fact tried to avoid votes. The only reason he ran was because lawyers were not allowed to advertise, and so would-be attorneys had to find creative ways to tell the public who they were. His efforts got the attention of Merril Reller, who was already established with an office, and they set up a practice together. Reller respected John's vast knowledge and his ability to inspire through carefully chosen words, a skill Reller lacked. Reller was a knowledgeable, and even shrewd attorney, was great with money and investments, but when it came to speaking, he was deficient in charisma, often rambled and had difficulty getting to the point.

The two shared an uncanny ability to connect with people, though each did it in his own way. John was like a master thespian, changing the manner in which he spoke to match the person he was talking to. If it was a well-educated person from elite society, he utilized his extensive inner library of words. If it was a blue collar worker, he could talk with them about cars, or football, for which he was a passionate fan. If it was a farmer, he could relate to them from his own experiences. Reller, on the other hand, was completely transparent. He was always very genuine, and never altered his personality for any person. Sometimes he said things people didn't want to hear, but his sincerity was clear, and people appreciated and respected his candor.

John had a trademark style in court that involved asking a witness a series of questions that seemed innocent enough so they would answer freely. He would then turn the questioning to a different subject for a while before returning to the subject at hand. He then used the answers from the innocent questions to trip up the witness. For instance, when an officer on the witness stand once said he knew what time something had occurred because he always noted the time when he looked at a clock, John asked him to describe the clock. The officer described it, and John said, "So it looked like the clock behind you." The man glanced at it and said yes. John took him through a series of irrelevant questions, then turned suddenly on the man and said, "Now when you looked back at the clock a few minutes ago, what time was it?" The man couldn't answer, and John won the case.

He was a quiet man, often distant, even from his family. He chose his words carefully, condensing them to a powerful, brief core that spoke more than most people could utter in a whole speech. His lessons to his children were short and to the point. His sense of humor was dry, and sometimes misunderstood.

When he once came home with a switch blade, evidence from one of his trials, he held it up in front of his family at the dinner table. "Does anyone have any enemies?" he asked. Five-year-old Ben raised his tiny hand, and John allowed him to look it over. The next day, when the switch blade was missing, his wife panicked, and even rushed to the school thinking Ben had taken it to show and tell, but John had returned it to the office.

John had only one suit, and often mismatched socks, unless Ruby happened to notice them before he left. When he felt something needed to be done, or if someone was in need, he often helped without telling anyone. Once, when an elderly woman in town died, the family learned that John had been paying her mortgage for years, ever since her husband had died so she could continue living in the house they had shared. They saw hints of other charitable ventures, but John would not tell them anything more, not even his wife.

Although he could quote any line from the Bible, John was not a religious man, none of his family had ever been. One of his brothers even ran a well-known agnostic newspaper. But his wife was a staunch Seventh-day Adventist, and John agreed to raise their children under the faith, though he did not follow many of the practices himself. Seventh-day Adventism was a strong proponent of health, and though he didn't drink, he smoked like a chimney. And even though the television was supposed to be off for much of the weekend, John refused to give up watching the fights and Sid Caesar on Friday nights or the Cornhusker football game on Saturday mornings.

He liked to keep things simple. He was conservative with his money, a product of growing up during the Great Depression. When one of his sons asked him about going into the stock market, John warned "stocks are something where you give someone your money and they give you a piece of paper that says they have your money."

Moralistic and with a deep sense of justice, John's practice gained a reputation of integrity even among his rivals in court. He believed strongly in the Constitution, and could explain every portion of constitutional law in detail. He especially believed in every person's right to representation in court, and that such representation came with a certain responsibility to fairness. It was not up to the attorney to trick the law, but rather to use the law to express his client's point of view. He abhorred it when other attorneys bent the rules. He especially hated it when police officers abused their power, and he saved his own tricks for moments when he knew they were lying.

John's office was small, crowded, and modest. Though he had won many awards and graduated at the top of his class in both college and law school, the only thing he had framed on his wall was his high school diploma, which he told friends he had placed up proudly so that "people will know I'm educated." The office was so diminutive, in fact, that he often met clients at Virginia's, a nearby café. He told them that it was because meetings there could be a lot more informal, but in truth there was more space in a booth than there was in his entire office. Although he was primarily a divorce attorney, handling half of the divorces in the region, he also took other cases that fascinated him. Before Caril, his most famous case was when he represented a girl who was charging Errol Flynn with statutory rape, a case made all the more ironic because Ruby was friends with Flynn's agent.

John was typically seen driving older, less elegant cars around town because he always made sure Ruby had the nice car. The only car she did not like was a limo he had received as payment from a mortuary. But she drove it because it fit their six children, who enjoyed the car because they could enter through the "dead man's door." Their family had grown so large by this point that John was fond of saying, "Now count the kids while I'm gone."

Things were going well for them, but John still pined for the country. The city was too confining for his spirit, and he longed for a large yard and quiet surroundings. So he and Ruby compromised on a house they had built just south of town in the solitude of the woods just one mile away from the prison where John sometimes had to visit his clients. It was a tranquil, one-story abode with a basement furnished with shag carpet. It was charming, and slightly rustic both inside and out. Ruby adored antiques, collecting items from all over the world. John's contribution usually involved gifts from clients who could not afford his services and paid through a bartering system.

John paced through these rooms relentlessly whenever he had a lot on his mind, speaking in a low growl to himself, smoking his cigarette and rolling a silver dollar through his fingers so much that the facing wore off. He occasionally flipped it in the air, usually unconsciously, and always caught it, sometimes behind his back without ever looking up or breaking his pace. There were even times in the middle of the night when Ruby would wake from sleep to the sound of John pacing the floor, the occasional 'ding' ringing from the coin and the low, barely audible rumble of his voice. Sometimes the coin hit the ceiling, causing not only a thudding noise, but leaving an indentation. Over the years, the ceiling in the living room was pocked by numerous scars. When Ruby at last had enough of this, John was banished to the woods, which was fine with him. The fresh air cleared his mind, and he was able to think his way through problems.

He needed it now more than ever. With most of the city against him, he had received more death threats than he could count for merely accepting the job as Caril Fugate's attorney, and now he actually believed in her innocence - a belief that would cause innumerable troubles for himself, his family and his law practice. Merril Reller had been very supportive. He never once questioned John's decision to accept the case, and he even took the rest of the practice's work load so John could focus on Caril's defense.

John had appealed the court's rejection of his request to move the trial to juvenile court. Professor Belsheim, the Dean of Wesleyan University who had first been appointed to represent Caril, helped John try to convince the State Supreme Court that Caril, being a minor, by law was entitled to have a trial in juvenile court, but the appeal had failed. They were going to try her as an adult. What now troubled him more was the court's refusal to allow Caril a different venue. John knew she would never receive a fair trial in Nebraska, the emotions were simply too strong. Everyone had drawn their own conclusions based on the fears they had felt during the murders. Executing Charlie simply wasn't enough for them - they wanted more. John tried to mitigate this and hastily requested the date of her trial be pushed to the following spring when tempers had cooled. The State Supreme Court denied this request, too, claiming that they were doing what was in Caril's best interest by giving her a speedy trial.

The name McArthur was becoming synonymous with Fugate, and even Starkweather. Some of the McArthur children were met with open hostility from strangers, occasionally from friends, and even from teachers in school. Even at Virginia's, which was owned and managed by Caril's cousin, they were met with unwelcome stares, and fewer people walked up to John. Ruby also had difficulties. She had always placed great importance in her social circles, but now she was met with scorn by friends and other members of the community.

John's family was still receiving death threats in their home. Their youngest daughter, Linda, merely thirteen years old, had answered the call of one of the threats. The voice on the other end asked how her father could defend Caril Fugate, and before she could answer he told her that he was going to kill the entire McArthur family.

Linda was petrified. The whole family was frightened. But the kids trusted their father, even worshipped him, and they had faith in his convictions. Though four of the kids were now in their rebellious teen years, they knew what he was standing for was important, and they stood with him, though it often meant humiliation among their friends.

John began to get mail right away, most of it negative, but some of it very curious. Many news organizations wanted to learn whatever they could. He wrote back to only a few. To a Mrs. Frances Herling of Santa Cruz, California, he wrote:

*I find in this case a large number of people who think it is not possible for this young girl to be guilty of anything. On the other hand I also find a large number of people who are sure she is guilty because of something they read in the newspapers or heard on the radio. As far as I am concerned both points of view are wrong. I have examined into this case somewhat and I am unable at this time to form an opinion. I think the fair thing to do is to reserve judgment until both sides have been fully heard.*

John knew that he needed to turn public sentiment in Caril's favor, both for her sake, and for the sake of his family. But first he needed to learn more about the girl herself. Her family was mostly dead. At her school, many children were claiming to have known her, and hateful rumors were spreading about what a rotten child she had been, but the truth was that she had been timid and unpopular. Most kids at her school had never even noticed her until she became headline news and they learned that she was their classmate.

Some of the only people who had really spent time with her after the murders were the police in Wyoming. They had seen her at her most vulnerable, when she had first escaped from Starkweather. John decided to take a trip to talk with them, but he wanted to bring someone along.

\*     \*     \*

James was known by many as "The Road Runner" because he was so thin and liked to run everywhere. He was neither suave nor popular. He was studious, mature beyond his years, and passionate about his interests, especially history and English. Having grown up with a speech impediment, he did not have his father's gift for oration.

This difficulty had caused him to pull back until his junior year of high school when he went away to boarding school and made it on his own for a time. He had returned with a renewed sense of confidence, and he enjoyed debating with teachers at his Seventh-day Adventist private school. He spoke at their level more than he did with other students, with whom he often did not have a lot in common. His favorite topic was English, in which he often traded puns and sparred over semantics with the teacher, Jerry Wiley. Wiley admired and respected James' father, and saw many of the same qualities in his student.

Alternatively, James' religion teacher, Neville George, was openly critical of James' father in front of the students. He belittled James, and lectured about what a terrible thing his father was doing. He said that people like Caril didn't deserve representation, and anyone who dared to defend her shared in her guilt.

James was patient and said nothing. But when he received an F on a test where others who had plainly done worse got A's, James fired back. He stood up, interrupted class, and confronted Mr. George in front of the other students. Like a veteran attorney, he demanded the teacher show just cause for having given him a low grade. Mr. George tried to brush him off, but it only made James bolder. He knew that if George could stand by his claim, he would have already sent him to the principal's office, so he continued to insist that he prove that he deserved to get such a low grade. Mr. George did not admit to doing wrong, but later James found his grade changed to an A.

James was growing more interested in following his father's footsteps and becoming a lawyer, which was discouraged at his school. Seventh-day Adventism taught that attorneys were nothing short of crooks, and advised its members to steer clear of the profession for moral reasons.

But now sixteen years old, James wanted to know more about his father's job. John took him once to visit Caril. James was nervous and didn't know what to say, but John reassured him by saying, "Just ask her anything. She's very open." And James found that to be the truth. They were close in age, so they could relate in many ways. They were also similar in that they were a little shy at first, but they both opened up a great deal as they got to talking; she in a more direct and forthright manner, James more animated and fervent.

When John invited James to go with him to Wyoming, he jumped at the chance. It was a full day's journey across the flat middle of the state, and then northward across the Sand Hills where John had grown up. James had been here before when he was younger to visit his grandmother, but he found a new appreciation for the area that comes with age. Most importantly, he saw it now from his father's point of view. This was the first time in his life when he'd had so much time alone with his father. James had grown up in the middle of the family with five other siblings vying for their father's attention. Now, in the placid air of western Nebraska, he met the quiet man that was his father, and knew him for the first time as a person. There was a certain understated excitement that overcame John when he spoke of his native soil. He told James that the land in the Sand Hills was unique, formed over millions of years in a fashion unseen anywhere else in the world. He described the different areas, how the sharp gullies of the Wild Cat Hills to the south differed from the rippling, smooth slopes of the north.

John also opened up about his passion for his work; his love for the theory of law, which he referred to as "the practical application of philosophy." Being an attorney was not just a job to him, it was a responsibility. He saw himself as a protector of the Constitution. He didn't always like his clients and sometimes knew they were guilty. He *represented* a client, but he *defended* the Constitution, and his clients' rights were a part of that equation; which meant he had a responsibility to not only stand up for their rights, but to do it honorably.

John's and James' path followed the route Charlie and Caril had taken several months earlier. It was a grand adventure for James, who collected the silver dollars that were given as change at the old-fashioned hotels where they stayed. It was as though they were heading back in time. The further they went, the more it seemed like the old west. People even dressed in cowboy boots and hats, something James had only seen in the movies.

The last stretch of road between Douglas and Casper, Wyoming was an empty two lane highway. This was where Charlie had killed his last victim, and Caril had run and jumped into Officer Bill Romer's squad car.

John and James began their interviews with Romer. He seemed very sympathetic to Caril, describing her as frantic and eager to get away from Charlie when she had jumped into his car. At first, Romer had not been able to distinguish what she was saying until he made out the word "Starkweather," and then he had frozen, scared stiff by the prospect of coming face to face with the infamous mass murderer. When Charlie jumped into his car and drove away, Romer had called ahead to other officers in Douglas, about twenty miles away, and they took up the chase from there. Romer was confirming everything Caril had said, word for word. Their interview was then cut off by a phone call Romer had to take.

When he hung up, he apologized to John and James and said he had to go somewhere. About two hours later he returned and explained that a man had committed suicide inside his brand new Buick. Romer had to go to the car to investigate, but he asked John if they would like to go with him. John still had things he wanted to talk with Romer about, so he and James joined Romer.

James never forgot the sight. The Buick, polished and new on the outside, was filled with blood on the inside. Small chunks of brain and bone still clung to the ceiling. The man had literally blown his own head clear off with a shotgun.

After Romer concluded his investigation, he and John resumed their conversation about Caril. His story continued to coincide identically with hers. He told them he drove Caril to Douglas and placed her in the jail. She asked about her parents several times. Were they safe? Were they hurt? He didn't answer, he just told her to remain calm, that everything would be okay.

John later spoke with Earl Heflin, the sheriff who had run Charlie to ground, and his wife. He was a law man straight out of western movies, with a swagger and a directness akin to John Wayne. He had told Starkweather to get down on the ground, and when Charlie refused, Heflin had fired between his legs. Starkweather dropped in an instant. Even though Caril had been a prisoner inside their home, the Heflins also were very sympathetic toward her. They told John and James it was clear to them that she had not been with

Charlie willingly. She was shaken up, very distraught over everything that had happened, and relieved that it was all over. But she continuously asked for her family, which the Heflins didn't know how to answer, so they left it for the Nebraska police, who were on their way.

When Nebraska's Sheriff Karnopp and his wife Gertrude showed up along with Detective Eugene Masters and Elmer Scheele, the Heflins were surprised at how much they were set against Caril. They immediately began describing a hardened, evil criminal who didn't even remotely resemble the timid, frightened girl they had in their jail. They told the Heflins that Caril had killed her parents, and helped Charlie kill many others, and brushed it off when the Heflins informed them that Caril had asked if her family was okay. The Heflins became confused as to why they were so insistent on painting Caril in a negative light.

Back in Lincoln, Scheele, Sheriff Karnopp, and his wife had made a number of statements to the newspapers, claiming that Caril had said and done some things while the Heflins were in the room, and both Earl and his wife said that those statements simply were not true. Gertrude Karnopp in particular had claimed that the Heflins had made statements against Caril that they wouldn't have said, and besides, Mrs. Karnopp hadn't even been in the room. This was especially unsettling for John since these statements were being printed as fact in the Lincoln papers and believed by most people in Nebraska, some of whom would inevitably wind up in the jury.

John talked with them about the note they had found in the pocket of the jacket Caril was wearing. The Heflins told John that the note had been written by Caril and said she was a prisoner and asked for someone to "get help." It could have been proof that Caril was trying to escape. Scheele had asked the Heflins to mail the note to his office. They did, and the note then disappeared forever.

As James and John went throughout Casper and Douglas they experienced the exact opposite of what they experienced in Lincoln. People everywhere believed Caril had been Charlie's hostage, and they did not understand why the Nebraska authorities were so set against her.

By the time they were finished in Wyoming, James was completely convinced of Caril's innocence. As they took the northern route back to Lincoln, stopping in to see one of John's clients on a farm, James realized that he had grown in ways he had never expected, seeing a side of his father that is typically reserved only for close friends. His respect for him abounded as a man, as well as a father. And just as importantly, his own desire to follow in his footsteps was solidified.

*     *     *

With his interest in his father's business peaked, James was now very attentive when he drove past the police station and the penitentiary before he reached home. He knew who many of the officers were and he saw them enter and leave on their various shifts. He got to know a lot of the schedules and the usual procedures.

Then one day something just seemed out of place. He saw a deputy sheriff's car pull out in front of him. He recognized the driver, Les Hansen, someone he knew quite well. But the passenger in the back seemed unusual. He had bright red, almost orange hair. James had seen only two people with hair that shade, Lucille Ball and Charlie Starkweather. It certainly wasn't the former, and Charlie was supposed to be in solitary confinement. James couldn't believe his eyes. Bringing Starkweather out of his cell would be a major breach in police procedure and a huge scandal. He drove up closer to get a better look, expecting to be mistaken. But the closer he got, the more certain he was that this was Charlie in the back of the police car ahead of him. Suddenly the police car sped up, pulling away from James. His teenage curiosity getting the better of him, James accelerated to get a look at the passenger. The police car sped up even more, and James took chase. It was an unusual pursuit, a 16-year-old boy in a shiny Ford chasing a squad car down a one-way street. James knew that he could be in trouble for doing this, but James knew that an officer would not pull him over while he had a prisoner in the backseat, especially if that prisoner was who James was certain it was.

Without warning, the officer quickly pulled over to the left and stopped. As James sped by, he looked over and spotted the man in the backseat staring back at him. It was the steely eyes of Charlie Starkweather following him as he passed; James was certain beyond any shadow of a doubt. He slowed down and watched through the rear view mirror. He wanted to see where these officers were taking Charlie. They started their car very torpidly, and now the pursuit reversed, with James driving slowly in front, hoping for the officer to pass him so he could get another look.

James reached a line of barricades at South Street. Ninth was closed for several blocks, so James took the detour around. He continued at a snail's pace, hoping the police car would come down that road and pass him. He watched in the rear view mirror as the police car reached the corner. But instead of turning, it drove around the barricades and onto the closed road.

James sped up, racing around the detour until it brought him back to Ninth Street on Van Dorn where the barricades ended. There he waited, looking down the road under construction. It was rough and torn up. Any car driving down it would surely have had to slow down. But after he waited for several minutes, it became clear that the police car had already gone by while he was taking the detour.

James continued down Ninth Street until it led him past the penitentiary. He peered into the parking lot. Unable to spot Starkweather, he continued home. There he told his father about what he had seen.

"Oh, you must be mistaken," John told him with a chuckle. He explained that it would be not only highly irregular for them to do such a thing, but very illegal. He couldn't imagine any reason why they would take a man on death row, especially Starkweather, out for a drive. James insisted, but no matter how much he swore about what he had seen, John simply didn't believe him.

*     *     *

John continued to take his walks in the woods with his dog, flipping his coin, talking to himself, and thinking.

His wife Ruby was now collecting 'True Detective' magazines that featured Caril and Charlie's stories in it. Most of what was reported in every periodical was based on rumors and often lies. It was hard for the public to know the difference, and they didn't try. Caril was being successfully painted as a hardened killer, as evil and twisted as Charlie.

It was well that Reller had taken charge of all the rest of the cases, as this one was sucking up all of John's time and energy. They were still receiving death threats and weren't surprised one day to find a rock with a note attached to it in their front yard. When one of the children brought it to John, he assumed it was another threat, but it turned out to be a request for representation. The inmates of the nearby prison had learned that this famous attorney lived only a mile away, and that his house was along their route to go to work on a farm where they picked tomatoes and corn. En route, one of them had attached a note to a rock asking for John to represent him and had thrown it onto the front lawn. John passed the note on to Reller so he could take care of it while John continued to concentrate on the case that seemed impossible to win.

Public sentiment was so greatly against Caril that John knew they didn't have a chance locally. Even if John could find a jury of people who could side with Caril, they could not return home to families who were convinced of her guilt. Scheele and his team were using the media to convict her before the trial had even begun. They sent out press releases, held conferences, and made statements about their side of the story. Most of what they said was based on information Charlie was feeding them, though they didn't reveal that he was the source. Since no one could object to these statements, they had gone into the public record, and the minds of the people.

John wanted to keep everything in the courtroom. He considered airing the dirty laundry of the law into the public to be tacky and inappropriate. He didn't even advertise beyond a two inch picture of his building in the yellow pages. The last thing he wanted to do was begin a war of words through the media. But he also knew that the jury would be chosen from the people of the community, and if one side of the story was being presented to them before the trial began and not the other, Caril wouldn't stand a chance.

Ninette Beaver had been pushing him for months to grant an interview with Caril to her boss at KMTV, Floyd Kalber, but John had refused. He was turning down all interviews. Merril Reller stood by him on this, but as the prosecution continued to try Caril in the press, he began to see the necessity of what had to be done. This had turned into a case of international importance. News organizations from every state, and even other countries, were reporting what came out of the Nebraska papers as fact. Although he'd been denied a change of venue, John hoped that, should the verdict come back as guilty, he would appeal it out of Nebraska where he could get a more unprejudiced forum, and he didn't want the entire country against her. So at last John agreed to allow an interview, but only one. He didn't want Caril to endure the ordeal multiple times, so, though he would allow other cameras and reporters to be there to record the event, only one reporter would be able to actually speak with her.

The only question was who would that one person be? Every reporter in the world wanted this interview. Top anchormen from the highest news media in New York were clamoring for the opportunity. The most important thing to John was that it be someone impartial who would give Caril a fair chance to tell her side of the story. He was not trying to coddle her, nor bend the truth. John wanted to be up front and honest, and he knew Caril would do just that. But most reporters had proven that they had made their minds up long ago with whatever side was more sensational and sold more newspapers. He wanted someone with enough integrity to go after the truth instead of ratings, and that was hard to find. But John knew just the person.

# Chapter Six
## Ninette Beaver

Ninette Beaver never meant to go into journalism. She had been a sociology major from Iowa. She expected to raise a family with her husband, like most women in the 1950s. When she was 28, a friend asked her to cover for him at the Des Moines Register while he recovered from an illness. The position was supposed to be temporary, but as the year passed, they kept her on. She was one of the first and only female members of the staff. Yet no one at the paper had any qualms about her working there. She was simply one of the guys.

When television journalism came along, neither Ninette nor the other members of her paper took it very seriously. Television was not only a new medium, it's very future was uncertain. Few people across the country could afford one, the image was small and blurry, and its intended use was entertainment. Respected journalists such as Edward R. Murrow were making the jump, but it would be a long time before people would take the medium seriously enough to get their information from a box. They typically turned on the TV to watch Jack Benny or 'The Honeymooners'. If they wanted the news, they'd read the paper.

In Omaha, the television station KMTV had lost a reporter, and they needed someone who lived in Iowa to cover Council Bluffs, which sat across the Missouri River. They were a small station, just getting started. They didn't even have sound equipment for their field reporters. Yet, when they asked Ninette to cover Council Bluffs for them, she could hardly refuse this opportunity to explore a new field. And the position was temporary, so she could dabble her feet without dedicating her life to it.

Though it was new and exciting, Ninette's experience did not convince her that TV could compete with the well-established, reliable newspapers and periodicals. The equipment, what little they had of it, often broke down, and only one or two people knew how to run it, let alone fix it. In general, it seemed that the staff was making it up as they went along, which, in many ways, they were; and they did it with the few resources they had available. They were all pioneers in a new and strange world.

Again, she was one woman among a large team of men in a highly male dominated career. But, like with the Des Moines Register, no one made any mention of it. She was simply their Iowa correspondent, and everyone respected her. She occasionally met people on interviews that had difficulty accepting a female reporter, but it was rare. Her biggest challenge was getting used to making stories within a certain length of time rather than a certain size margin on the page. Words were treated differently, much of it based on who was speaking rather than the typeface.

Soon she was brought into the Omaha office to work, and another temporary assignment turned into a career for her. There, she assisted most of the men who anchored the broadcast or went out onto the field. She worked closest with Floyd Kalber, one of the chief anchors. She delivered teletype, made phone calls, ran errands, and was rarely out in the field anymore. At last the staff received their first microphones and other sound equipment the reporters could use on location. Only one man, Jim Roberts, actually knew how to use them. He was still training the others on the equipment a week after they had received it when the Starkweather murders occurred.

In the aftermath of the tragedy, every reporter of every media wanted to interview the Starkweather family, but all were refused.

Ninette sat in the car with Jerry Hansen, a reporter she was assisting, in front of the Starkweather home on the north side of Lincoln on a cold, February day. They were only a few blocks from the courthouse and jail, where Charlie was being held.

Guy and Helen Starkweather's son was only 19-years-old, and now he was the most reviled and feared criminal in the world. This would not be an easy interview. And now it was Jerry's job to ask them how they felt. Ninette had borrowed a camera from a competitor's station. This was common during the days when there were more story ideas to go around than cameras, but if they had known Ninette was going to the Starkweather home, they may have insisted on tagging along, which is why she had not mentioned it. But she knew that showing up at the door with the cameras would be too intrusive. Also, she thought that perhaps the Starkweathers might open up to her more than they would to a man, so even though she was supposed to be there as Jerry's assistant, she suggested that she talk to them first. Jerry agreed, and Ninette approached the house. She had no idea what she would say.

She knocked on the door and waited. When the Starkweathers answered, they were not as Ninette had expected. Though from a poor neighborhood, they had pride in their home, and in the way they dressed. They were a very average, normal couple, though very distraught. Helen Starkweather, a petite woman with tight blonde hair, looked as though she had not gotten much sleep lately. Her husband Guy, gaunt, with a dark mustache and angular features, stood close, ready to jump to her defense if need be, though he had been worn down by the past several days as well.

Ninette told them who she was, and that she'd like to talk with them about their son. They told her that they didn't have anything to tell the press. "I understand perfectly," she responded, "but I had to ask. That's my job." Then, after a polite pause, she asked, "I wonder if you could let me use your phone. I promised my sister that I'd call her as soon as I got here from Omaha and I think she might be worried." They invited her in and Helen led Ninette to the kitchen where the phone sat, then waited while Ninette dialed. "Hi, Joanne!" she said when her sister answered. "I just wanted to let you know that I'm in Lincoln safe and sound."

Her sister was silent. She had seen Ninette fifteen minutes earlier, just before she left for the Starkweather home. "You're in trouble," she said. "Do you want me to call the police?"

"Oh, no. Everything's fine. We were just late getting out of Omaha."

"Okay," Joanne answered. "Let me guess. You're at the Starkweathers' house and you're trying to keep your foot in the door."

"Right."

"I hope you choke. But call me as soon as you get out of there."

"Right. I'll see you this afternoon." And Ninette hung up. She thanked Mrs. Starkweather, who offered her a cup of coffee.

"Why, thank you very much," Ninette said. "I really could use a cup."

They sat down at the kitchen table along with Guy. "I'm really sorry we had to pester you folks this morning, but it's part of our job, you know," Ninette told them in her amiable, yet forthright manner in which she always excelled. "I guess you'll be hounded by reporters from now on. They'll be asking all sorts of questions about your son and how you feel about what happened. I know it will be difficult."

Helen nodded. Ninette observed her and knew this was the moment to ask.

"You know," she said, "one thing about a television interview is that you are the one saying what you want said, in your own words and in your own way. It's not so hard, really. We could just sort of talk, the way we're talking now."

A few minutes later, the camera was set up in the dining room and Ninette was holding the microphone as she sat talking with Guy and Helen Starkweather. They opened up to her as they had not done with any other reporter.

\*       \*       \*

John watched the interview on TV. He was fascinated, as many people were, by how normal the Starkweathers seemed. But he was also impressed with Ninette's forthright integrity. KMTV had also struck John as a station of higher principle, and this was one woman who was more interested in the truth than in jumping to judgment.

Though she was now at the center of what was happening, Ninette continued to try to get an interview with Charlie for Floyd.

She worked for him, and never tried to build her own career through it. Nevertheless, Guy and Helen trusted Ninette more, and they did a second interview exclusively with her. She visited them every day, whether by phone or in person, and they promised to get her boss an exclusive interview with Charlie. They talked with him every morning, but he never granted it. Instead, he was meeting with Lincoln Journal reporter Marjorie Marlette, and Dr. James M. Reinhardt, a professor of criminology who was writing down his findings about Charlie to later be published in a book.

Charlie told Reinhardt about visions he saw, such as when he would walk in the woods and the flowers would sing to him. Charlie fantasized about killing all the people on earth, then living in peace with the animals. According to Reinhardt, Charlie believed that, though he walked among men, he did not belong to their world. To him, the world of men was symbolized by the expensive Cornhusker Hotel restaurant in which others sat and ate fine food while he could only stand outside in the cold Nebraska wind and gaze through the window. He continued to explain that Charlie had planned to have Caril with him all along, and by leading a life of crime, he could be free of their families, his job, and everyone who looked down on him.

Charlie told Reinhardt that there was nothing he loved more than the feel of a gun in his hand, and he bragged about what a good shot he was, despite his bad eyesight, and that he shot from the hip rather than taking aim.

He also opened up about his childhood to Reinhardt, about his family of six brothers and one sister. He told him about his earliest memories of getting to know people outside his family, when he went off to Saratoga Elementary School. He described the isolation, the relentless teasing about his hair, his bow legs, and his speech impediment. He described his first day, when he went into a toy house where two other children were playing. The other children left the house and went to the teacher, telling her that Charlie had bullied them and made them leave. He was made to sit at a table alone, and for days after that, even when children could sit with him, they chose not to.

Marjorie Marlette, who usually went by Marj, seemed to grow sympathetic to Charlie, as reflected in her writing about him. She quoted a poem that Charlie wrote for his mother, "The stranger asks no craeter clory till life is through than to spend one minute in wilderness." As her compassion for Charlie grew, her acrimony of Caril swelled. She presented what Charlie said as truth, including blaming Caril for causing the entire murder spree. She also turned on Reinhardt, reporting that he occasionally asked embarrassing questions of Charlie in an attempt to anger him and elicit a vengeful response. Whether this was true or not is uncertain, as much of what Marlette reported was unsubstantiated, but there are parts of Reinhardt's book that, like Marlette's writings, do not sound like Charlie's voice.

Ninette, meanwhile, only saw Charlie during his trial. She was there every day listening intently to the proceedings. She spotted John McArthur sitting in the front row taking copious notes on the yellow legal pad he always had with him. He wrote in pencil until long after it had worn dull and flat. She also saw his son James in the press box with the reporters on occasion. He appeared to Ninette to be bright, enthusiastic, even bubbly. Highly animated, James would move his arms around as he described details of his father's work. Ninette knew that her best chance at getting to John was through James, and she spent as much time talking with the teenager as she could.

After Charlie's conviction there was a break for several months before Caril would be tried. Many of the reporters were taking their vacations because they knew they wouldn't have a chance once the Fugate trial began. Her case was much more complicated than Charlie's, and would require more time. Ninette took the opportunity to get to know John better. She began calling and visiting his office, asking him about details regarding the Starkweather case and studying legal terminology.

She was impressed with how strongly he believed in Caril's innocence. John explained to Ninette that it's not just a matter of what happened. It was about her state of mind at the time. She was a frightened girl whose mind was manipulated by a vicious killer, a man who had recently been her boyfriend. Ninette tried to convince John to allow an interview between Caril and her boss. She believed in John's strong convictions, and earnestly thought Caril should have a chance to tell her side of the story.

One day Ninette blurted out to him, "John, people have made up their minds already about whether the girl is guilty or not. And the longer you keep her out of sight, the more suspicious they become." Merril Reller joined the discussion, standing by John's decision as he often did. Ninette found herself having to confront both of them with the truth she felt they were not seeing.

"Look," she said, "if the girl has a story, you should let her tell it. Nobody knows anything, except that she was with Starkweather. The longer you wait, the more people will think that she's using this time to concoct something. Why don't you let Floyd interview her? He'll get the story out of her and everybody will believe it."

They shook their heads. She wasn't convincing them. They didn't want to try this case through the media. Even if it would be effective, it wasn't ethical.

"Besides," she continued, "you know that everyone is saying she's pregnant. It's been over six months since they were captured and, if you don't let people get a look at her pretty soon, you'll never be able to stop those rumors."

They continued to say no. Ninette left them believing she had failed, but in truth, she was beginning to get through to the two lawyers.

Then McArthur and Reller were hit with a new surprise. The facility where Caril was being kept cut her hair against her will. It made her look fifteen years older. The psychiatric ward had the right to make an inmate shorten her hair in the name of hygiene, but there was no reason to believe that hygiene was an issue in this instance. John was infuriated. There could be no doubt now that the entire legal system was more interested in convicting her than it was in discovering the truth.

The hair cutting incident came just before her arraignment, so there was no time to grow it out again in time to remind jurors that this was the youngest child in United States history to be charged with first degree murder.

Now she would be fighting for her life. If found guilty, she would receive either life in prison, or the death penalty. She could legitimately be executed before even reaching the proper age of being tried. The actual charge was accomplice to the robbery and murder of

Robert Jensen. It was a shrewd move by Elmer Scheele, as it would be much easier to prove, and at the time, a person convicted as an accomplice to murder received the same sentence as the killer. And that's exactly what Charlie wanted. Speaking from his cell, he declared, "When I go to the chair, I want Caril sitting right there on my lap!"

The charges were announced on television. As Ninette watched the network report from the local station, she knew that John had no choice. He had to put Caril in front of a camera to tell her side. Certainly, John had to know how important public opinion was, especially considering the fact that the jury would be chosen from that public.

She continued to make the hour long drive to Lincoln where she encouraged John to accept the interview with Floyd. John continued to respectfully turn her down. He knew what opening such a Pandora's box could do. Never before had a legal case been opened to the public in such a way, John didn't want to be the first.

By mid-October, Ninette had all but given up. Caril's trial was in ten days, and John had still not acquiesced. She didn't even try to go to Lincoln. Instead, she called it a day at 2:00. If she hurried, she could get home before her kids returned home from school.

She had just gotten to the stairs when the phone rang in the newsroom. 'Let someone else answer it,' she thought as she stepped down the stairs. She had worked hard enough to get to both Charlie and Caril to no avail.

Jerry Hansen ran down the hall and looked down at her from the top of the stairwell. "It's for you, Ninette," he told her.

"I've gone home," she answered.

"You better take it," he said. "It's Merril Reller."

Ninette didn't take her coat off. This would be quick and she'd leave, but she tried to sound friendly on the phone nevertheless.

Reller told her that he would give her the interview. She stood up, surprised. "But it has to be a press conference," he said.

Ninette was silent, angry. She had been trying to get an exclusive for Floyd.

"It won't be a regular news conference," Reller told her. "We don't want that child badgered. So we've worked out our own ground rules. Anyone from the press can attend, but only one person will be allowed to ask Caril questions."

"All right, Merril," Ninette said. "I want you to let Floyd do the interview. I've worked so hard on this; you can't let me down now. Floyd'll be the one to ask the questions, right?"

"No," said Reller.

Ninette's heart sank, but she didn't give up. "You have to let Floyd do it! You know he's the best interviewer around and I've really worked very hard on this and you just can't let me down. I don't think I'm asking too much for you to let him do it."

"No," said Reller. "John and I have talked about it. We're going to have *you* do the interview, Ninette."

*       *       *

No trial had ever been under such public scrutiny as this one. For the first time, a defendant would be questioned on television and it would be aired throughout the country and abroad into the homes of more people than any other previous television broadcast since television's invention. It was the beginning of a new era for both the news media and the law.

John had sent out a notice five days earlier that told newspapers, radio, and television stations, "If you care to avail yourself of this opportunity, I suggest that you have your cameras set up a little before 1:00 p.m." The interview was set for two days before the trial was to begin.

John was all too aware of the importance of this event as he waited in a private room with Caril, Merril, and James shortly before 1 pm on October 20th. He didn't know who was more nervous, himself or Caril. Ninette and Floyd were escorted into the room to see them. Ninette had reason to be nervous as well. Still young and relatively inexperienced, she had been thrust into the middle of the most coveted journalism position in the country. The ground rules that John had set stated that only she could ask questions. Other reporters could hand her notes with questions they wanted her to ask, but she alone would decide which ones to pass along.

Jealousy and resentment abounded coast to coast. This was something reporters worked their whole lives to cover. News men from the major networks would now have to timidly hand their questions to a woman from Iowa and hope that she would choose their questions to ask in her own inexperienced way. They would later criticize the conference in their own papers, and some referred to Ninette as a "girl reporter."

Marjorie Marlette, who now found herself taking a backseat, would later criticize Ninette relentlessly, making spiteful jabs whenever possible. What Marlette did not seem to realize was that John had not given Marlette the job because McArthur and Reller knew that she, as well as many other journalists, were looking for a sensationalized story of a hardened criminal. Thus far, in their previous writings, they had not allowed facts to get in the way of a good story. Marlette and many others certainly wouldn't change this tactic now, and he knew they would not be fair to Caril if they had been the ones to interview her.

Even Ninette's own station, KMTV, had tried to talk John into giving the interview to Floyd, their most respected and experienced reporter. John admired Floyd. He watched his show every night and relied on him for information. But he had dealt with Ninette many times. She had spoken with James and had gotten to know the Starkweathers. She engaged with people on a personal basis, and what was more, she could connect with Caril the way no man could. He knew that she was fair, and that Caril would be most comfortable telling Ninette about what happened. Far from feeling resentment, Floyd felt incredible pride in this young prodigy. But other reporters surely would not.

Ninette and Caril froze for a moment, seeing one another for the first time. They were both celebrities to one another. Each had seen the other on newscasts, but this was the first time they met face to face. What really shocked Ninette was how small and fragile Caril seemed and, when Caril began to speak, how timid she was. Her eyes were wide and blue. Her smile was bright and child-like.

When Floyd entered the room, Caril told him excitedly that she had watched him on television. James stepped up to the famous news man and shook his hand vigorously, telling him what a fan he was.

Floyd was taken slightly aback. Teenagers were not his usual target audience. Ninette looked at the two teenagers, James and Caril, both close in age, yet miles apart in their experiences.

But upon looking at the mousy girl, Ninette could hardly believe she had been involved in such a disaster. She looked more like a person who would be afraid of her own shadow. And then it occurred to her what John had been saying, that this was a girl who was heavily influenced by Starkweather's aggressiveness. Ninette could see how such a tiny adolescent could be easily coerced into just about anything.

"You'll be a television star yourself soon," Merril told Caril as he gestured toward the camera Floyd was holding. He shared a closeness with the girl that not even John had achieved. Merril was as warm and open as John was introspective. Though John was good at talking to people on their own terms, he lacked Merril's charm. Merril was also very good at reading a person's emotions, and thinking of their needs. He had brought a sweater for Caril to wear. It was bright blue, Caril's favorite color.

Floyd pointed the camera toward Caril and her two attorneys to get some B-roll. "Just talk to each other," he said. "This camera doesn't record sound, so you can say anything you like."

"Ohhhh. I'm so nervous," Caril giggled. She looked up at John, a towering figure over her. "Aren't you nervous, Mr. McArthur?"

A master at hiding his true feelings, he never looked nervous. But now he looked down at Caril with a slight, yet confident smile on one side of his mouth and said, "Yes, I'm nervous." And he was. Not because of the interview; he had the utmost confidence in both Caril and Ninette. He was still afraid of the serpent he was letting out of the bag by allowing this press conference to take place. He was afraid what this was going to do to the future of the profession he loved so much.

Before they went into the news conference, John gave Caril one warning. He told her not to let the press rattle her. Not to allow their questions to make her lose control of her emotions. He didn't want her to give them anything they could use as fodder to say she was wild and out of control. It was a belief Caril already shared. Her mother had always been stoic, and believed that a show of emotion was a sign of weakness. She had taught Caril that when someone made her angry or sad, she was to hold in her emotions and remain firm and strong. It was a matter of pride as well as survival.

When they opened the door to enter the conference room they were met by bright flashes of camera bulbs and a hoard of photographers crammed together asking Caril to look in their directions. Ninette looked at Caril and saw the winsome, youthful smile of a girl quickly dissolve into the scowl of a frustrated woman, and when they sat at the table, all sweet innocence had disappeared. No longer was the hair the only thing that looked old about her. She had curled up inside herself. The advice John had given her would haunt him for years to come, because from that point on, many remembered the stoic face more than what she said.

John explained the rules to the crowd of reporters and they reacted as Ninette had expected. "That's the way it's going to be," he told them firmly. "Otherwise, we'll call the whole thing off." The reporters sat down like scolded children, muttering.

Ninette started by asking about her relationship with Charlie. "Now, Caril, before this all began, didn't you go out with Charlie Starkweather for quite a while?"

"Yes, I went with him the year before, and then I told him that I never wanted to see him again, but he came back." Her words were short and clipped. Her face was stern and solid. The light, amiable girl Ninette had met a few minutes before had disappeared and been replaced by a talking statue. "And that Sunday, I told him to leave and I told him I didn't ever want to see him again."

"Why?" Ninette asked. "What had brought you to this conclusion? Why didn't you want to go with him any more?"

Caril looked slightly away from Ninette. Her face wrinkled in an angry fashion. "I think he's crazy."

"Do you still think that?"

"Yes, I do."

"Did you ever break down and cry and beg Charlie to let you go? Or anything like that?"

"Yes. I cried all the way... He kept telling me that if I didn't do what he said, he would make one telephone call and they would all be killed."

Ninette continued to ask her questions regarding how she felt about what was going on. Ninette knew that John wanted to clear the air of rumors, so she brought up the pregnancy. "Since nobody's seen you since your capture, there's been a rumor you were pregnant and secretly had Charlie Starkweather's baby."

"No, I've never been pregnant, and I've never had a baby, and I'm not pregnant now." The words were robotic. Ninette knew that it was because Caril was uncomfortable and frustrated, but she wasn't sure how it would come across to the public.

She asked Caril when the first time was that she heard about her parents' death. When she was captured. When the police officer was at the door, why hadn't Caril told him what was happening? Because Charlie was waiting behind the door, and Caril didn't want anyone to get killed.

She continued to walk Caril through the events, and Caril answered with the same answers she had given John, but in that curt, defiant fashion that did not go over well with audiences.

"Have you thought about the outcome of the trial?" Ninette asked. "For instance, have you thought, if you were convicted, that you might go to prison, or you might even go to the electric chair? Have you thought much about that?"

"Yes, I have," Caril answered, and she looked directly over at the other reporters in the room. "And I don't really believe that I have anything to worry about. The Lord knows I'm innocent, and I know it, and the people who are involved know it, too."

# Chapter Seven
## The State of Nebraska v. Caril Ann Fugate: The Prosecution

Prior to the advent of television, courtrooms were a major source of entertainment, and were thus built like theaters, with high ceilings, long rows of seats, and even balconies. Once television came along, attendance to these trials dropped, and by 1958 most of the time these seats were only half filled. But now people crammed into courtroom number one, the largest of the courtrooms in the Lincoln courthouse, to be able to watch what was being referred to by many across the country as the trial of the century.

The jury was comprised of seven men and five women, and had been selected in a day and a half. They had been whittled down to thirty by the prosecution. John was to bring this number down to twelve. He did so by asking about their childhoods, a line of questioning that caught most people off guard. Ninette, watching from the press area, knew John's strategy by this point. He wanted the people on the jury to identify with Caril and see her as someone who shouldn't even be tried as an adult. John also asked if the potential jurors were ever threatened with a deadly weapon, and he typically passed those who either had, or knew anyone who had, which led many to understand that he would also be defending Caril on the basis of being kidnapped.

Nobody knew it, but McArthur was not supposed to be the one choosing the jury. Though John had prepared for most of the proceedings, Merril had done the research and the preparations for the jury selection. Reller stood to begin the questioning, but Judge Spencer immediately had him report to his chambers, where they spoke in private. When they returned several minutes later, Reller whispered to McArthur, "Why don't you take this one," and sat down in the second chair, the one behind lead council, thus stating that John would be leading the proceedings. John was taken by surprise. A little off balance, he asked questions that he knew his partner was going to ask, and did the best he could to get a favorable jury. It was only later that he learned that Judge Spencer had told Reller that he wanted only McArthur to handle the proceedings. "I gave the case to him," he told Merril. He had assigned two attorneys to Starkweather, and two attorneys were on the prosecution's side against Caril, but Judge Spencer would only allow one to represent Caril. Though such an action far exceeded the authority of the bench, if John fought it, it would take a lot of time and effort away from the task at hand, which was already far bigger than anything he had ever tackled. They would instead use it on appeal, assuming it ever got that far. For now, Reller would sit with Caril and help comfort her throughout the trial.

John had wanted to ask more questions of the potential jury members, but he was limited in the type and number of questions he was allowed to ask and kept as directly to the point as he could. He asked if they had already come to a conclusion of the case. Of course, just about everyone in town had, but John believed that those who would admit to it would be extra prejudicial, and so they were excused. One potential juror declared that she knew Caril was guilty, and nothing in the world would change her mind. She was, of course, immediately excused.

James hurried in after school every day, rushing to the courthouse, then entering through the back and making his way through the "bar," a short wall that sectioned off the business area of the court from the spectators. He sat in a spot that had been saved for him all day among the reporters with whom he had gained a rapport.

He was sitting among national news organizations, foreign correspondents from other countries, all listening intently to one of the biggest stories in the world. And his father was the star. He wasn't far off from Ninette, who noticed him watching anxiously, nodding, and learning. He knew his father's strategy, to get as many jurors who might identify with a girl's fear in a time of crisis. Ninette knew it, too, and she wondered if it would work against such incredible odds.

Her interview with Caril had been reported all over the world, and had run on the Today Show the day after it had aired on KMTV. Judge Spencer had been furious. He had not objected to any of the times the prosecution went to the media, but when John tried to present Caril's side of the story to the public, it was suddenly objectionable. His animosity grew when the interview aired nationwide, and people in other parts of the country began to realize there was another side to this case. He had little to worry about, however, as locals mostly discounted Caril's words and noticed only the rock solid indifference in her emotionless face.

When the jury selection was complete, William Fugate, Caril's biological father who watched the proceedings with his new wife and daughter, proclaimed to a reporter with relief, "I don't think I could have picked a better bunch myself. If I was on trial, that's the jury I'd want."

Nevertheless, William, and the rest of the surviving Fugates, were outraged that Caril was not being allowed to have both her attorneys represent her. They signed an affidavit requesting Reller be allowed to help, but Judge Spencer only allowed him to sit with Caril and John.

The trial began on Wednesday, October 29, 1958. As with Charlie's trial, the prosecution and the defense sat across from one another at the same table. Elmer sat with his long team of prosecutors and their folders of evidence stacked before them. On the other side sat John with his yellow legal pad and dull pencil, and Merril sat next to Caril. She was dressed in her favorite bright blue sweater and skirt and her girlish bobby socks. Occasionally, Caril grasped Merril's arm for moral support whenever she grew angry about something that was being said.

Elmer Scheele rose and reminded the jury they had "been going on for a better part of three days, you have been selected to hear the evidence as presented by both sides in the trial State versus Caril Ann Fugate." He then reiterated the details of the case, describing much of what had come out during the Starkweather trial. He described how they had fled the Bartlett home together, stopped for gas, gone to Bennet, and finally arrived at the Jensen car where Robert and his girlfriend Carol were killed, and the car was stolen. "The case will depend," Scheele said, "on whether you find that Caril Ann Fugate aided and abetted Charles Starkweather in the commission of this atrocious crime." He reminded them that Caril had held a gun the entire time they were in the car, that she had pointed it at Carol King, and had done nothing to stop Charlie. He told them that Caril "willingly and actively accompanied and assisted Starkweather" and that she had "ample opportunity to get away from Starkweather."

"Evidence will show," he said, "that Caril Fugate took money from Robert Jensen's billfold... and aided and abetted in the robbery of Robert Jensen." He finished by telling the jury that it would be necessary to go through all of the murders in order to show that Caril had willingly accompanied Charles Starkweather during his crime spree.

This came as good news to the many spectators, who had been curiously awaiting more information about the murders, and were less interested in the tedium of details in a robbery. But it didn't sound like it would be a long trial. If Scheele could present evidence to prove what he was claiming, this should be an open and shut case. He had already proven the robbery through Charlie's trial. He merely needed to show that Caril was there willingly to put her away for life, or to put her in the electric chair right after Charlie.

Then McArthur rose and began presenting his case. "There is a basic problem that has been overlooked here," he began. "This girl was introduced into this horrible sequence of events by opening a door and having a gun stuck in her face." She was a frightened girl who had been thrust into this chain of events, he said, and she too had been victimized. Her own family had been killed, though she did not know it at the time. He told the jury something that was not widely publicized, that she had been claiming all along that she did not know her family was dead, and she had gone along with Charlie to save their lives. "Must we condemn Caril," he said, "for failing to do what no one in Nebraska could do; stop mad killer Starkweather?"

As for the police, John told them this was all a ruse to cover up their own mistakes. They needed a scapegoat so people would not recognize their incompetence at having missed Charlie in so many instances. There was, in fact, an investigation being held to discover just why the Nebraska police had missed Charlie so many times, and how the chase had been so mishandled. "The facts in this case are grossly misunderstood by the public," John said, and then reminded them of the murder of Robert Colvert at the beginning of December. Even though the police had repeatedly been told that Starkweather had been responsible for the killing, they had done nothing to bring him in, or even to investigate him. "The mistakes were repeated in the other murders," he continued, "and it became necessary for them to make Caril an accomplice of Starkweather." He told them that relatives who tried to warn the police that something strange was going on at the Bartlett home were told by the police to go away because it was "none of their business."

And now, he said, the police "expected a higher degree of bravery than could be expected from most of us." If she had done what they claim she should have done, she "would have been Charlie's twelfth victim." He told them that Caril acted as any child would, and implored them to see it through the eyes of a fourteen-year-old girl.

He concluded, "Must we condemn Caril for failing to do what no one in Nebraska could do: stop Starkweather?"

*   *   *

The next morning the prosecution began making their case. Scheele started by questioning Robert Jensen's father, Robert Jensen Sr. He established many of the same things they had gone over in the Starkweather trial, his son's relationship with Carol King, the type of car he drove, and Mr. Jensen went over the painful details of that night when Robert didn't come home. Most importantly, Scheele entered into evidence the wallet that was stolen from Robert, which proved that this was a homicide in the perpetration of a robbery.

There was little that John could cross examine. The man had been through the brutal loss of his son, and he blamed Caril Fugate for it. But John did ask about Robert's health. "Did he have the strength of a boy of that age and size should have?"

"Yes, he did."

"He had the full use of his limbs?"

"Yes, sir."

"And in your judgment was he a boy of the good courage that a child of that upbringing would have?"

"Yes."

Carol King's father was next. Scheele again established the details of what was known. Mr. King described the jacket his daughter had owned, which Caril Fugate was later found wearing. The jacket held a similar importance to the wallet.

On cross-examination, John again asked about her physical height and strength. Her father said she was average for her age. He also asked about her intelligence and was told she was the top of her class.

When Scheele called William S. Romer, the Wyoming officer Caril had run to, John thought he now had an ally on the witness stand. As the questions began, he answered pretty much as he had when John had talked with him in Wyoming, except that he gave himself more credit for chasing Charlie down. In Wyoming he had stated that he had not seen Charlie fighting with another man in the road until Caril jumped into his car, but now, in court, he claimed that he had seen the scuffling before she got there. He also claimed to have chased after Charlie before deciding that Sheriff Hefflin could take care of it, and returning to the man who had been shot. In Wyoming, he had stated that he had radioed ahead and stayed with Caril.

Scheele almost accidentally revealed the hole in Romer's story when he was asking about the scuffle in the road. "And what did you do then when you saw this girl running towards you?" Romer didn't know how to answer. He had just claimed that he had seen the fight before Caril got to him. That made Caril less of a victim, certainly, but it also made him incompetent. If he saw two men wrestling over a fight in the middle of the street, why didn't he do anything? His new story was already unraveling.

"Well, I..." Romer stammered.

Scheele seemed to have realized the mistake and quickly covered it up with, "What did *she* do?"

"She came and got into my car."

So far, the changes in his story were minor. But then Romer went on to drop the bombshell John had not expected. In Wyoming, Romer had claimed that Caril had been hysterical until they heard over the radio that Charlie had been captured. But now, when Scheele asked if she had said anything to him while the chase was taking place, Romer said, "She told me that she had seen Mr. Starkweather kill ten people."

"And what did she say?"

"She said she had seen him kill her mother, her step-father, her step-sister and a boy and a girl, and a farm hand and three other people."

Everyone at the defense side of the table froze. Caril leaned forward biting her lip as though stopping herself from shouting out in disgust. John simply glared at the man who was lying under oath. He knew that someone must have gotten to Romer between the time he had spoken with him in Wyoming and the moment he testified. Someone had convinced him to lie on the witness stand. It was the very sort of thing John hated above all else, the sworn protectors of the law breaking it. The law was sacred to John, and those who abused it that were supposed to be defending it were more despicable than the criminals they fought.

Romer then began to describe walking to the body inside the car, but Scheele interrupted him. "Did Caril Fugate tell you any of the details of the killing of these people that she said she had witnessed?"

"Yes, sir."

"Including the deaths of her father and mother. Her step-father, her mother and her step-sister?"

"Yes, sir."

"Did she say whether or not she had been present when her mother, her step-father and her step-sister had been killed?"

"Yes, sir."

"I'm going to object to this as leading," John interjected.

"It is leading," Judge Spencer agreed. "The objection is sustained."

Scheele asked several more questions, and when he was finished, he returned to the counsel table. "You may cross-examine," he said to John.

McArthur rose quickly and marched deliberately at Romer. He stared him down for several seconds. Romer looked back at him, giving no sign of remorse, no explanation for the change in his story. At last John spoke up. "Did you get the impression she was afraid of Starkweather as long as he was on the loose?"

"Yes, sir, I did."

He asked Romer about Caril's state of mind when she entered the car. "You have used the expression that Caril Fugate was hysterical and that she was crying, as you have described her. Was she at that time in what you would consider a state of shock?"

"At the time I thought so, sir."

"You felt that she was in shock?"

"Yes, sir, I did."

He asked him details about when he had come upon the fight between Charlie and Joe Sprinkle, when he had "captured" Caril. John had Romer explain the details, how he had been stuck behind a milk truck and had not seen the fight until Caril was already running to him.

"Now, what was Caril Fugate doing at the first moment that you saw her?"

"The first moment I saw her?"

"Yes."

"She was running to my car."

"She was already running at that time?"

"Yes, sir."

"Are you able to say whether she started from any of these vehicles or from any certain place?"

"No, sir, I am not."

"You don't know that. Was she at any time within your view armed?"

"No, sir."

"Now was she at any time within your view aiding or abetting Starkweather in any way?"

105

"No, sir."

John had him describe his own car. Though it was unmarked, it was clearly a police car, and Caril had run straight to it once she recognized what it was. She had in no way avoided him or run from him. It was an important point to make. All of the newspapers reported that Caril had been "captured" along with her "boyfriend" Charlie. People believed Romer was a hero who brought in the teeny bopper criminal. But according to all other witnesses on the scene, and his own original statements to John, Romer had hesitated before chasing Starkweather. After Caril blurted out who it was that was fighting in the middle of the street, Romer wavered a few more moments while Charlie ran back to his car. Caril shouted for him to take chase, but Romer continued to vacillate until Charlie was heading east, at which time Romer finally called ahead to Douglas to have others stop him there. Finally, he claimed that he took chase for a few miles before giving up and turning back around to investigate the abandoned car where Charlie's eleventh victim lay dead. On the stand, Romer denied hesitating, claiming that he had not been able to get around the truck in front of him and another car that was stopped nearby. John moved on to the interrogation Scheele had conducted with Caril the following day.

"Now Mr. Wise was the Justice of the Peace?" John asked.

"Yes, sir."

"Who asked him to be there?"

"I believe Mr. Scheele asked him to be present."

"It wasn't Caril that asked him to be there?"

"No, sir."

"Was Mr. Wise called in, in any sense to advise this girl?

"I believe he was called for that purpose, sir."

"Mr. Scheele called Mr. Wise to be the advisor to Caril Ann?"

"To know that the girl – he called Mr. Wise, I believe, to, so that Mr. Wise could verify that Caril had been advised of her rights."

John had Romer run down the list of everyone else that was present. Then John went back to the Justice of the Peace who was there to advise Caril.

"Did he advise her?"

"I don't remember."

"You don't recall whether he advised her at all?"

"I don't remember what he said to her."

"Do you know whether the contents of this was discussed?" John was referring to the waiver of rights to fight extradition.

"Yes sir, it was."

"I notice it recites 'To answer charges pending or yet to be filed against me.' Was anything said about what kind of charges were filed or yet to be filed?"

"I don't remember, sir; I know that there was, she was told that there was charges pending, but I don't..."

"Was there anything said about first degree murder charges filed, or would be filed?"

"Yes, sir."

"How does it happen that wasn't put in the thing that she signed, do you know that?"

"I don't know, sir." John knew he would answer this way, but he asked it so as to bring the jury's attention to the fact that, had anyone mentioned this fact to Caril, it probably would have also been put in writing.

"And what's this about where she says 'I exonerate all authorities in Douglas, Wyoming and in Nebraska here for any blame, compulsion or interference in this connection?'"

"I don't know, sir."

"What was the blame and compulsion and interference that they had used on her?"

"There wasn't any, any..."

"Well, why was she asked to excuse them from that then?"

"That I don't know."

"Sir," John went on, "to be fair, weren't they just trying to get something on, over, her signature, so that she would never be able to assert the rights that were taken away at that place?"

"I don't believe so."

"You don't think that; you think that this, a fourteen year old child in a state of shock, was treated fairly, do you?"

Romer had said earlier that she had been in a state of shock. John had employed one of his trademark tactics on him, to ask the witness about something that he would answer innocently enough, but would then prove John's point later on when he used the witness's own words to make his point. Romer could not take back what he had said. All he could do was say, "I think she was."

There were several questions in cross-examination which detailed the interview with Caril, and the investigation of the cars after Charlie had left. The most notable piece of information was that the .22 rifle that Caril had carried during the murder spree was both jammed and unloaded. Had she tried to use it on Charlie, as so many people thought she should have, it would not have worked.

When they returned from recess the other shoe dropped. Earl Heflin, the sheriff from Douglas, Wyoming, revealed what had been found in Caril's jacket pocket. James, sitting in the crowd watching, had been waiting for the note to appear; the one where Caril asked for help. She had told John that she intended to leave it in a bathroom where someone could find it. Heflin had told John that he mailed it to Scheele, but Scheele claimed never to have received it.

"Now, Sheriff," Scheele began, "would you now take the envelope which the reporter has marked Exhibit 29 and remove the contents from it and tell us what the contents are, if you know?"

"Yes, sir."

"And will you tell us what it is, sir?"

"These clippings were found in the jacket pocket that Caril Fugate was wearing at the time."

They were photographs from newspaper clippings that described the murder of Caril's family. Having them in her pocket implied that she actually knew about their deaths. The note she had written asking for help had been in her pocket, but it had mysteriously disappeared; while these photos, which had been in the same pocket, *had* been found.

When Scheele officially introduced the clippings into evidence, John cut in, "Objected to as no proper and sufficient foundation and not specifically connected with the defendant, they are prejudicial..." His voice was trailing off into a rant of disgust.

"John, you are talking to yourself. I can't hear you," Judge Spencer said.

John raised his voice, "Prejudicial and inflammatory, insufficient evidence that they were in the knowledge of the defendant."

"Overruled; it will be received," Spencer said.

John was at a loss for words. Scheele had always been a respectable DA and an honorable man. For him to employee such back-alley tactics seemed out of character. These practices, while legal, were beneath the dignity of both Scheele and especially the position he held.

There was an important factor to consider, one that perhaps explained why Scheele was so willing to bend the law for his own purposes. By this point, the Fugate case had attracted international recognition. Reporters from Japan, London, and many other countries were filling the hotel rooms of Lincoln and watching from the press section. Domestically, the story was featured on the nightly news and on nationally syndicated newspapers every day. The eyes of the world were watching what should be a slam dunk for the police in convicting someone they believed was guilty. The newspapers had already tried and convicted her as she made the trek across the state with the sheriff. Now, if the prosecution failed to convict Caril, they would look incompetent. Worse yet, people would turn to the police and once again question why it had taken them so long to catch Charlie, and why Caril had to be the one to at last run to a police officer's car before he was caught. But if they succeeded, the careers of the major players would be set. Scheele himself was looking to become a judge, a promotion that could easily happen should he win this all-important case.

The next few days saw a stream of witnesses testifying their views of what happened. The most damning testimony for Caril were accounts of the time they spent at the Bartlett home after her parents had been killed. A local grocery store clerk stated that Charlie had shopped at his place alone. Two of Starkweather's relatives said that he had visited them on a couple occasions for several hours. Charlie's brother Rodney described going to the Bartlett home twice. The first time was to get his rifle back, and when he saw Caril at the door, she looked sick rather than frightened to him. He returned again with Caril's brother-in-law, Bob Von Busch. Caril's sister testified about her visit, and Caril's stand-offish behavior, but then Barbara also described how, as she was about to leave, Caril had leaned out to her and explained that their mother was in real danger, and she needed to stay away for a while.

The officer who responded to Bob and Rodney's call when Caril had sent them away also testified. He told the court he had knocked on the door for some time before Caril answered. "As soon as she opened the door I asked her 'what the trouble was here.' She said, 'Well, there isn't any trouble.' And I said, 'Well, we got a call that some people weren't allowed to enter the house.' She said, 'Oh, that was my sister and brother-in-law and a little baby.' And I says, 'Well, how come they couldn't come in?' She says, 'Well, I told them that my mother and father and little sister had the flu,' and she said especially the little girl, she said 'My mother said my sister had a little baby and she didn't want her to come in the house and catch the flu.' And I asked her if there was any trouble between them if they had an argument or anything; she said, 'No, we didn't.' She said, 'They just left after I told them they couldn't come in.'"

On cross examination, John asked, "Did you know at that time that Caril and this brother-in-law had always been very close to each other?"

"No, I didn't know him at all."

"Did you know that when he was going with Caril's sister that Caril always was taken along?"

"No, I didn't."

"Well, did you know that it was the brother-in-law that was making the complaint that Caril wouldn't let him in?"

"Not at the time I didn't know."

"You didn't know that?"

"No."

"Did you by any chance check back to find out why the brother-in-law would be disturbed about not getting in and Caril claiming that there was trouble with him?"

"No, I didn't."

"Well, from what you have learned since are you now aware that if you had of done that you would have known that Caril was trying to warn you for something that she couldn't say?" Scheele objected, and it was sustained, but John had gotten his point across to the jury. Caril had been trying to send out signals that the police were not catching on to.

Other witnesses that saw Charlie on the road testified that she had been left alone several times. A service station attendant stated that Caril had remained in the car alone while he raised it on the grease rack. Charlie had left her alone while he went into the office for close to a half hour. "He gets out and buys himself a bottle of pop and the girl a bottle of pop, and he gives her a bottle of pop and he goes up front in the office, around through the alleyway, and up into the office, and stands looking out the window. Well, he was nervous, or, I mean, he just didn't appear right, the whole works didn't come up right, so I stood where I could watch him and the cash register, because I thought I was going to get hooked." His story was corroborated by his associate, who had been working that day and also saw Caril stay in the car. Both also felt a threatening presence about Charlie and were afraid he was going to rob the station. On cross-examination, John asked one of the employees, "You kept him under surveillance at any time while he was near your cash register, is that true?"

"Yes."

"And when he asked you to break a twenty dollar bill did you refuse him because you would have to admit that you had that much money?"

"Right."

"And when a customer asked him to cash a ten dollar check, did you refuse him for the same reason?"

"Yes – well, wait a minute, for Starkweather's benefit?"

"Yes, that's what I mean, we'll call it Starkweather's demeanor and appearance."

"Yes, I mean, he was still there in the office."

"You weren't wanting to stir up some trouble with Starkweather in your place."

"Other than to knock him in the head for stepping on my wax was the only thing."

"Well, I'll say this, sir; looking back aren't you rather grateful that Caril didn't stir up some kind of a fuss about Starkweather?"

"Well, I'm grateful nobody did."

Two employees of a second service station testified that Caril had left the car and gone into a restaurant to buy hamburgers. The waitress in the restaurant testified that Caril had bought the hamburgers and could have left whenever she wanted. John also asked these service station attendants if they had felt a threatening presence from Charlie. They testified that they did. One went so far as to say he thought Charlie would rob them, too. As for Caril, almost everyone who saw her stated that she looked tired.

Then the judge dropped the largest bomb in the courthouse. "Let the record show," he said, "that the prosecution has filed an application for an order for the production of a witness, Charles R. Starkweather..." From that moment forward, none of the spectators heard anything that was said on the witness stand. They were watching the door, waiting for the biggest celebrity in Nebraska to be led into the room. When the time came, the doors opened dramatically and all eyes turned toward it to see the man himself, surrounded by eight officers, standing in the middle of the doorway. He strode inside as though he owned the place; as though no death penalty could strip away his pride.

Caril buried her face in her hands, her body shaking. At last she pulled her head up and looked at him wide eyed. Her hand reached out and found Merril's arm. She grasped the sleeve of his jacket hard, twisting the fabric. Charlie never looked at Caril as he passed by her. He spoke quietly with the court reporter, then sat down and made himself comfortable in the witness chair. Elmer Scheele stepped up and questioned him. Though he had been the man to convince a jury to end Charlie's life, Charlie didn't seem resentful or bitter. In fact, he continued to have the same adoration for the man.

Charlie spoke very quietly, so quietly that the court continuously had to ask him to speak up, about the morning before the murders. He said that he had gone to the Bartlett home, had argued with Mr. Bartlett several times before returning again and waiting in the back yard for Caril to get home from school. When she did, she began arguing with her parents and he entered.

"Did she ask you to leave again?" Scheele asked.

"I don't remember what she said."

"Did she slap you?"

"Yes."

"And then what happened?"

"I hit her back."

"And then what happened?"

"She screamed, and Mr. Bartlett came in."

"Speak a little louder," Judge Spencer said.

"She screamed."

"Then when Mr. Bartlett came in, what happened?" Scheele asked.

"We got in a fight," Charlie answered.

"And in the course of that fight did you do anything to Mr. Bartlett?"

"Yes."

"What did you do?"

"I shot him."

"What with?"

"The .22."

"Your brother's .22 rifle?"

"Yes."

"And did you do anything to Mrs. Bartlett?"

"Well, I shot her, too."

"With the same gun?"

"Yes, but I didn't kill her."

"And did you do anything to Betty Jean?"

"Yes, I threw a knife at her."

"Now what knife did you throw at Betty Jean?"

"It was a hunting knife."

"Whose hunting knife was it?"

He continued to describe the murders indifferently and kept to the account he'd given at his trial. He explained that Caril was in another room when he killed her father, but that she was in the room when he killed her mother and baby step-sister.

"Now then, what did you do after this all happened there at the Bartlett home?"

"I cleaned it up."

"And what did you do with the bodies?"

"I put Mr…"

"I can't hear you," Scheele said.

"I put Mr. Bartlett in the chicken shed and Betty Jean and her mother in the outdoor house."

"When you were cleaning up what was Caril Fugate doing?"

"Nothing."

"Well was she there all the time?"

"Yes."

"What was she doing?"

"Watching TV."

"How long did it take you to clean up there at the house and get the bodies out of the house?"

"Well, it was about 4:30 when I started and it was about a quarter of 8 when I quit."

He described leaving briefly to go to the store and said that Caril stayed at the house alone. Scheele asked if she had been tied up, and Charlie said she hadn't been. He described going to several places over the next few days while Caril remained in the house alone and unimpeded. He could not remember anything that she was doing when he returned, or anything that they did together in the home during those days, nor did he explain why she did not go with him or desire to go to the store herself, or for a walk, or anything at all, but he insisted that Caril was not tied up.

He then described the list of people who came to visit, each one growing more and more curious as to why the family had disappeared and why Caril was there all alone. Every time, Charlie claimed to be in another room where he could hear the conversations, but couldn't make out the words. That is, until Caril's grandmother, Pansy Street, came to the door and would not be allowed in. "She said she knew I was in there and was going to get the police."

"Then did she leave?"

"Yes."

"What did you do after Mrs. Street left?"

"We left."

Charlie described to them how they sneaked out the back, then retrieved Charlie's car from his friend and left Lincoln. Charlie stated that Caril had again been alone with his friends at one point. He next confirmed what others had testified to, that they had gone to a couple service stations, gotten a couple burgers, maps of Nebraska and Kansas, and headed south.

Before they reached Kansas, however, Charlie changed his mind suddenly and turned east toward Bennet. He described driving through town, then onto the property of his friend August Meyer where he promptly got his car stuck in the mud. Scheele stopped him and asked him about the drive toward Bennet. "Did she say anything to you about the hamburgers?"

"Yes."

"What did she say?"

"She said she didn't like them."

"Did she say anything else?"

"Yes."

"What?"

"She said, 'We ought to go back and shoot them.'"

He described going to the storm cellar, which he called a cave, and checking it out, then walking up to August Meyer's home to ask for help getting his car unstuck.

"What did he say?" Scheele asked.

"He said he had to change his jacket, or something. I don't know what it was."

"Now was Caril with you in your presence at all times when you were there at the August Meyer farm?"

"All during the whole time?" Charlie asked.

"Yes."

"No."

"Well, when was that, that you were separated?"

"Just before I shot him." Charlie spoke so casually and it came out so suddenly that it was hard to recognize the gravity of what he said.

"And where was she then?" Scheele asked.

"I don't know."

"Did she know what had happened to..."

"Now just a minute," John interrupted. "I'm going to object to Mr. Scheele telling his witness what to say here."

"Rephrase your question, Mr. Scheele," Judge Spencer said.

"Did she see what happened there?"

115

"Yes."

Charlie said that after he shot August Meyer, both Caril and he had gone through the house looking for weapons. Then they left the farm and drove around, seemingly aimlessly, in and out of Bennet. The car got stuck and a man came along to help them push it out. Scheele knew the story so well by now that he led the questions rather than asking them. John objected multiple times that Scheele was telling the witness what to say.

At last they reached the point in the story that he and Caril were being tried for, the murders of the two teenagers.

"He rolled the window down and asked if we was lost, and something, and I told him, 'No, my car went over the ditch.' And he asked me if it was a Ford, and I said, 'Yes.' 'A black one?' And I says, 'Yes.'"

"Now were you carrying any weapon at that time?"

"Yes."

"What were you carrying?"

"A .22."

"Was it loaded?"

"Yes."

"You mean the .22 rifle that you got from the Meyer farm?"

"Yes."

"Was Caril Fugate carrying any weapons at that time?"

"A .410."

"And was it loaded?"

"Yes."

"What happened then after you talked to Robert Jensen there?"

"I asked him if he'd give us a ride into Bennet."

"What did he say?"

"He said... I don't remember if he said anything or not, he just opened the back door."

"Was there any conversation at or about that time concerning the guns that you and Caril Fugate were carrying?"

"Yes."

"Will you tell us what that was?"

"I don't know the exact words."

"Generally."

"Well, he… as I was getting in, I got in before Caril, and he grabbed the front of the .22 barrel and said he'd take this; and, and I don't remember if I said anything or not, but, yes, I said it wasn't loaded. And Caril spoke up and said 'We don't walk around with loaded guns.'"

Charlie said that he sat behind the Jensen boy and Caril sat behind the King girl. Charlie told them that he needed to use a phone, so Robert took them to a pay phone in Bennet. When they got to it they saw that it didn't work, so Robert offered to take them to the house of a friend where he could use their phone. "I said, 'Look, you do as we tell you before somebody gets hurt.'" Charlie continued on, saying that Robert didn't believe that they'd shoot him. Then he said that Caril spoke up. "She said, 'You do as we tell you or you'll find out, and I'll shoot this girl to show you that we will.' Them ain't the exact words, something like that." Charlie had Robert drive toward Lincoln, then suddenly had him turn around and drive past Bennet into the country, where they stopped at the "cave."

"Now was there any conversation concerning a billfold?" Scheele asked.

"Yes," Charlie answered.

"When did that take place?"

"After we went through Bennet."

"Was that between the time you left Bennet and got to the cave?"

"Yes."

"Will you tell us what was said about that?"

"Caril asked if, if I'd already asked him for his money, and I said 'No.'"

It was what Scheele was searching for. Caril Fugate, the mastermind behind the plan who had manipulated this man into robbery and murder. "Was she holding any weapon in her possession at that time?"

"She had a .410 laying there."

"Was it loaded?"

"Yes."

Charlie described in detail how Caril had taken the billfold, taken the money, handed the billfold back to Robert, then put the

117

money into Charlie's billfold.  Judge Spencer then told the press that if any of them needed to leave to meet a deadline, they were welcome to.  No one moved.  They hung onto Charlie's every word.

After getting off track and being led back by Scheele again, John said, "Now I'm going to object to this again.  He ought to let the witness do his own talking."

Judge Spencer sustained it and Scheele had to let Charlie stand on his own.  "Then, well, just tell us what, where he drove the car," Scheele said.  Charlie described them parking the car, then getting out.  Caril stayed by the car while Charlie led the couple to the cave.  Scheele asked several times if Caril said anything, and Charlie said that she had, but he didn't hear what it was.  He wasn't paying any attention to her.

"What did you do after you got there near the cave entrance?" Scheele asked.

"Told them to go on down."

"Did they go down?"

"Yes."

"Then what happened?"

"They come back up."

"Who came back up?"

"Bob Jensen."

"Where was Carol King at that time?"

"Right behind him."

"And what happened after that?"

"He knocked her down."

"Knocked who down?"

"Carol King."

"And what did he do then, you mean he bumped into her?"

"Oh, he just kind of pushed her out of the way."

"What did you do?"

"And when he was coming up I was shooting away."

"Did you shoot the rifle at him?"

"Yes."

"More than one time?"

"Yes."

"Then what happened?"

"He fell back down."

"Then what happened, what did you do after that?"

"I went on back down in the cave."

"How long were you down in the cave?"

"Not very long."

"Where was the King girl when you were down in the cave?"

"She was still up there."

"Was she lying down or standing?"

"She was standing down there."

"How long were you down there with the Jensen boy?"

"Not very long."

"Then what did you do?"

"I went back up to the car."

"Went where?"

"Back over to the car."

"Where was Carol King when you went to the car?"

"Right where she was standing."

"Where?"

"Just a little bit out of the entrance to the cave."

"And after you got to the car what did you do?"

"I got a flashlight and reloaded the gun."

"Where was Caril Fugate when you came back to the car?"

"Sitting behind the steering wheel."

"Was she holding anything?"

"The .410."

"Was it loaded?"

"It was the last time I knew of."

"What did you do then after you reloaded your .22 rifle?"

"I went back to the cave."

"How long were you in the cave then?"

"Not very long."

"And where was Carol King while you were down there?"

"She was still out, standing up."

"Where was Caril Fugate?"

"I don't know."

"Now after you came back out of the cave then where did you go?"

"I told Carol King to go on down in the cave, and I went on over to the car."

"Did Carol King go on down into the cave?"

"I don't know."

The story was beginning to become absurd, but after so many objections from McArthur, Scheele couldn't lead his testimony anymore. "What did you do after you went over to the car?" he asked.

"I was so nervous I went over in the ditch."

"Did you start the car up?"

"No."

"Did you start the motor to the car?"

"No."

"Where was Carol King when you went back to the car?"

"I don't know."

"I mean, Caril Fugate?"

"She had moved over on the passenger side."

"In which seat?"

"The front seat."

"What did you do then after you got into the car with Caril Fugate?"

"Released the emergency brake and started to back down, and went over in the ditch."

"You got stuck?"

"Went over in the ditch."

"What did you do after that happened?"

"Got out and looked at it."

"And then what did you do?"

"Cussed like mad."

"And then what?"

"Caril Fugate got out, and we walked up to the cave."

"Who walked up to the cave?"

"I and Caril both."

"Caril Fugate."

"Yes."

"What did you do after you got back up to the cave?"

"Told Carol King to come on out."

"Was she in the cave when you got there?"

"Not all the way down, no."

"And did she come out when you told her that?"

"Yes."

"Then what did you do?"

"I gave the gun to Caril and told her to watch her."

"Gave the gun to Caril?"

"The .22."

"Which .22 was that?"

"The .22 pump, August Meyer's."

"The one that you just reloaded?"

"Yes."

"And what did she do then?"

"I don't know what she did."

"Did she take the gun from you?"

"Yes."

"And what did you do?"

"I went back down to the car."

"And what were you doing down at the car?"

"Trying to get it un... out of the ditch."

"Did you get it out of the ditch?"

"Later on, yes."

He described how Caril and he had used several articles, blankets, boards, etc. to help the car get out of the ditch. He described in great detail placing everything in its place just as the police later found it. It was a description of the location straight out of the police records without any mistakes. But it left out the most important detail, how the life of a healthy young girl had been so brutally ended. Scheele didn't ask a single question about the event, as though he didn't want Charlie to make any more mistakes.

"I don't remember which way we went, but we got back on the highway," Charlie said.

"What did you do after you got to Lincoln?" Scheele asked.

"We just drove around for a while and then we just parked and went to sleep."

When they woke up a few hours later, they drove around the neighborhood. Charlie said that he told Caril to pick out any house she wanted, and she picked the Ward home. He was not very specific about the Ward home. He said that when they entered the house there was a morning newspaper and another came in the evening. He said that the maid was hard of hearing and that he and Caril communicated with her by shouting and writing notes. He described things they took, such as money and clothing; that Caril had warned him when Mr. Ward was pulling up, and when they left they put shoe polish in Charlie's hair to change his appearance.

Court recessed, and when they returned, Scheele walked Charlie through some of the details from before, when they had left the Bartlett home, things that happened at the cave, and when they drove to Lincoln. He again glanced over the time at the Wards', then went through the drive from Lincoln to Wyoming. Charlie claimed that he left Caril alone several times as he went into various gas stations, and that a police car followed him a short time in Douglas, Wyoming, but did not recognize him since his hair was darkened with the polish. With the story told, the State rested its case and it was the defense's turn to question Charlie. McArthur asked for time to examine Charlie's testimony before cross-examining, and the judge granted it, ordering Charlie to return the following day.

The next witness took the stand, but most people didn't notice him for the first couple minutes. They instead watched Charlie being led out of the room. The witness on the stand was Dr. Vance Rogers, President of Nebraska Wesleyan University. He had sat in as an observer on February 1 when Caril was questioned in Wyoming by Assistant District Attorney Dale Fahrnbruch. This time, Dale Fahrnbruch was questioning him, and though he was trying to establish that Caril was questioned fairly, Rogers offered little new information, and testified that Caril had seemed "terribly frightened" during the entire interview. He also established that Caril had been very cooperative, and had answered every question without hesitation.

The prosecution had called this witness to testify about some of the things Caril said, and to establish that the prosecution had been fair in their questions to her. It was highly irregular to ask someone who had represented a girl to testify against her. Dr. Rogers explained several details from the interview, and painted an image of an intimidated, frightened girl overwhelmed by a team of men. He went on to describe how they had to interrogate her without informing her that she would be charged with murder, and without offering her any real legal counsel. They also never introduced the written records of the interview, which McArthur immediately began asking about upon cross examination. "Doctor, do I understand that there was no written record made of this transaction?"

"Not to my knowledge."

"And the persons you have named were the only ones there?"

"To the best of my memory, yes, sir."

"Caril's father wasn't there?"

"No."

"Nor any member of her family?"

"No."

"Did Mr. Fahrnbruch say anything to Caril about filing a first degree murder charge against her?"

"Not in my presence that I can recall."

"Did he say anything to the effect that there had been a first degree murder charge filed against her?"

"Not in my memory."

"Did he make any statement to this girl that he intended to ask for her electrocution?"

"No."

"Did he ever tell her within your hearing that whatever she said would be presented to a court and a jury as evidence against her?"

"No."

With that, court was adjourned, and the spectators left, eagerly awaiting how McArthur would handle Charlie on the stand the following day. That night John paced the floor at home flipping his coin and talking to himself. Only two people really knew what had happened during those two fateful weeks, and they would both be in the courthouse the next day. His questions would have to be precise.

The next day the crowds were so thick with people wanting to get a look that it was difficult to get into the building. As John and Elmer and their teams arrived, most people looked past them. Caril grabbed a lot of attention, but Charlie was the main event. Every photographer wanted him to look his way, and every reporter wanted him to answer his questions.

In the witness chair, Charlie studied John McArthur's face, fascinated by the angular strokes of his chin, nose, and cheeks. It was a face with a lot of character. Charlie had to almost squint because he was not wearing his glasses.

"Charles," John began, "do you know who I am?"

"Yes."

"You saw me at your own trial, did you not?"

"Yes."

"Have you ever talked to me before this present moment?"

"No."

"Charles, do you prefer that I call you Charles, or Mr. Starkweather, or Chuck, or do you have…"

"It makes no difference," Charlie said, relaxing. Many expected John to be aggressive with Charlie. After all, he was the star witness against his client. But John instead took the same tone he had always taken with his clients and spoke to Charlie in a non-patronizing and respectful manner. It wasn't something Charlie was used to.

John began by asking about Charlie's weight, a question that seemed to perplex Charlie. So far, the questions he had been given had all been rehearsed. Now he didn't know where it was going. He spoke very quietly, and when John asked him to speak up, Charlie responded by telling him he could barely hear him as well.

"It's hard for you to hear me?" John asked.

"Yes."

"I'll do the same. I don't know whether everyone heard or not, but do you know your present weight?"

Charlie answered he didn't know what his weight was at the moment, but when he had been sent to prison, he had been weighed, and it was one hundred and sixty-four pounds.

John asked about the car Charlie drove. "What color was it when you bought it?"

Charlie answered under his breath.

"I think I'm talking louder than you are now," John said.

"Blue," Charlie said, raising his voice.

John began asking him about the car. "Do you remember of Caril asking you why you painted it?"

"She might of."

"Do you remember of Bob Von Busch asking you?"

"He might of."

"Do you remember what you told those people?"

"No, I don't."

This was going a different direction than most people thought. McArthur wasn't asking about Caril, about the murders, about anything that seemed to have anything to do with this case.

"Do you remember where you told them you painted it?"

"I don't recall if they asked me or not."

"Do you remember telling them why you painted it?"

"No."

"Charles, do you remember telling anybody that you had painted your car because a bunch of boys got drunk and spotted it with different colors of paint?"

"I don't recall."

"You do not remember that?"

"No."

"Charles, why did you shoot Robert Jensen?"

It was sudden, and out of nowhere, but within Charlie's comfort zone. "He come back up the steps," he said.

"And what is the expression that you have used in the past as to your actual position you were in, do you recall?"

"What do you mean by that?"

"Well, I'll restate it. Has it been your position and have you said that you killed him in self-defense?"

"He come back up the steps, yes."

"Yes. Was it your feeling at that time that you were killing Robert Jensen in self-defense?"

"It was."

"And is it at this time your feeling that you killed Robert Jensen in self-defense?"

"No."

"What do you now say was your motive?"

"Well, I was in the wrong."

"I beg your pardon?"

"I was in the wrong."

"At that time, when you actually shot him, did you feel that you were in the right?"

Charlie sat there quietly. He nodded his head very slightly.

McArthur persisted, "At that time, when you actually shot him, did you feel that you were in the right?"

"Yes," Charlie answered at last.

McArthur asked him about killing Robert Jensen. Charlie claimed to have had no intention of killing him until Robert came at him on the stairs.

"What did you intend to do when you took him to the cave?" McArthur asked.

"Leave him in the cave."

"And at that time Caril Fugate was in Jensen's car, was she?"

"As far as I know, I wasn't paying no attention to her."

McArthur said he assumed Charlie couldn't see her because it was night, but Charlie said that he could see, even though it was night, he simply wasn't paying attention to her.

"Then when you and Robert Jensen walked from his car to the cave you had no intention of killing him?" McArthur asked.

"No."

"Your intention at that time was to leave him in the cave and take his car, would that be correct?"

"Yes."

"Did you at any time tell Caril Fugate that you intended to kill Robert Jensen?"

"No."

This one word in many ways killed the State's entire case, or at least should have. She was charged with aiding and abetting in the murder of Robert Jensen. But if she had no knowledge that Charlie was going to kill him, then she could not have been aiding him in the murder. The questioning had only begun, and McArthur had already gotten the most important admission out of Charlie by asking him questions that seemed as though they were about one thing, but turned out to be an admission to something else, and Charlie had walked right into it.

"As far as you know," McArthur continued, "did she have any knowledge of your intention to kill Robert Jensen?"

"I don't know what she was thinking."

"She was in the car and you were over to the cave when the intention came into your mind, is that true?"

"I don't know whether she was in the car or not, I wasn't paying enough attention to her."

"That may be true, at least, she was far enough away that you didn't see her?"

"Yes."

"And when you decided that Robert Jensen was coming for you, is that when you made the decision to shoot him?"

"Yes."

"And is that when you did shoot him?"

"Yes."

"Did the intention to shoot and the actual shooting occur just about the same moment?"

"Yes."

"Then there really was no way that Caril Fugate could aid or abet you in any way in that killing was there?"

"Now, Your Honor, that I object to," Scheele said. "That's calling for a conclusion."

"Sustained," Judge Spencer said.

"Well, I'll ask you this then, Charles," McArthur said. "Did Caril Fugate take any part whatsoever in the killing of Robert Jensen?"

"That again, Your Honor, I object to as calling for a conclusion and invading the province of the jury," Scheele said.

"You may answer," Judge Spencer said to Charlie.

"Would you repeat that?" Charlie asked.

"I'll ask Mr. Shamberg to read it," John said.

As the question was repeated, everyone waited with baited breath. No matter what else Charlie had said about every other murder, Caril was only being charged with aiding and abetting this particular one, so all of his testimony was worthless unless he said "yes" or "maybe."

"No," he responded. She had not aided and abetted him in any way.

McArthur continued, asking about when Charlie killed Robert Jensen. He asked him details about where Jensen was on the stairs, and where Charlie was in relation to him. He asked about the type of gun he used, and what it took to prepare to fire it. John picked up the rifle from the evidence table and showed it to Charlie. A shudder ran through the audience, afraid to see Charlie so close to a gun again. "Can you see this?" John asked, holding up the rifle.

"Yes, sir."

"And what is it?"

"A rifle."

"Do you know what kind?"

"Not from where you are standing, no."

"I beg your pardon?"

"Not from where you are standing."

"You can not tell what kind of a rifle it is from where I am standing?"

Charlie was allowed to look closer at the gun. The watching crowd was now visibly shifting in their seats. Charlie reached forward to get a better look and John pulled it away. "Now, Charlie, you can appreciate that I cannot *give* you the gun," McArthur said.

Charlie smiled slightly and sat back in the witness chair, answering the question, "A .22 pump." John asked several questions about it. Charlie had claimed to shoot Robert every time while Robert was still standing. Yet, it was six shots, and it took a lot of time to pump the gun between each shot, so McArthur couldn't understand how Robert stayed standing for all six shots. Charlie didn't have an answer for that. He couldn't see completely clearly.

"Charles," McArthur said, "is it hard for you to see from where you are?"

"I can see."

"Can you see me?"

"Yes."

"Can you see the jury?"

"Yes."

"Do you know Mr. Masters, Eugene Masters?"

"Yes."

"Can you see him?"

"No."

"You can't see him at all?"

"No."

"Would you try…"

"No."

"You can't make him out in this courtroom?"

"No."

"You know the man on sight?"

"Yes."

"Can you see Caril Fugate?"

"Yes."

"Can you see her now?"

He looked at her coldly. She shifted uncomfortably in her seat. "Yes," he said.

"What color dress is she wearing?"

"Blue."

"Can you see well enough to know that?"

"Yes."

"Do you wear glasses?"

"Yes."

"And you could see better here if you had them on?"

"Yes."

"Would that be true?"

"Yes."

"Are they in the courtroom?"

"Yes."

John turned to Judge Spencer and said, "I'm going to ask that he be permitted to wear them."

"Your Honor, I don't feel like putting them on," Charlie said.

"You'd rather not wear them?" McArthur asked.

"Yes."

"Charles, would you rather not see what's going on here?" McArthur said.

"There ain't nobody in here that I want to see," he responded.

Judge Spencer soon took a break for members of the press to go make reports. People were glued to their seats. When they began again, Charlie answered every question so quietly people could hardly hear him, and he had to constantly repeat himself. John asked about the murder of Caril's step-father. Starkweather claimed that each member of her family had come at him, and it was all in self defense.

"And at that moment it was your belief that unless you killed him he'd hit you with a hammer, is that true?"

"Yes."

"And is that still your belief?"

"Yes."

"And, Charles, why did you kill Mrs. Bartlett?"

"I shot Mrs. Bartlett, but I didn't finish killing her."

"Well, why did you shoot her?"

"Mr. McArthur, in these murders, I wish not to talk about them," Charlie said.

"I beg your pardon?" McArthur said, a little taken aback.

"These murders, I wish not to talk about them."

"I can understand that, I can understand that very well, but you realize that if there wasn't a reason I wouldn't ask you."

"She had a knife in her hand."

"And was Mrs. Bartlett then threatening you with a knife?"

"A little bit."

"Well at that time was it your belief that unless you killed Mrs. Bartlett that she'd attack you with a knife?"

"I shot her, but I didn't finish killing her."

"Well that isn't exactly my question, Charles."

"That's what you said, you said if I killed her."

"Well I'll restate it, and if my questions anytime aren't clear, of course you can't answer a question that you don't understand, so you just say so," McArthur said. Then he continued, "My question is this; when you shot Mrs. Bartlett did you think she was going to attack you with a knife?"

"Yes."

"And, Charles, why did you kill Betty Jean, the baby?"

"I didn't kill Betty Jean."

"Didn't you say yesterday that you did?"

"I said I threw a knife at her, I didn't say I killed her."

"Well, I'll put it this way then. Why did you throw a knife at Betty Jean?"

Charlie recoiled and said very quietly, "I don't know."

"I'm sorry, I didn't hear it," McArthur said.

"She was screaming," Charlie answered.

"Betty Jean was screaming, is that true?"

"Yes."

"Charles, at that moment that Betty Jean was screaming was it your belief that the right way to stop that screaming was to throw a knife at her?"

"Yes."

"Is it also true, Charles, that you shot Robert Colvert on December 1, 1957?"

"Yes."

"And why did you shoot Robert Colvert?"

"I was holding the gun, but I didn't shoot him."

"Well was there anybody there besides you and Robert Colvert?"

"No."

"Well, would you just tell us briefly the circumstances, how you happened to be there?" McArthur asked.

"No," Charlie responded suddenly.

"You don't want to do that?" McArthur asked, again surprised at the audacity.

"No."

"Well, Charles, would it be correct to say that you went into that Crest station where he worked and made him drive your car out there while you held the shotgun on him?"

"Yes."

As McArthur continued to question him, Charlie admitted that he had not intended to kill Colvert until it happened, something else that was important for McArthur to establish.

Then Charlie switched gears in a way no one expected. McArthur asked, "Is this a fair statement then, Charles, that you have never killed anybody unless they made some kind of a, of an attack on you first?"

Charlie did not respond.

"Do you follow my question?" McArthur asked.

"Well," Charlie said very quietly, "they were in the right."

McArthur had to have the answer repeated to him to believe what he had heard. It was an amazing moment for Charlie, for him to make such an admission of responsibility, but this trial was about Caril, so John said, "Yes, but that isn't my question; my question is, is it true that in every instance where you killed anybody, you wouldn't decide to or you wouldn't kill them until they had made some movement toward you?"

"Yes," Charlie answered, still quiet, reflective.

"That is correct, is it not?"

"Yes."

"And you, you still feel that way at this time?"

"They were still in the right," Charlie said.

"They were still in the right," McArthur agreed, "but is your memory still that in each instance if they'd have left you alone they wouldn't have got hurt?"

"Yes."

"That is correct," McArthur said. "And has it been your position and is it still your position that every time you killed anybody the actual killing was when you were defending yourself?"

"Yes."

"That is correct, is it not?"

Charlie was quiet again.

"Charles," McArthur said, shifting gears again to a less judgmental tone, "how did you feel after you killed Robert Colvert?"

"Not very good."

"And how did you feel after you killed Robert Jensen?"

"The same way."

"Well I didn't quite get the…"

"I said not very good."

"And is it true that any time you killed anybody you felt bad about it?"

"All except one," Charlie said.

"Do you mean there's one person you killed that you still feel that you did the right thing with?"

"I don't feel I did the right thing, but I don't feel sorry for him."

"Well, who is that?" McArthur asked.

"Marion Bartlett."

McArthur asked a few questions about Charlie planning to kill Marion, then said, "Charles, have you always told your story about these several deaths in the same way?"

"No."

"Have you told various law enforcement authorities a number of different versions as to each death?"

"Yes."

"And have you given the various authorities perhaps as many as seven or eight different accounts of how each death occurred?"

"They are not all different."

"I beg your pardon?"

"They are not all different."

"Well isn't it true that there isn't any single death that you have told about as happening in the same way?"

Charlie didn't answer. He had changed his story about what had happened seven times in the first week alone, and it kept changing every time someone asked him about it. McArthur asked Charlie how it made him feel when he lied about things like this.

"I ain't much of a liar," Charlie said.

"Well I'm not suggesting that yet anyway, but I'm just trying to find out when you do, when you do tell a lie about one of these deaths, how do you feel about telling the lie?"

"Well, I don't stop to think how my emotions are."

"Does it make any, does it give you any feeling at all, is what I'm getting at?"

"I just got done saying I didn't stop to think how my emotions are."

"Well, I know you haven't, but will you just do that now, will you give that a little thought and tell this court and jury?"

"Well, you're asking me how I felt, and I just got done saying I don't know how my emotions were."

"I see. Then you just do not remember about that?"

"I didn't think much of it."

"Well, Charles, did it occur to you that when you lie about something as serious as murder it might get somebody in a lot of trouble?"

"What are you trying to get at?"

"Well I'm just asking you, there's nothing secret about this…"

"Are you saying that I lied when I said if Caril killed somebody?"

"I'm not accusing you of anything."

"That's what it sounds like."

McArthur had his question about how his lying could get someone in a lot of trouble read aloud.

"I suppose I could," Charlie acknowledged.

"Well did that thought enter your mind when you told these false accounts?"

"There you go again."

McArthur went on to ask Charlie point blank why he was testifying against Caril. Charlie answered that Scheele had asked him to come.

"Charles," McArthur said, "you know there was nothing that anybody could really do to you that would hurt if you really refused to come up here and talk, did you?"

"No, I don't."

"I beg your pardon?" McArthur asked.

"No, I don't."

"Well, did you feel that…" McArthur paused for a moment. It had been a strange answer he hadn't expected. "What do you mean by that, can you tell us?"

"Well, you just got done saying that I, what did you say…"

"Well, I think we're confused again, Charles;" McArthur said, "but what I'm trying to find out was did you think that they could make it miserable for you if you refused to come in here and talk?"

"Well, I figured that they could make me do it."

"Well what did you think would happen if you just refused?"

"They'd just come out and get me and take me in."

McArthur asked about Charlie's appeals that were coming up, and established that a good reputation with the county attorney would help in these appeals. Then he went on to the statement Charlie had made about Caril. "Did you ever make a statement that you'd like to have her on your lap if you got electrocuted?"

"Well, I'll tell you one day my attorney came out and told me that, and I told him I wouldn't mind doing it; my attorney brought it up first."

"Well, at least…"

"I agreed with him, yes."

"You agreed with your attorney that Caril Ann ought to be electrocuted; would that be a fair summary of it?"

"Yes."

McArthur continued along this line of questioning before suddenly turning to the murders again. "Charles, why did you shoot August Meyer?"

"Mr. Meyers took a shot at me." He said that August came out of his house with a gun, stepped off the porch, and took a shot at Charlie with a rifle. This was the same rifle Charlie had earlier told Scheele he wasn't able to find after August was dead. Now Scheele asked him to speak up. If there was going to be a new story, he needed to know what it was.

"Well as far as you know," McArthur questioned, "did he just do that without any reason?"

"He had a reason," Charlie said.

"Well do you know what his reason was?"

"Yes."

"And what was that?"

"I think he was a little suspicious of something."

"I beg your pardon?"

"He was suspicious of something."

"Did Mr. Meyer say anything to you about his reason for taking a shot at you?"

"No."

McArthur persisted. He asked Charlie how he knew August was suspicious. Because he had a suspicious look on his face. Where did he get the gun? He had gone inside claiming he was getting a coat.

"And is that the time that he had that suspicious look?" McArthur asked.

"Yes," Charlie answered.

"Now when he came out of the house, did he have his coat on?"

"Well, I was looking the other way when he come out; he had a coat on, yes, but I didn't notice when he came out."

"I see. And when he came out did he have a gun in his hand?"

"I didn't see that neither."

McArthur continued asking about details that Charlie continued to contradict. "Well, what did you see?" McArthur asked.

"What do you mean what did I see?" Charlie snapped back. He was getting flustered. "You mean afterwards or before?"

John remained cool and collected. "I just want to know what you can tell us about his taking a shot at you, Charles."

"Well, I didn't want to talk about these crimes."

"I appreciate you don't, and I don't either."

"Well, a little bit ago I told you if anyone I shot, I told you I thought I was doing it in self defense."

"That's true."

"Then you come up with this deal here."

"No, I just want you to explain it a little bit more so the jury will understand what you were faced with."

"He just shot at me, that's all."

"All right. Now I want a little more detail; did you see him shoot at you?"

"I turned around, yes."

"All right, and did he say anything…"

"No…"

"…before he shot?"

"No."

"Could you see if the gun was pointing at you?"

"It jammed on him."

"Did it go off?"

"It jammed on him."

"Well, I'm not much of a gunsmith, Charles, and I don't know whether it could go off in a jam or not."

"It didn't go off."

"Well, actually when you think of a man shooting, don't you think of a bullet coming out the end?"

"A bullet came out the end before it jammed on him."

"Well, did it make a noise like an ordinary…"

"Most guns do." Charlie was getting impatient and angry.

"Well, yes, I'm asking about Meyer's gun when he shot."

"It made a noise."

"Yes. Do you have any idea where the bullet went?"

"What do you mean where the bullet went?"

"Well, I'm telling you something, Charles, when you talk about the gun jamming that gets me mixed up."

"If you're talking about where the bullet went, it went past me."

"Then when you speak of the jamming, that didn't keep that one bullet from coming out the end, is that right?"

"Well, he fired once, then when he went to push that lever down it jammed on him then."

"I see. Then the first shot went off, you might say, in a normal way."

"It went off, yes."

McArthur asked him details about the guns. He knew that, since Charlie was up for appeal, he would fix his story to make himself look as innocent as possible. This would cause him to contradict certain facts the jury already knew, and Charlie didn't disappoint.

McArthur asked him again about the Jensen murder and Charlie said it was Jensen's own fault he was killed because he had said something and turned on Charlie at the stairs. He didn't know what Jensen had said, but at first it was because he hadn't heard him, then it was because he didn't remember. As they went through the story, Charlie continued to protest, saying he had gone over this with Scheele, and McArthur asked him politely to bear with him. Curiously, Scheele never objected to any of the line of questioning. At one point, McArthur even asked Charlie if Scheele had coached him on his story, but Charlie said he hadn't. When he described riding in the car with the two teenagers to find a phone, McArthur asked whom Charlie intended to call. "The law authorities," Charlie said. McArthur asked why he would want to call the authorities, and Charlie told him that he wanted to give himself up.

McArthur asked if Jensen "knew who you were when you flagged him down?"

"I believe he did."

"Yes; you had the opinion or you felt that Robert Jensen recognized you, did you not?"

"I did."

"Now I'd like to have you tell the court and jury what happened there to give you the opinion that you were recognized by Robert Jensen."

"I told that yesterday."

"Well, I'm kind of dumb, Charles; will you tell me that now?"

"Well, he stopped and he opened the window and asked me what was the matter, and I said 'my car went over in the ditch' – now these might not be the exact words though; but he, he asked what kind of a car it was, and I said 'Forty-nine Ford.' And he said, 'A black one?' and I said, 'Yes.'"

McArthur asked if that was when Jensen had recognized him, and Charlie said that it was when they were in Bennet.

"And will you tell us what gave you that opinion?" McArthur asked.

"I also told that yesterday."

"Well; there's a little of it I didn't hear, Charles, your voice is awfully low."

"Well, he said he couldn't drive to the telephone booth because the phone didn't work, he would have to drive to the man that owned it. And I told him not to do that, and he said he didn't think that we would shoot."

McArthur asked why he had decided not to call the authorities.

"I wasn't going to let them be heroes and take us in," Charlie said.

McArthur asked about more details, bringing up various contradictions, then he read from earlier statements Charlie had made to Scheele in official interrogations.

He got to a point in the Ward home where Charlie had claimed to have cut out newspaper clippings with Caril. "Question: Did Caril know at that time what you had done to her mother and step-father and step-sister? Answer: Well, I think she knew something was wrong, but she didn't come out and say it, didn't talk. Did you answer that way?"

"Yep."

"Question: Well, did she specifically ask you about it? Answer: No; after we left her home she never did talk about it. She had heard something about it on the car radio Monday night. Do you recall that?"

"Yes."

McArthur had already covered his bases on this one. He had checked into the records of the radio station Charlie had claimed to be listening to, and they had not reported this news at the time he claimed to have heard it, or any time near it. In the statement, Charlie went on to explain that he had cut out all references to Caril's family having been killed before giving them to her. McArthur asked Charlie to confirm that he had made that statement, and Charlie did.

He asked about more details, and Charlie continued to answer affirmative until at last he said, "Well, that whole statement that you are reading is a bunch of hogwash."

"Just like everything else you've been saying," John muttered.

"Now, John," Judge Spencer scolded.

He asked about details at the Ward home, establishing that Mrs. Ward had been free to wander the house, yet she had never left, or gone to warn anyone, just like Caril hadn't.

"And as far as you know there was nobody but Mrs. Ward on the second floor, isn't that true?" McArthur asked.

"Yes."

"And as far as you know that telephone was in working order?"

"Yes."

"Charles, do you know why that lady didn't make a phone call to somebody?"

"No."

"Charles, wasn't that lady so terrified she couldn't have dialed one number?"

Charlie claimed that she wasn't, but the question remained open. Why had this woman, left alone on the second floor for close to an hour, neither sneaked away, nor called anyone, nor signaled to a neighbor? And if she, a mature, healthy adult couldn't do it, how could Caril have done it?

"She could talk anytime she wanted to," Charlie said.

"Yes, she could talk, but what I'm asking you, do you know what you would have done if she had?"

"I don't care what she did, she wasn't going to talk."

"Do you know…"

"She was worried about not getting to the cops, she wasn't going to."

"You're not answering me; what would you have done if she had?"

"She wasn't going to do it."

"Well, of course, you realize that she wasn't going to talk and everybody knows she didn't talk, but what I'm asking about what would you have done if she had?"

"I wasn't worried about her talking, I wasn't worrying about what she did, she wasn't going to talk."

"Well, you're kind of dodging me a little bit."

"No, I ain't."

"Do you know what you would have done if she had?"

"Well, I wasn't worrying about her doing it, so I didn't think about it."

"So it didn't enter your head?"

"It didn't enter my head."

There was a specific reason McArthur used those exact words. They had been the words Charlie used when describing the incidents leading up to the murders of everyone else. Killing them, "hadn't entered his head" until the moment he did it. Killing Caril "hadn't entered his head," but who knows what would have happened if she had crossed him, as he perceived Robert Jensen, August Meyer, Mrs. Ward, or any of the other victims had?

By this point, Charlie seemed to know that McArthur was on to him, revealing his hypocrisies and contradictions, so he simply claimed to not remember anything more that he had claimed in the past.

So McArthur returned to his current explanation of what happened. He asked Charlie if Caril knew what he had done to Robert Jensen and Carol King.

"She knew about it," Charlie said.

"Well did you tell her about it?"

"No."

"I beg your pardon?"

"No."

"Did anybody know about it besides yourself at the time it happened?"

"At the time it happened?"

"Yes."

"No."

"Well when you say Caril knew, we have to assume that if she wasn't there either you told her or you told somebody else that did tell her; will you clear that up, please?"

"She knew I was there."

"I beg your pardon?"

"She knew I was there after it happened."

"Well how did she find it out?"

"She read my mind."

After a recess, McArthur brought up the letter that Charlie had written to his parents soon after he had been captured in which he told them not to blame Caril because she had nothing to do with the murders. Then he wrote a hand written statement Charlie had written:

*My name is Charles R. Starkweather. I'm making this statement at my own free will. There has not been any threats or force used against me or have any promises been made. I realize that I did not have to make any statement of any kind. Any statement that I may make may be used against me. I have been told that I have a right to contact an attorney.*

*On Tuesday, eight days before now, I went down to the Bartlett home about 1:30 in the afternoon and Betty got into a fight over Caril, and she said for me not to come down any more to see Caril, and I said something to her and she did not like it, and she hit me about three times. It was something about Bob Von Busch, and his wife who is Caril's older sister. They have been wanting Caril to break up with me so she could go with someone Bob knows.*

*"At the time me and Betty got into the fight I had my brother's gun with me, and because me and Marion was going hunting that afternoon, and Betty hit me, and I hit her back, and she let out a loud*

*cry. And Marion came in and hit me and was pushing all over the
room. Then he picked up a hammer and was going to hit me with it,
and then I ran into the other room and put a bullet in the gun. He
come running into the bedroom where I was, and he, and was just
about ready to come down with a hammer, so I let him have it, I think
it killed him right away.*

*"Then Betty came running out with the knife that I had with
me. I did the same to her, but it didn't kill her right away, so I had to
hit her. Then Betty Jean start yelling so loud that she could wake up
the whole town, so I hit her, and I do not know how many times I did.*

*"I wrapped them up and put them in the little house out behind
the house. Caril came home about 4 of that afternoon. I told her a
line that they were somewhere. I was going to tell her about what
happened, but I was letting it go by, and before I said anything the
days went by so fast I never did say anything to Caril."*

Charlie said the whole statement was untrue. Then McArthur
went through the statement Charlie gave to Scheele soon after that,
comparing it with the written statement. It was the closest Charlie
ever came to repeating the story verbatim. Charlie continued to deny
the entire thing, claiming that his current account was what was true.
When McArthur finished, Charlie simply said, "I told you this
morning I couldn't remember the answers."

"Your answer is that you don't remember?"

"Well, I could have saved you trouble of reading."

McArthur turned to the murder of Lauer Ward. "Would you
tell just briefly what he did?"

Charlie was silent for a time, then muttered something very
briefly.

"I beg your pardon?" McArthur said.

"No."

"You mean you can't recall?"

"I told you this morning I wasn't going to talk about it."

He said the same thing about other murders and refused to
answer any more of McArthur's questions regarding the killings.

McArthur turned very suddenly to another subject. "Charles, has Sheriff Karnopp been a frequent visitor to you at the penitentiary since your trial?"

"No."

"How long has it been since he's called upon you other than to bring you down to this trial?"

"That's how long."

"Well, how long back?"

"Well, from the end of my trial until the time he come and got me."

"You haven't seen him in the meantime?"

"No."

"Isn't it true that you have always felt rather friendly toward Mr. Karnopp, that is true, is it not?"

"Yes."

McArthur ended his cross-examination soon after that.

Scheele immediately started on his own damage control, asking Charlie if he, or anyone in the police department, had told Charlie what to say. Charlie said no. He asked him a few more questions about details pertaining to his arrest, and when he was brought back to Lincoln. Then he said, "Now, Charles, why did you not tell the entire truth to me when I asked you questions about those matters that were taken down by Mr. Shamberg?"

"I told you that once before."

"Well will you tell me now?"

"I was protecting Caril Fugate."

Scheele walked him through his story again, wisely skipping the Meyer farm, but clearing up his statements on the other events. When they came to the Ward home, there was some confusion about from which newspapers he had cut portions out. McArthur rose and asked the court's permission to question Charlie on his knowledge of the articles. Judge Spencer granted it, and as McArthur asked Charlie to describe what parts of the paper he had cut out, they did not match the first clippings that were offered into evidence, so they were removed. Then, as Scheele asked him about a second group of clippings, they again did not match Charlie's own description, so when McArthur objected, they were again tossed out.

Scheele was more careful with the third group of clippings. He first described them to Charlie so he would not confuse them. "That's objected to as leading, and he's already said he doesn't know anything about them, can't identify them;" McArthur insisted. "Now he's asked to compare them with something else that he couldn't identify." Spencer overruled his objection, and allowed Charlie to look at the clippings. Now, of course, Charlie was able to identify them as pictures Caril had seen from articles that said that her family was dead. He claimed that Caril knew her family was dead all along, and that they made up the story about her being kidnapped together.

"When did you both make that story up?" Scheele asked.

"Sometime during that week."

"While you were staying at the Bartlett home?"

"Yes."

"And what is the truth with reference to the story of your holding Caril your hostage?"

"That ain't true."

"Was that story made up too?"

"Yes."

Scheele had Charlie go over the story of killing Caril's parents again. Charlie explained how Caril was involved, and embellished even more. This time he claimed that Caril grabbed the gun from Charlie and asked him to let her "blow her (mother) to hell." McArthur objected throughout the testimony, but the judge overruled every objection.

When McArthur got his redirect examination, he asked if he was telling the truth now, on the stand. Charlie said yes. McArthur asked him again about his previous statements which he was now contradicting, and Charlie again called the previous accounts "hogwash." Then McArthur said, "Every time you have made a statement or made a confession or signed something in the past have you told the people that you gave it to that it was all the truth?"

"A few of them."

"Well did you ever deliver one and tell them it wasn't the truth when they delivered it?"

"No."

"You have always said it was the truth at the time, haven't you?"

"Yes."

On his re-cross examination, Scheele brought up the letter Charlie wrote in the Ward home that claimed both he and Caril had committed the murders, and that they would die together. McArthur didn't object to the letter. In fact, he seized upon it on his own re-cross examination, asking Charlie that, if they both wrote it together, why didn't Caril sign it? In fact, why didn't she write the letter, since she had the better penmanship? Charlie wasn't able to answer any of the questions, but insisted she had told him what to write.

After that, they were both finished with Charlie, and he was returned to the penitentiary.

Next on the stand was Gertrude Karnopp, the wife of the Lancaster County Sheriff. She spoke about when she first met Caril. "The first words that were said to me about the events during that time was when Caril asked me, 'Are my folks dead?' And I didn't answer immediately. And she said, 'Who killed them?' And I believe my answer was, 'Don't you know, Caril?' And she told me that the first that she had known about it was when Mrs. Warick, the Scottsbluff County sheriff's wife, had told her in the jail at Gering." Caril told Gertrude about being in the car when Robert and Carol were killed, that Charlie had gone into the "cave" with them, been in there several minutes before she heard two gunshots, then came out several minutes later saying that the girl was dead, but the boy was still barely alive. She then talked about the murders of the Wards, before she returned to the subject of her family.

"She talked about her family at various times during the day, and she mentioned that she didn't like her stepfather very well, that he was very strict with them... And she also talked about one time, she started talking about a fight that had taken place at their home when Charles came in and her mother was washing, and that they had gotten into a fight, and then Charles said some bad things and her mother said some bad things is the way she put it, and Charles grabbed at her little sister, as I remember her saying it, and then she stopped talking about this fight. She also showed me some pictures that she had of her mother and father and her little sister."

Scheele presented the newspaper clippings and Gertrude said those were the photographs that Caril had shown her.

"She also at one time said that the papers said that those three bodies that were found where they were shot, but they weren't shot outside, they were shot in the house."

"Did you ask her anything when she said that?" Scheele asked.

"Yes, I asked her which three bodies she meant."

"What did she say?"

McArthur objected to this whole line of questioning as it was a statement without any official court reporter, attorney, or any kind of secondary witness present. But the objection was overruled.

Gertrude continued, "She waited a moment and she says, 'Mr. Meyer's body was shot in the house and drug out there,' and then she refused to talk to me."

Mrs. Karnopp went on to claim that Caril had told her she had practiced throwing knives, that she had callously gone through her mother's purse after she had been killed, and that she had given guns to Charlie when he asked for them.

By the time John got up to cross-examine, Gertrude had presented what was essentially Caril's confession for the jury. He began by asking her if Caril had ever told her why she had taken part in helping with the murders.

"She told me that her folks had been taken someplace and that something would happen to them if she didn't do what Charles said to," Mrs. Karnopp said.

"Then the whole gist of her conversation there was that she was acting under compulsion, wouldn't that be fair?" McArthur asked.

"That was," she said.

"Mrs. Karnopp, you were here as I recall it when Sheriff Romer testified?"

"Yes, sir, I was."

"You heard Sheriff Romer?"

"Yes, sir."

"And did you notice that every time he quoted Caril on this witness stand, he quoted her as referring to her stepsister, do you remember that?"

"I didn't specifically, no, sir."

"You didn't notice that. You do know, however, that Caril has never had a stepsister, don't you?"

"Well, I know she has a sister and she had a half sister."

"This little child that died was a blood sister?"

"Would be a half sister to her, yes."

"Sure. Not a stepsister. And isn't this true, Mrs. Karnopp, that as of that period of time it was the radio and the newspapers and the television that was referring to the little child as Caril's stepsister?"

"Well, it's possible."

The rest of the cross-examination involved Caril's various interviews with the police, and how much legal counsel she was allowed. Gertrude did not know every detail, but she did know that Caril only had a lawyer present late in the interview processes.

The next witness was Dr. Edwin A. Coats, who had also been present when Caril was questioned. Again, the prosecution established that she was treated fairly, and the defense questioned whether she was given legal counsel.

Two more people testified about Caril giving her statement in the same way before Gertrude Karnopp retook the stand, followed by her husband. Sheriff Merle Karnopp testified that he had received the newspaper clippings that had allegedly been found in Caril's coat. On cross-examination, McArthur asked him about the note Caril had written asking for help. Heflin had mailed it along with the clippings, but Karnopp claimed that he never received the note.

At the end of the week, McArthur requested a mistrial on the basis that Charlie had refused to answer his questions even though he had answered the prosecution questions. The motion was denied since John had not asked the court to force Charlie to answer.

On Monday morning, Officer Eugene Masters took the stand and told about the conditions of the Bartlett home when they investigated it. They found blood stains in several locations, and of course the bodies in the chicken coop out back, but he also found several places where rope had been used to tie someone down, then cut.

Next, the jury was able to hear Caril's story for the first time, but not from her lips. Audrey Wheeler, who took shorthand notes during Scheele's first "informal visit" with Caril, was called to the witness stand. McArthur objected on the grounds that Caril was not questioned with a lawyer present, was not offered a lawyer, and was not informed that there would be charges against her. The objection was overruled and Scheele began questioning Wheeler about the day of the visit. "Who was present at that time?"

"Mrs. Karnopp, Dr. Coats, Mr. Fahrnbruch, Caril, and myself."

"And during the course of that conversation did Mr. Fahrnbruch make any explanations to her?"

"Yes, he did."

"And will you tell us generally what they referred to, please?"

McArthur objected, but it was overruled.

"Well," Audrey began, "he first explained to her that she would be taken to the county attorney's office that afternoon, at which time an opportunity to visit with them before she was taken over to the County Court for arraignment."

McArthur objected again, and it was overruled.

She continued, "Well, he told her that this was a very serious charge; she said she understood that. He told her that she would be taken to County Court and arraigned, explained that charges that would be filed against her, which would be first-degree murder and murder committed in the perpetration of a crime. He asked her if she understood that, and she said she did. He then told her, asked her, if she knew that at the time these things were going on they were wrong, and she said she did... And he told her that she could have an attorney if she wanted one, that at the preliminary hearing it would be up to her folks or friends to provide such an attorney... Mr. Fahrnbruch asked her if she had been told by you in Wyoming that she could have an attorney... She said yes."

"Did she say whether or not she had asked me or anyone else to provide an attorney for her?" Scheele asked.

"She said no, she had not."

Scheele concluded his questioning.

John McArthur stepped up. "Miss Wheeler, wouldn't you say that the way you have related this conversation is quite misleading?" he asked abruptly.

"I don't understand what you mean by misleading, Mr. McArthur."

John held up his copy of the transcription she had written. He gestured to her own copy of the notes that she was holding and told her he would read from his copy.

"By Mr. Fahrnbruch, 'And did Mr. Scheele explain to you, and he did explain to you in Wyoming, did he not, that you could have a lawyer if you wanted one?' And the answer was 'Yes.' And the very next question, 'And you told him at that time that you did not want a lawyer?' And the answer, 'No, I never. I didn't know what he meant at that time by that. I thought he meant by the District Attorney.' And the next question and answer, 'Did you want a lawyer at that time?' And the answer, 'Yes.' And the next question and answer, 'And you want a lawyer now, is that right?' And the answer, 'Yes, but who would take it?'"

Miss Wheeler admitted that this was the actual transcription. It became suddenly very obvious why Elmer Scheele had asked her to recite the testimony by memory rather than read the transcript. What Scheele did not know was that Audrey Wheeler had contacted John after the visit and informed him that something was amiss. The transcript they were reading from had literally been cut off at the bottom with scissors. Audrey recalled that, after Caril asked, "Who would take it?" Dale Fahrnbruch had said, "Well, you understand that I can't get you an attorney." She couldn't remember exactly what else had been said, but Audrey told John that Fahrnbruch had told Caril that she was basically "on her own." When John looked at the missing part of the transcript, he found what Fahrnbrook had said after Caril had asked who would take her case.

Fahrnbrook had told Caril, "In the County Court it is up to the person being charged or it is up to her friends to get a lawyer. After the preliminary hearing and if you are bound over to the District Court then you are entitled to have a lawyer appointed by the court." In other words, he was saying that she would not be given an attorney unless the case went to district court, which was not only confusing for anyone, let alone a scared fourteen-year-old child, but was also entirely untrue. The missing portion of the transcript also revealed that Scheele had told Caril if she pled "not guilty" things would "only go bad for her."

Scheele then offered Caril's statement into evidence. McArthur objected stating that, as he had just shown, there was no attorney present, nor was an attorney offered. His objection was overruled and Scheele began to read:

*"Caril, this is Miss Wheeler, a Court Reporter, and you know Mrs. Karnopp and Dr. Coats?"*
*"Yes."*
*"Caril, you and I have talked a couple of times here, and you and I and your father talked this afternoon, is that right Caril?"*
*"Yes."*
*"We discussed at that time, and talked over about taking this statement from you with the Court Reporter present, is that correct, Caril?"*
*"Yes."*
*"And you told me at that time that you would be willing to do that?"*
*"Yes."*
*"You also asked me at that time if there would be a trial?"*
*"Yes."*
*"And go to court, and I told you there would be?"*
*"Yes."*
*"And you understand that this can be used in court, this statement that we are taking? You understand that?"*
*"Yes."*

Scheele was establishing that he had warned Caril that there would be a trial, and that this statement could be used in that trial, which to some onlookers seemed as though he had warned her. But to look at it closely, one sees that he had not stated what trial, and whom it would be used against. As far as Caril knew, this was still about Charlie's trial, and it would be used against him.

The statement began with them establishing her age, where she went to school, where she lived, who her family was, etc. They moved on to her relationship with Charlie. Her brother-in-law had introduced them a year and a half earlier, and she had dated him ever since. She wasn't certain of Charlie's age, but they had spent a lot of time together. Scheele then asked her if she knew anything about the elderly man who was killed near Bennet. She said she did.

> *"What do you know about it, Caril?"*
> *"Well, I know who killed him."*
> *"And what man are you referring to?"*
> *"Mr. Meyer."*
> *"And who did kill Mr. Meyer?"*
> *"Chuck Starkweather."*

He asked her how she had met August Meyer, and she told him that her brother-in-law had taken her and her sister out there hunting a long time ago. Scheele asked about the day Charlie killed Mr. Meyer. Caril said that Charlie had told her he was going to meet some other boys out at the farm.

> *"Now, after you got out to the farm, what happened out there, Caril?"*
> *"Do you want me to tell the story?"*
> *"Yes."*
> *"I am all mixed up. I don't know whether I can tell it straight or not now."*
> *"Just tell it as best you remember it."*
> *"Well, we went out there and pulled up in the drive, and we got stuck, and then we got out of the car and tried to get out, but we couldn't, so we went down to – what do you call that place, a bomb shelter or what?"*
> *"Was that on the way in to the Meyer farm?"*
> *"Yes."*
> *"And what happened then?"*
> *"We got out of the car, and we couldn't move it because it was stuck, and then we went down in to that place."*
> *"When you say you went down in to that place, you mean the bomb shelter?"*
> *"Yes."*
> *"And what was down in the cellar?"*
> *"Some old school books."*

She said they stayed in the storm cellar for about a half hour before coming back out and walking up to the Meyer farm. Charlie told Mr. Meyer that they needed horses to get his car unstuck. They headed to the barn.

"Then Mr. Meyer said, I don't know what he said. Then we started to walk back to the house, and Mr. Meyer started to go in the door, and I saw him raise the gun and heard a shot."

"Who did you see raise the gun?"

"Chuck."

Caril described how Charlie told her to watch for cars while he dragged the body inside. Going through Meyer's things, Charlie found some money and several guns which he took. He also found new clothing which he put on, and told Caril to put on some as well, but Caril refused. Charlie ate some of the food in the kitchen, but Caril didn't want any.

"What did you do after he had eaten this food?"

"Well, I kept saying let's go, because I was scared."

"What were you afraid of?"

"I was afraid of Mr. Meyer, because he was dead, and I was scared."

After that, she could not recall very well the order of things. She remembered going to a couple of service stations, getting the car fixed, and getting some food, but she couldn't remember if that had been before they went to the Meyer farm or after. She sounded as though she was in shock over the murder, but Scheele never asked about her emotional state. She said when they returned to the Meyer farm, Charlie looked in the window and said that the white sheet he had placed over August had been removed, and that they better leave because it looked like someone had discovered the body. They drove back into Lincoln, and along the way Charlie pointed out the house where he said her mother was being kept.

Caril was trying to elaborate on that when Scheele interrupted her, "Did you get stuck at Bennet and leave a car there on the Meyer farm?"

"Yes."

"What happened at that time?" he asked.

"We got stuck there."

She described being picked up by the two teenagers, who took them into Bennet so they could use a phone, but it didn't work, so

Robert Jensen began to drive them to another phone when Charlie pulled out his gun and pointed it at his head.

Caril's statement continued: *"He said – he told him to keep going or he would blow his head off. I think that's what he said. The boy said, you wouldn't do that, or I don't think you would do that, and Chuck said, do you want to find out buddy. He said something about buddy, and then the boy kept driving."* Charlie informed Robert that he was going to take his car from him, then he had him pull up beside the other car that Charlie had gotten stuck in the mud.

*"Chuck told the boy to get out, and I pointed the gun at the girl. I put it on the seat back, like that (indicating), and told her to get out."*

*"You mean you pointed the gun at the girl and told her to get out?"*

*"Yes. I just waived the gun across the seat like that (indicating)."*

*"What did you tell her at that time?"*

*"I told her to get out."*

*"Why did you do that, Caril?"*

*"Because he told him to get out."*

*"He told the driver to get out?"*

*"He told them both to get out."*

Charlie then walked the two teenagers into the storm cellar. Caril heard two shots, then a half hour later, Charlie returned, and began to drive out, but got stuck again. Caril helped him get the car unstuck again.

*"Did you get out then?"* Scheele asked.

*"Well, he told me while he was getting it out, if he got it out that he would take me home, and he told me he would take me home because I had seen enough and heard enough."*

Charlie drove toward Lincoln. Along the way, Caril found some school books in the car and threw them out the window.

Back in Lincoln, Charlie circled Caril's house, but, spotting the police, he drove on. He again took Caril past the house where he said her family was being kept, and reminded her what would happen if she left. He got tires from the house, then continued on around the corner where they eventually entered the Ward house.

The courtroom took a short recess, and when they returned, Scheele stepped them back to the time they were with the teenagers. *"Was there anything else taken from them?"*

*"Yes, there was $4.00."*

*"And how did that come about?"*

*"Well, Chuck asked them if they had any money, and the boy said yes, he had $4.00, and handed his billfold to Chuck, and Chuck handed his billfold and the boy's billfold to me. I took the money out of the boy's billfold and put it in Chuck's, and handed Chuck's billfold back to him, and handed the boy's billfold back to the girl, because he asked me to."*

They returned to talking about the Ward house. After sleeping in their car, Charlie and Caril entered the house. Mrs. Ward and the maid were there. Despite their intrusion, Mrs. Ward was very hospitable. Caril was still tired, and she went and slept on the couch. She didn't remember much of what else happened.

When she woke up, she was offered pancakes, but Caril still wasn't hungry. She instead went back to sleep.

At this point, Scheele asked her about several details including the layout of the home, what several of the people had in their possession, and what they were wearing. Caril tried to remember, but couldn't. The day at the Ward home was a blur, as she was in and out of consciousness. When at last she woke up and stayed awake, Charlie came down with a bloody knife and told her to wash it. The knife had come from Caril's mother's home.

*"Now, what did you do after you washed the knife off?"* Scheele asked.

*"He told me to go upstairs and sprinkle some perfume around."*

*"Why did he tell you that?"*

*"He said he could smell the blood."*

He asked about some details regarding the perfume, then said, *"After you sprinkled this perfume around and put the bottle back, what did you do then?"*

*"Then I went downstairs, and I think he asked me – I think he told me to go in the closet in the man's room and see if there was any coat or jacket."*

After that, Charlie wrote notes to the maid and had her get supplies for them, then flushed the notes down the toilet.

*"Now Caril,"* Scheele said, *"did you ever have a gun in your hands while you were in the Ward house?"*

*"Yes."*

*"And what gun did you have in your hands?"*

*"The .22."*

*"And was that loaded at that time?"*

*"Yes."*

*"And what did you do with that gun, Caril?"*

*"Well, I pointed it at the maid."*

*"And why did you do that?"*

*"Because he told me to."*

Charlie had Caril watched for Mr. Ward's return, and she called to him when she saw Lauer pulling into the driveway.

*"What did you go in the bathroom for?"* Scheele asked.

*"I just went in there. I was scared."*

Caril came out a few minutes later to find Mr. Ward moaning on the floor, and the maid sitting against the wall. Charlie took the maid upstairs and told her that if anyone else came to the door, he would shoot her. He then tied her to the bed using the bed sheet, her feet on one end and her hands to the other. She asked them to turn on the lights because it was scary in the dark, but Charlie refused.

*"And then what happened?"* Scheele asked.

*"I was looking out the window, and he started stabbing her, and she started screaming and hollering."*

*"How many times did he stab her?"*

*"I don't know."*

*"Do you know what he stabbed her with?"*

*"Yes, my mother's knife."*

*"Did he say anything while he was stabbing her?"*

*"I don't know. He put a pillow over her face."*

*"Did he stab her more than once?"*

*"Yes."*

*"Would it be more than twice?"*

*"Yes."*

*"How do you know that, Caril?"*

*"I heard it. Every time he stabbed her, she moaned."*

*"About how many times did she moan?"*

*"Well, more than five."*

*"And did her hands continue to be tied to the top of the bed?"*

*"No, she broke them loose."*

*"When did she break them loose?"*

*"When he was stabbing her."*

*"And how about her feet, were they still tied to the bottom of the bed?"*

*"Yes."*

*"And then what happened after he got done stabbing her?"*

*"He said he didn't think she was ever going to die, and then he said to shine the flashlight over there and he cut the strips holding her legs, and covered her up."*

She held the flashlight to him, but she continued to look away. After she could hear he was finished, she looked at him. His shirt and right arm were covered in blood. He told Caril to get him a new shirt and she did. They cleaned up, then Charlie looked for money and told Caril to do the same.

*"Now Caril, while you were in the house there, did you look at any newspapers?"*

*"Yes. I didn't look at it. There was a newspaper there, and he had it and cut out some pictures."*

*"And did you cut out any of the pictures?"*

*"Well, he cut part of them out and I cut the rest of them out."*

*"What pictures did you cut out?"*

*"The pictures of him and I."*

*"You cut that one out?"*

*"I helped cut that one out. He cut part way and I cut the rest."*

She described several other clippings, including some of her family, that were cut out.

*"In any event, either you or he cut them out, is that right?"* Scheele asked.

*"I think he cut them out,"* Caril answered.

*"Were they in there when you cut out the picture of you and Chuck?"*

*"I don't know. I didn't get to see the paper. He wouldn't let me see it."*

*"You cut out the other picture, didn't you?"*

*"Yes."*

*"Were those, the pictures of your mother and dad and little sister in the paper when you cut out the big picture?"*

*"No, they weren't in the paper. I didn't see them."*

*"Either you or he cut them out?"*

*"Yes."*

*"Do you know which one?"*

*"I think he cut them out, or I think I cut them out."*

Just before they left, the phone rang. Charlie told Caril to answer it, and she did. Scheele didn't ask her to whom she spoke, just how long she had talked. She told him it had been about a minute before she hung up and they left, heading west toward Washington. Charlie had a brother who lived there, and they would stay with him.

She then described stopping in Wyoming when Charlie shot the man sleeping in his car. He told Caril to get into the backseat of the car, and she did. Charlie had some trouble starting the car, so he shook the man, hoping he was still alive. Charlie tried again and got the car moving. She told Scheele they had driven it a little ways, and then Charlie got out of the car. *"I was in the back seat,"* Caril said, *"and he got out and ran back to the Packard."*

*"What did he run back to the Packard for?"*

*"He was going to put it in the place where the other car was."*

*"Is that sort of a secluded place, or a place where it was covered up and couldn't be seen?"*

*"No, you could see it."*

*"Then what happened?"*

*"I don't know whether he started it or not. I was in the back seat, and this man drove up behind the Buick and started walking towards Chuck, and I was trying to tell him to go away. I motioned for him to go away, and shook my head at him, and once he stopped, and then he started walking towards Chuck, and Chuck pointed the gun at him and told him to help release the brake and he wouldn't get hurt."*

Caril said she had tried to start the car she was in, but she couldn't get it started. Charlie pointed the gun at the man who had pulled up and told him to help Charlie move his car into place. The man grabbed the gun and they wrestled over it.

The court took a recess, and when they returned, Scheele started over from the very beginning, when Caril first got home to find Charlie there.

*"I came in, and I opened the door and walked in, and he was standing behind the door... He told me – he said for me to sit down on the couch, or chair, and then I asked him where my folks were, because they were out there and they were gone, and then he told me that story... He told me my folks were over to that old lady's house where he had the hot rod, I guess that's what you call it, and he said if I done what he told me, then they wouldn't be hurt. I asked him how they got over there, and he said he had come in and my mother had told him to get out, and he asked them if they were going along peacefully, and he said my mother kept telling him to get out, and they grabbed my little sister, and then they asked him if he was going to come peacefully, and he said they would."*

Caril asked Charlie to let her talk to her family, but he refused, assuring her that they were indeed safe. They watched a late night movie, and she went to bed. He stayed in the chair part of the night, then crawled into bed with her. The next morning a friend came over to walk with Caril to school, and Charlie had Caril send the friend away.

She described being tied up with rags and sheets whenever he left to do errands. Whenever someone came to the door, she told them to go away because everyone was sick with the flu. When the police officer came, she woke Charlie up, then told the officer the same thing she had told everyone else. On each of these occasions, Charlie was either in another room, or behind the door with a gun in case they came in. The two most adamant people who tried to gain entry were Caril's sister and grandmother. Her sister didn't go away until Caril got mad at her and told her to leave if she knew what was good for her.

She only told one person that Charlie was in the house, and that her family was being held hostage, Charlie's sister. Charlie had been in another room and Caril spoke quietly to her, but his sister merely looked at her strangely and walked away.

The questioning soon turned to very delicate matters. Scheele began to ask Caril if she had had sex with Charlie. Caril didn't seem to understand what he meant, and he began to graphically describe each step. Had he put his penis into her sexual organ? *Yes.* How far? *Not quite an inch.* It had hurt, and she told him to stop. The questions persisted about various positions, various things Charlie had tried. Caril claimed she had told Charlie to stop each time because it hurt. Scheele then asked her if they had sexual relations on the way to Wyoming, and she said she thought so, but she again seemed confused by the questions.

"*Now Caril,*" he began again, "*I believe you also told me earlier day before yesterday or yesterday morning, that you told Charles on the way to Wyoming you loved him, is that true?*"

"*Yes, I think so.*"

"*And did you tell him that on more than one occasion?*"

"*Yes.*"

"*And what was your reason for telling him that?*"

"*I was afraid he might kill me.*"

"*And did he ever tell you, when you were back here during those few days, did he ever tell you to kill him?*"

"*Yes.*"

"*And when and where did that take place?*"

"*I was sitting on the davenport.*"

"*And what did he say?*"

"*Well, he throwed the gun at me and told me to go ahead and shoot.*"

"*And what did you say?*"

"*I told him, don't be so silly.*"

He asked about details on the road. She described writing the note that later disappeared. It had read, '*Help. Police. Don't ignore.*'

"*Do you know where that note is at this time?*"

"*It should be in my blue coat; my old coat.*"

Then came the most damaging part of the entire statement, Caril's admission that she could have gotten away.

"*Now then, Caril, you told me the other day that you had several opportunities to leave Chuck?*"

"*Yes.*"

*"In your own mind, when did you have those opportunities?"*

*"When I went to the mail box. I don't know for sure."*

*"Well, did you think that at the time that you talked to your sister and her husband when they were in the cab?"*

*"I had a chance then."*

*"Did you think at that time that you had a chance?"*

*"Yes. And I know when the policemen were there. I opened the door and let the dog in, and then I was going to go with them, but I didn't."*

She was asked about several other details, including hearing a report on the radio about three bodies being found at her house. They had been in the car on the way to Wyoming, and as soon as the report came on, Charlie turned it off. Scheele ended the questioning by saying, *"Now is there anything else, Caril, that you know of about any of the cases; the Colvert case, the Meyer case, the Jensen case, the Carol King case, the Mr. and Mrs. Ward or the maid cases, that you haven't told me about?"*

*"Yes,"* she said. *"I didn't know he was going to kill any of them."*

Court was adjourned. As everyone was filing out, Ninette found James. "That statement sure looks bad for your dad's case, Jim." James told her that it's not the way it sounded. His father had explained it was a matter of intent. "Caril will answer any question you ask her, Mrs. Beaver, you know that," James said. "She's very honest and will tell you anything. I remember the first time I met her; I was worried about maybe saying the wrong thing. But Dad told me I could ask her anything at all and not to worry about it. That's the way she is. She doesn't make excuses for herself or try to explain why she did something. She just answers whatever you ask her. The reasons make all the difference."

"And when do we get to hear the reasons?" Ninette asked him.

"When Dad starts his case," he answered. "That should be soon. Mr. Scheele said that the statement would end his case."

Early the next week, the State did indeed rest its case, and it was time for John to make his.

# Chapter Eight
## The State of Nebraska v
## Caril Ann Fugate:
## The Defense

It was a stressful time for John, though he did his best not to show it at home. It wasn't that difficult; hiding his emotions came naturally to him. But he paced more often, flipped his coin, and ran it through his fingers faster. He talked to himself throughout his long walks. Some mornings his family awoke to hear him pacing, growling under his breath, or arguing with himself in the mirror while he shaved.

His children rarely saw him. They were used to his leaving at five in the morning, appearing at dinner time, then disappearing to return to work for the evening, but during the weeks of the trial, John didn't even come home for dinner most of the time, returning after the children had gone off to bed. And on many of those nights he hardly slept, but wandered the house thinking aloud. Usually mild mannered and patient, John was intense and short tempered during the weeks of the trial. Much of the family gave him room. His regular habit of reading from a history book for an hour each night before heading to bed was often replaced with more pacing, more thinking, and more frustrated growling. Someone had left a Bible on the doorstep recently, a hint to John that if he only found God, he would realize that

Caril was guilty, and he wouldn't commit this terrible sin of defending her.

He always brought home his briefcase and left it where he could get to it if he needed to. John Jr, now eighteen years old, was always curious about what was inside, and one morning, before his father left, he opened it just enough to sneak a peek. Inside were photographs of the murders. Bodies were contorted in ways John Jr. didn't know were possible. It was the most horrific thing he had ever seen. He shut the briefcase quickly. If that was the business his father was in, he didn't want to have anything to do with it.

*     *     *

The defense began with their star witness, Caril. Typically it is not a good idea for someone to be a witness at their own trial, but Elmer Scheele had already read her statement, and he had done it in his voice, reading from a statement Caril had made when she was merely intending to tell what Charlie had done, and not explaining the reasons for her own actions. She marched to the witness stand rigidly and sat with her back straight and her chin forward. She was raised to be proud, brave. But, as in her interview, it was coming across to the spectators as defiant.

"Will you tell us your name?" McArthur began.

"Caril Ann Fugate," she said, her words like sharp jabs; no expression on her face.

John tried to counter this by asking about her various schools, and what she did in them. She described a regular schoolgirl existence.

He moved on to her relationship with her family, asking her about their vacations up into the Sand Hills. It was the only trip she had ever taken, she had never seen very much outside of Lincoln. Emphasizing her youth, he asked about her age, about recent national events, such as World War II and the Korean War. She knew little about them except what she had learned in history class.

He asked about what she did at the hospital where she was being kept. She played cards sometimes, but most of the time she volunteered to help the nurses. The person these questions revealed was in stark contrast with the stone faced person sitting in the witness chair.

Then John got to the point. "How did you feel when Charles Starkweather walked into this Courtroom?"

"I was scared to death of him."

John asked her how well she got along with her family. She viewed her mother and step father the way any young teenager would; she resented the discipline they placed on her, but she respected them. Her half-sister, whom she referred to as her "baby sister," she adored.

"How did you feel when that baby sister was born, Caril?"

"I felt like a million."

"What were your feelings toward that little girl?"

"I would do anything for her."

He walked her through her friendships, showed photographs of her with her friends and had her talk about her church membership, for which she was once given an award for service. During this he performed another one of his maneuvers for which John was known. When talking about one of the photographs, he said, "…does it correctly show what it purports to show there?"

"Yes, sir."

Then he asked, "Do you know what 'purports' means?"

"No, sir."

It was a seemingly unimportant piece of evidence, but John had just made the most important point of the case. Caril was easily manipulated into answering positively when someone in authority asked her something, even if she didn't understand. It was just that easy to get her to go along.

John asked her about her relationship with Charlie. She said that he often told her that he was a sheriff, and was fond of telling her about his adventures rounding up Indians on the prairie. They mostly went to movies, out to eat, and rode horses. He liked to dress up like a cowboy and build on his own personal mythology. They were together for about six months. Her step-father never liked Charlie, but her mother put up with him. Charlie then broke up with Caril, but they patched things up. Then Caril broke up with Charlie the Sunday before all of the trouble began. "He came down and he came in the house, and we were doing the washing; and he started spouting off about different things and accusing me of going out with other boys, saying nasty things, and I told him to leave and not to come back and I didn't want to ever see him again. And my mother was out in the kitchen and so was my little sister, I went out in the kitchen and I told my mother that I told him to go away, and she told him to go away. And his face turned red, and he got mad about it, and he was hitting his hand with his fist. And he asked me if I never wanted to see him again, and I said, yes, I never wanted to see him again. And he says, 'All right,' and hung around for a few more minutes and he went out the door and slammed it."

John asked her about the night the teenagers were killed. Caril was scared and tired. She had hardly slept throughout the week they were in the house, and she hadn't slept since they left it. Charlie was keeping her standing by holding her by the arm.

"Now how did you happen to be carrying your father's gun?" John asked.

"After he hit the dog with it he told me I was to carry it until he could get it fixed."

"Get it fixed?"

"Yes, sir."

"What was the matter with it?"

"He said it broke something after he had hit Mr. Meyer's dog with it." John had her establish again how many weapons Charlie was carrying, and the fact that her weapon didn't work, while his did. He asked her if she had seen any houses or cars while they were walking. She hadn't. She described the Jensen boy and the King girl picking them up much as it had been described before. Caril said she was so afraid of Charlie doing the same thing to all of them as he had done to August Meyer that she remained completely quiet.

They got to the telephone and Robert said it didn't work. "When Robert Jensen said he thought he ought to go see this man about the telephone, he took it down and pointed it to his head... Charles Starkweather told him to keep driving, and Robert Jensen said he thought he ought to go see this man."

"Did you see what Carol King did when the gun was put up against Jensen's head?"

"She stiffened out."

"What did you do?"

"I started to cry."

"Why?"

"Because I thought he was going to shoot him like he did Mr. Meyers... I said 'Please don't hurt him,' and he told me to shut up."

"What did Robert Jensen say if you can remember at that time?"

"I think he said something about 'Do as he says,' or, 'Do what he says so we don't get hurt.'"

Later, as they were driving, Charlie told Robert to give him his money. He handed him his billfold, then Charlie handed it to Caril and told her to take the money out. She hesitated, and again, Robert told her to do as Charlie said so no one would get hurt. So she did, and she gave the billfold back to Robert. When they got to the storm cellar, Charlie told them to get out. Robert obliged, but Carol King hesitated. Charlie told her to point the gun at King and tell her to get out, which Fugate did. "I said she better get out so she doesn't get hurt." John took the gun she had been holding from the witness table and asked her to show everyone how she held it. People in the court began to move uncomfortably. Some stood to leave.

The gun wasn't loaded and the judge called out, "Everyone remain seated in the courtroom, please." The audience calmed down and people took their seats. John handed the gun to her and had her demonstrate how she had held the gun. She showed him, then said she put the gun down and climbed into the front seat where she waited while Charlie took them to the cellar.

After Caril described hearing the shots, John asked, "Caril, why didn't you jump out and run away?"

"I couldn't move, after I heard the shots I couldn't move."

It was silent for a long time until at last Charlie returned. "He was saying foul language and said one of them was dead and one of them wasn't, and he was going to let him die."

"Did he say which one of them was dead and which one wasn't?" John asked.

"I'm not sure, I think he said Robert Jensen."

"Did he say anything about Carol King?"

"No, sir, he didn't say anything."

"Did he tell you why he shot either of them?"

"No, sir."

"Did you ask him anything about it?"

"I asked him why he did it."

"What did he say?"

"He didn't say anything, he just – and said…" She was getting emotional now; one of the few times during the trial she revealed something behind that hard expression.

"All right," John said. "What did Charles Starkweather do then when he came back and said that?"

"When he first came back he opened the door and stuck the gun in first… He stuck it in, and I thought I was going to get it, and then he laid it in the back seat."

They drove to Lincoln. Caril found books in the car and threw them out. "I knew somebody would find them and start looking for them."

John brought up the subject of the note Caril had written. Since it had disappeared somewhere with the police or county attorney's office, his only way to present it as evidence was to have Caril talk about it. She had written it while the car was hoisted up at the mechanic's. She knew Charlie could not get into the car while it was up there, so she pulled a pencil and paper out of the glove compartment and wrote "Help. Police. Don't ignore."

"Do you know where the note is now?" John asked.

"It should be in my blue coat pocket in the right hand pocket." She had tried to pass it to the waitress at the restaurant, but Charlie had walked in before she was able. After that, Caril was simply too scared to try to pass it along.

She was, in fact, too frightened to do just about anything, even talk. She was silent as they got back to Lincoln and saw the police at her house.

"Why didn't you jump out and run?"

"He had the knife with him."

"Which one was it that you were most afraid of?"

"The knife."

"Did you want to get away, Caril?"

"Yes, I did… but he always told me that if I ever got loose my family would be killed, and it would be my fault."

She described being taken to the house where Charlie said her family was being kept. It was near there that they pulled over and slept for a few hours. Caril became so tired talking about it that most answers now became "I don't remember," so she was excused to be brought back again at a later time.

Dr. Erwin Zeman was called in to testify about the autopsy on the body of Carol King. He told them that the cause of death was a gunshot wound to the right side of the head behind the right ear. There had also been brush burns on the back of her head from having been dragged, as well as a lot of bleeding and internal damage. But the worst part was something no one had been prepared for, even though they had known there was rape involved. Carol King had been stabbed several times in the vagina, once so deeply that it had gone through the internal walls into the rectum. The jury was horrified. Caril's face remained rigid and impassive.

Next, McArthur entered into evidence the testimony of Dr. John O'Hearne, the psychiatrist who testified for the defense at Starkweather's trial, who had been interviewed outside of court. O'Hearne had stated that Charlie was too mentally ill to be believed, and that any testimony taken by him should not be taken seriously. This had originally been submitted as evidence to defend Charlie from his own admissions of guilt. John was hoping that this jury might at least recognize his insanity enough to not believe his testimony.

In a few rounds of cross-examination and redirect, Scheele tried to prove that Charlie's testimony was reliable, and McArthur tried to prove that it was not.

John then called to the stand three witnesses who testified that the Wards and John Colvert were all strong and healthy people. His point was that if these people could not overcome Charlie, how could someone as small as Caril hope to take him down. John did not dare to call members of the Jensen or King family. They had made up their minds that Caril was guilty of killing their boy and girl, and would answer in any way that would implicate her.

McArthur then called to the stand four friends of the Bartlett family who all testified that the family had been close, that Caril loved all of them, especially her little half-sister, who she bought clothes for with her baby-sitting money.

An aid at the state hospital testified that Caril was still very efficacious even after the terrible events. She helped with the other patients, talked with them, made their beds. She was doing what she hoped to do when she grew up, be a nurse. This testimony was crucial since Caril was showing none of that friendliness in court. Looking at her, one would think she had been a hardened criminal behind bars for years, and was just waiting to get this all over with.

The star witness for the day was Pansy Street, Caril's grandmother. She testified, as the others had, that the Bartlett family had been warm and loving to one another, and Caril was no exception. John then turned the questioning to January 27, when she had taken a taxi to the Bartlett home.

"And what did you do when you got out there?"

"I-well, now, I don't know whether I told the taxi to wait or not, but anyhow he was in the drive, and I went up to the house, and I didn't even knock, I didn't get clear up to the screen door, that I know, and the door was opened. Now I don't remember by who or when or how... I seen Caril, standing, oh, about two feet back in the-which we would call the dining room... She looked awfully white to me... I think she stared right at me, stared terribly hard right at me... She said, 'Go away, Grandma, go home, Grandmom, oh, Grannie, go away,' and- Well, all the time that she was talking to me she kept stepping back in the middle of the dining room, which is a long room. They have a gas heater, and she kept stepping back towards the gas heater... I was trying to see whether she was crying or not, I can't remember whether she was crying or not, but I noticed especially, she put her hand up over her mouth, and as she stepped back toward that gas heater, it looked like, oh, she moved her fingers some way like they were pointing over in the corner, it looked at that time like she was."

"What did you say to her then, Mrs. Street?"

"Well, I wanted to see Betty, Mrs. Bartlett, and I kept begging her to speak to me... I was screaming... I was screaming for her to come to the door, I says, 'If you can't speak so I can hear you, just come to the door where I can at least see you.'... And she never come, I never heard no motion, and I never even heard Betty Jean make any motion, and, you know, if somebody was there Betty Jean would at least make a little racket... I got mad... I said, 'Well, if you won't let me in here I'm going to town and get a search warrant. I'll get in here.'"

"Where did you go then?"

"I went to the police station, took the cab right to the police station... I first stepped downstairs to the desk there and asked them something about getting somebody for me to go out to Betty's home, and they sent me upstairs... I went into a room... and there was a man sitting in there at the desk and I told him what I wanted... I told him I wanted somebody to go out with me and get in there so I could see what was wrong with Betty... he sent me across the hall in another room... I went over there and sat down and waited some time. Now I don't know, it seems an awful long time to me... They assigned two men to go out there with me."

"Do you know whether it was Officers Hansen and Fisher?"

"Well, all I know, one of them was baldheaded and he wasn't very nice."

"That would be Fisher; who was the other one?"

The spectators roared with laughter. The judge banged his gavel angrily and instructed them not to make any more noise, and that this was serious business.

Pansy described going to the house with the police. One of the officers climbed in a window and let her in the front door. They checked every room. Empty. The beds were made neatly and there was no sign of life, or any kind of trouble. The officers returned to the station, dropping Pansy off at a corner where she went to Caril's sister's apartment and called everyone that the Bartletts knew, then the hospitals. At last she had to go to work.

"After you'd left the Bartlett house and while you were being brought back by the police, did they have anything to say to you?"

"Yes... maybe I can't say the exact words but I can make the same opinion on it... They said, 'I would go home and I wouldn't stick my nose in my married kids' affairs if they didn't want me around.'"

"And then did you later on that same day find out what had happened to the Bartletts?"

"I went to work-yes, and I heard-when I went in, I asked Al, that's the man I work for, if he could have the radio on in the kitchen, and he said, 'Why, Pansy?' And I said, 'I'm expecting to hear trouble.' And he said, 'Okay,' and either on the five or six o'clock news I heard about it."

On cross-examination, Scheele tried to discredit her testimony about the home, but Pansy stuck to her story, and corrected him at every turn.

During McArthur's recross, he asked about Caril pointing at the corner. "Did it, at that time did you think about that meaning anything?"

"Yes, I did, I thought it was a very peculiar way for her to act like she wanted me to know…"

"Now just a moment," Scheele interrupted. "Your honor, I move to strike the commencement of the last sentence as not responsive."

The judge sustained it.

John reworked the question. "Had you ever seen Caril Ann act like that before?"

"No."

John asked one last question about the police. He observed in her answers that the route the police took to get to the Fugate house was very circuitous. He asked her if she knew why that was, and she said she could only imagine that they had no idea where the house was.

Hazel Heflin later testified about how Caril seemed very upset and frightened when she saw her in Wyoming. Mrs. Heflin had gotten a doctor to calm her down, and she fell asleep for a long time. When she woke up, she immediately began asking for her family. "She cried and screamed for her mother and little half-sister and wondered why they didn't call, and I said the phones are so busy now they couldn't call anyway. She said, 'Well maybe I can call a little later.' I said, 'Perhaps you can.'"

Her sister Barbara Von Busch later testified that Caril was very close with her family. She emphasized the fact that Caril doted on her baby half-sister like she was her own. Then she talked about the time she approached the house and Caril told her to leave.

"She told us to go back home because they were all sick, and I told her that I wanted to see mother, and she said, 'Go away, go away if you know what is best you will go away so mother don't get hurt…'"

"Did you wonder what she meant by 'mother getting hurt?'" John asked.

"Yes."

"Did you say anything to her about that?"

"Not no more because she got, oh, I don't know how to explain it, just kind of what you would call furious or something like that."

The Bartlett's neighbor was called next. She had returned at 4 pm the Tuesday of the murders. She heard no screaming, gunshots, or any struggling of any kind, contrary to Charlie's story, which claimed that this all happened in the evening after Caril had returned from school.

And then Caril returned to the witness stand. She looked pale, but still firm. John stepped up to her.

John began by asking about what happened at the August Meyer farm. She answered in the same clipped voice, her lips parting only enough to get the rapid-fire words out as efficiently as possible. She told the story the same way as she had in the statement. When Meyer went to get the horses to help with the car, Charlie suddenly shot him without explanation. She went through the entire event and the details matched what she had said in the statement Scheele had read. But this time she also added that Charlie slapped her, threatened her, and generally told her what to do.

She described being tied up in her home whenever he left. "He stuck my mouth full of a rag and then he tied it around my mouth and tied it in a knot in back," she said. "I couldn't breathe, I had to breathe out of my nose." When she asked why he was keeping her family hostage, he answered, "Because they know too much." He didn't explain about what, and Caril was too scared to ask.

"Caril," John asked, "did you ever make any other attempts to warn anybody or to send out some kind of message?"

"Yes, sir... when I wrote the sick note... I wrote-I don't remember what I wrote on it, but I said that they had the flu, and then I signed 'miss Bartlett.'"

"Now who is Miss Bartlett?"

"Well, my little sister can't write, but she's Miss Bartlett... whoever would read that note would know that my sister could never write and my mother would never sign the note 'Miss Bartlett.'"

She didn't feel she could get away from him at any time without putting herself and other people in danger. In Wyoming, however, she tried to start the car and get away from Charlie while he was in the salesman's car, but she couldn't get it started. While she was trying, Charlie came to her and told her to get into the other car. As she had said in her statement, she tried to tell Sprinkle, who then approached, to leave. "I stuck my head out of the window and I was motioning for him not to come, I shook my head and motioned with my mouth for him to go away... I kept whispering, I moved my lips, I didn't say anything, I didn't say anything, I just moved my lips and told him to go away."

John finished his questioning just before lunch. When they returned, Scheele began. Caril eyed him angrily. She had trusted him before with a child-like innocence, and now she understood the harsh reality of police work. She had thought they were on her side, had grown up believing the police were there to protect her. She knew better now. He questioned with calculated self-assuredness and she answered with cold firmness. She became more and more angry throughout the interview, her lips disappearing in a tight grimace when they closed, her answers shorter and crisper.

"Caril, do you recall first meeting me out in Douglas, Wyoming, in January?"

"No, sir, I don't."

"Do you recall having a conversation with me there in the kitchen of the Sheriff's house?"

"No, I don't."

"And do you remember that it was explained to you the procedure that could be gone through to extradite you to go back to the state of Nebraska to face trial?"

"I was told that I could go back of my own free will or else have the waiver and go back with the law."

"And you were also told that if you wanted to you could waive the extradition proceeding and go back with Nebraska authorities voluntarily, were you not?"

"Yes, sir."

"And didn't you decide yourself that you preferred to go back... voluntarily... without having the hearing before the governor of Wyoming?"

"I was told that I could either have it, go back freely and voluntarily, or else I would go back against my will."

"No, that you would have a hearing before the governor of Wyoming, and he would determine whether you would be sent back; wasn't it explained that way?"

"It was explained the way I said, that I could either go back on my own or go back with them."

"At any rate did you come back to Nebraska voluntarily and willingly?"

"Yes."

He walked her through the entire story again. Her answers were identical to those she gave McArthur. The difference was in the type of questioning. McArthur emphasized the desolation of where they went, and how strong others were who did not overcome Charlie or get away; Scheele emphasized the moments when Charlie was not around, and when Caril was closer to other people than she was to him, such as when she went into the diner and bought burgers. He also emphasized the fact that weapons were either close to her, or in her possession several times during the questioning. Caril often tried to explain further, but Scheele kept her to the questions at hand.

Scheele had done more research into Charlie and Caril's relationship than even Caril knew. He asked about a bank account that had been opened up in both of their names. Caril had known Charlie wanted to do that, but was not aware he had actually done it. He had given presents to Caril's parents that Caril didn't even know about.

Though Scheele successfully pointed out several moments when she could have possibly gotten away, he was unable to find any inconsistencies in her story. He then returned to the statement he had read earlier in the trial. He referred to it as the confession, but when McArthur objected, he was made to refer to it as a statement. He quoted from specific passages, reading them out of order to put them in the context he wanted. He began with her statements describing when Charlie taught her how to shoot a gun.

"I bet you're a pretty good shot," Scheele had said.

Caril had responded, "Sometimes." Taken out of context, and placed into the current circumstances, it sounded like she was a crack shot searching for a victim. He didn't read from the part where she said Charlie had taught her so she could go hunting with him, and that she really didn't like to carry a gun. Caril kept trying to interject this, but was interrupted by the next question.

"Did you at any time point a gun at the King girl and tell her to get out of the car?"

"I had to. Charlie Starkweather told me to."

"Well, if Charles Starkweather had told you to shoot her, would you have done that, too?"

"No."

McArthur objected, and it was sustained, but Scheele had made his point; though, in a way, he had made McArthur's point, also. Starkweather clearly had a hold on Caril and who knows what would have happened if he had actually told her to kill someone.

Scheele again asked her about the newspaper clippings. Caril claimed that she had seen some of the photographs, but had not read the articles. "Did you leave with him?" he asked.

"Against my will, yes."

"But did you leave with him?"

"Against my will, yes."

When Scheele concluded his questioning, the defense rested.

Scheele called a few witnesses for a rebuttal; a psychologist from the state hospital who said that Starkweather was disturbed, but not insane, and William Dixon, county attorney in Wyoming, who stated that he explained the extradition process to Caril and had told her that she was entitled to an attorney. Caril had said earlier that she hadn't understood why she needed one; that she didn't understand that she was going to be tried for these crimes, but she had already spoken, and was not able to answer to these allegations. Scheele had the last word on the matter.

With that, the State rested.

\*　　　\*　　　\*

It was Wednesday, November 19.  The courthouse was packed, and lines of people stretched outside the building into the frigid cold hoping to get a seat.  The press took their seats on the periphery.  James took the day off school to watch his father give closing arguments and sat in the press box near Ninette.

John began the closing arguments by describing Caril as Charlie's twelfth victim.  "The facts in this case," he said, "have been very misunderstood by the public."  They had been mislead by the county attorney's office to believe that there were mounds of evidence against Caril when, in fact, the only witness was the man that should be the target of their hatred, Charles Starkweather.  "The State is willing to see a fifteen-year-old child go to her death solely on the basis of testimony of a convicted killer," he said.

He asked when Caril could have gotten away from him with any certainty of success.  "When?" he demanded.  "When?  When Starkweather left her alone in a gas station, eight feet above the concrete floor?  When he sent her to buy hamburgers, telling her that he would be watching her, lurking she knew not where, ready to appear at any moment?  When her sister came to the door and he was there, out of sight, with a loaded gun ready to fire?  At August Meyer's farm, miles from town, the car stuck in the mud?  At the storm cellar with Starkweather somewhere in the darkness and the sound of gunshots still ringing in her ears?  At the Wards', in a neighborhood that owed its exclusivity to the distance between houses and the lack of traffic?  On the deserted street where they stopped to sleep in Lincoln at three in the morning?  From a moving car?  Charles Starkweather was known to be a deadly accurate marksman, both with a rifle and a knife."

His speech was not as emotional as Gaughan's had been for Starkweather.  John's passion showed primarily through his use of words.  He finished his first closing argument by reminding them to ignore Starkweather's testimony.  John pointed it out that his description of the events changed with each telling.  "I am convinced that Charles Starkweather is a madman."  He told the jury they had the choice to believe either Starkweather or Caril.  And with that, he sat down.

Elmer Scheele, who carried himself in much the same way that McArthur did, then stood before the jury to give his first closing argument. "There were several occasions when Caril could have gotten away," he began. His lips did not smile, but his air of tolerance encompassed an implied amusement. He told the jury that he would not go over each one in detail again, but he would mention the most glaring. "By her own admission, Caril Fugate had seen two policemen, themselves armed, experienced in dealing with dangerous men, dedicated to helping citizens protect themselves from danger, and Starkweather was asleep, what had Caril Fugate done? Had she welcomed the protection of the officers, who could save her from Starkweather? No, she had gone into the bedroom and waked Charlie, warning him that the police were coming." He admitted that Caril might have been doing this to protect her family, but then Scheele suggested that Caril could have whispered to the police officers at the door, even if Charlie was right there on the other side.

Scheele second guessed many of her decisions, stating all along the way that she could have gotten away, then turned to the jury's sense of duty. "I don't enjoy prosecuting her any more than you enjoy serving on this jury," he said. "I'd like to believe that a 14-year-old girl, an eighth grader, is incapable of performing the things the evidence shows this girl did in this case." But under Nebraska law, he continued, a fourteen or fifteen-year-old girl "knows the difference between right and wrong. We have no choice. We've got to fulfill our responsibilities and respective duties." He told them that, while Caril did not actually pull the trigger in Jensen's death, "she did aid and abet Charles Starkweather in the commission of this terrible crime." Under the law, anyone who aids and abets in the commission of any crime "is just as guilty as the principle offender."

Caril "was Starkweather's willing companion from the time she returned home from school on January 21 until the time of her capture January 29, eight days later," he said. "This is no ordinary fifteen-year-old girl we're dealing with. This has been shown in testimony offered by the State in her own statements and by her own appearance and conduct and demeanor while she sat in this courtroom on the witness stand." He was referring, of course, to Caril's stone-faced disposition which she still wore on her face as she listened to the prosecuting attorney.

He summarized the story as he saw it. Caril came home and argued with her mother about Charlie. Mrs. Bartlett ran at Starkweather with a knife, "and you know what happened after that," he declared, "in the presence of Caril Fugate!" Caril remained in the house while Starkweather completed the "gruesome, gory task" of disposing of the bodies. He turned to the killing of Jensen and King, reversing the order of the murders as he claimed, that Caril had allowed Charlie to kill King first. "While Caril Fugate did not actually pull the trigger which sent the bullets into the brain of Robert Jensen, she did aid and abet Starkweather in the commission of this terrible crime."

He then reminded the jury that, under Nebraska law, any person who aids in a murder is equally guilty as the person who did the actual killing, and that the best deterrent to crime and murder is to "convince people of all ages that there is a certainty of their apprehension and their conviction in court." He said that it was unprecedented to try someone so young for murder, but, "even fourteen-year-old teenagers must be made to realize they can't go off on an eight-day murder spree and get off because they are only fourteen. We have leaned over backward to give this girl a fair trial. Now, ladies and gentlemen, the time has come when she must face the consequences of her conduct. This fourteen-year-old girl is guilty of first-degree murder as charged. We must convince persons of all ages they will be caught, tried, and punished if they break the law. I ask for the conviction of first-degree murder for the robbery-slaying of Robert Jensen." It was notable that he had not asked for the death penalty. Instead, he said rather cryptically and conclusively to the jury, "I am perfectly satisfied to leave the question of the penalty up to you."

John at last rose for his final argument. He was slower, the strain visible on his long face. His shoulders struggled to straighten. Three long weeks had passed as this trial wore on, preceded by many months of preparation. And now it all came down to this. But when he began to speak, his voice bolted with confidence, even outrage. Scheele, a friend and colleague, along with his team of police and lawyers, had not only charged a girl who John now believed firmly was innocent, but they had trampled on the civil rights that he held so dear. He was made for this case, not because of Caril, but because of what he was truly standing up against, the thing he hated more than anything, a police force that abused its power to transfer its own blame onto a child.

"Caril Fugate was a victim of prejudice," he began. "The public indignation at law-enforcement inefficiency has settled on her." Her story was simple and understandable. In calmer moments, anyone would recognize it as such and would feel horrified compassion for the ordeal that this child had undergone. But the public was angry, angry at the law-enforcement system that had allowed Starkweather to escape apprehension after the murder of Robert Colvert, angry at the police who had been told again and again that something was wrong at the Bartlett house but had done nothing to correct it. And they were right to be angry. The law-enforcement officers had to find a scapegoat, and they found Caril. Far from protecting her, they persuaded a child who was under sedation to sign away her legal rights in Wyoming; they took advantage of her youthful ignorance to deny her the assistance of an attorney until they had secured a damaging statement from her that told only of her actions and not the reasons for her behavior. "I don't believe Scheele or his chief deputy Dale Fahrnbruch have ever seen Caril Ann Fugate," he said. "I think when they look in that chair they see Lucrezia Borgia or one of the witches out of Macbeth." The reporters looked up from their notepads in confusion. One of the correspondents from the New York Times turned to the man next to him and asked, "Who in the hell is Lucrezia Borgia?"

McArthur continued undeterred, stating that the police force felt "castigated unmercifully" for failing to apprehend Starkweather. "We have good police and a fine sheriff's office and the best county attorney in the state," he said, "but they were burning from the criticism which gave birth to prejudice." The lawmen "couldn't believe they had been so stupid, that a man would go on such a rampage while dragging along a little girl. The conviction of Caril Ann Fugate became a must." He said that Caril had "grown up a lot in the last year." But her physical and mental ability to escape had disappeared after Caril saw Starkweather shoot August Meyer in cold blood.

McArthur then attacked the oral statements that the prosecution presented against Caril, which he declared had been "the most invidious testimony of the trial." Procured under "suspicious" conditions, the statements deliberately omitted certain questions so as to make them misleading. "I regard a great deal of testimony regarding the freeness and voluntariness of her remarks a great façade of sham. There is also something hollow about the written statement Caril gave authorities. Caril poured out her soul when written transcripts were not taken, but did not elaborate when the written document was taken. When you read it and do not realize it was the third time over the ground, you do not realize something was wrong."

He reminded the jury of the several attempts Caril had made to warn visitors at the Bartlett home that something was amiss, but the warnings "ended up in the deadletter office at the police station." He pointed out that several members of both Caril and Charlie's family had gone to the police, but the police had simply told them to go away, and had not truly investigated. It had been those family members who finally found the bodies and had to lead the police to them. And Charlie had even driven right past them while they were inspecting the house. Caril was being prosecuted for "things she did not do" rather than things she did, he told the jury. Older, wiser, stronger people who came in contact with Charles Starkweather and defied him in any way ended up dead. "How could anyone expect Caril Fugate to do what others could not?"

He then settled into the specific case at hand. She was being tried for the murder of Robert Jensen. That was ridiculous, he said. The State's own evidence was questionable. It relied heavily on the story told by Charles Starkweather, a story that he had changed again and again since he had first told it. She could not possibly have aided in the killing, which, if his testimony was to be believed, Starkweather committed on impulse. There was no connection between the robbery and the murder.

Caril did not know her family was dead until after everything, he told the jury. "All the facts state it. Only Starkweather's often amended testimony says otherwise." As for Romer, he had claimed

Caril was hysterical and incoherent, but she calmed just enough to say incriminating things about herself before becoming hysterical again. It did not make sense. "He could not have heard what he claimed to have heard," John said.

He then turned to the credibility of the State's primary witness, Charles Starkweather. "I am convinced," John said, "that Starkweather is a madman." Only a madman could do what he did. Yet he was the chief witness against Caril. And even he, murderously insane, had not claimed Caril had anything to do with the killing of Robert Jensen. She had been in the car the whole time according to both of them. He reminded them that Charlie had raped Carol King, and that he was unlikely to have done many of the things he did in that cellar while Caril was present.

He reminded them of her age, and said that fourteen-year-olds are "obedient and gullible. But Caril did more than most children would have done to give the warning."

He implored the jury to put themselves into Caril's place, to try to imagine the effect on a young girl of what she had been through; thinking her family was in danger, traveling with a wild, angry young man who threw knives into walls for fun. Then, tired and hungry, she was taken by him to a deserted county road and to a farm where, for no reason, he shot a kind old man who was going to help him. When she saw Meyer killed, she became "a piece of putty in Starkweather's hands." Who could witness such senseless violence and become anything other than terrified? Later, she was alone in a car where she heard shots ring out somewhere in the darkness. By the time she reached the Ward's house, she had "no more will to resist than a three-year-old child. Whatever she did, however it might be interpreted, the fact was she acted out of terror."

"Who," he concluded, "adult or child, could be sure that he would be able to do otherwise?"

Having done everything he could for the girl, John finally sat down beside her.

Across from him, Elmer Scheele, angry at the jabs that had been pointed at himself and his police force, stood up. He accused McArthur of attempting to confuse the jurors for appealing to possible prejudices they might have against law enforcement personnel and also of making a "clever appeal" to the emotions and sympathies of the jurors instead of discussing the facts. Lacking evidence that Caril was forced to accompany Starkweather, McArthur had relied on the adage that "a good offense is the best defense." McArthur, he said, had then launched attacks on the police, sheriff, sheriff's wife, county attorney and "anybody and everybody" else that suited his purpose – to confuse the facts in the case. "The defense purposely avoided the facts by trying to lay the blame for the case upon myself and the police department."

He then began talking about his star witness. "The name of Charles Starkweather is without a doubt unpopular in Lancaster County today, but I can't change the fact that he is the only other living person besides Caril who knows the truth of what happened last January." He admitted that Starkweather had changed his story about Caril's participation in the murder spree several times, but Caril had, too. This was, in fact, not true, but McArthur had given his last final statement, and could no longer refute it.

Scheele told the jury that he had called Starkweather to the stand because he is the "only living person who knows what actually happened and what Caril's part was."

He went back to defending himself and his office, stating that McArthur had attempted to infer that "we took advantage of a 14-year-old girl. My office did everything possible to prevent any suspicion that the girl was abused from arising."

After defending his office again, Scheele finally asked the jury to find Caril Fugate guilty, leaving the punishment, whether life or death, in their hands.

*     *     *

The next morning the jury was to begin their deliberations. They would need to bring provisions to stay overnight, as they would not be allowed to go home once deliberations began. The judge gave them an hour long lecture on their responsibility. He reminded them Caril was being tried on two charges, first-degree murder and murder in the perpetration of a robbery. The jury could find her guilty or innocent of either or both charges. They could, at their behest, find her guilty of second-degree murder instead of first, which meant the murder was not premeditated.

He reminded them that Caril was not on trial for failing to report or prevent these crimes. These elements were only relevant in determining her state of mind at the time of Robert Jensen's murder. If she had traveled with Starkweather under duress, then she must be found innocent of both counts of murder. He reminded them that merely being present while a murder is committed does not necessarily make the person an accomplice to it.

Then he talked about Starkweather. "Extreme care and caution should be used in weighing his testimony. You will scrutinize it closely in the light of all the other evidence in the case and you will give it such weight as you may think it is entitled to have, keeping in mind the credibility of such a witness." He finished by instructing the jury to "meet responsibility fairly and courageously," and telling them that the verdict "must not be influenced by any personal or other consideration."

The case was handed to them at 10:01 a.m.

*       *       *

It was ten months to the day since Caril's mother and stepfather had been killed. The world was moving along outside the town of Lincoln, and news shows and papers were ready to follow them. Jimmy Hoffa's union fight with the government was going all the way to President Kennedy, the Soviet Union had begun to grant Berlin its independence the same day that the Fugate case began, and it completed the process the day the case was handed to the jury, and a major effort was underway to save more than 70 miners who were trapped in Nova Scotia when a tunnel collapsed.

It was a crisp, sunny day, which was a relief to the majority of reporters who milled about on the lawn. The jury deliberated throughout the day, and as it grew late, most of the reporters and other hangers on moved indoors.

Ninette was climbing the stairs when she came upon Merril Reller. She smiled widely. "I understand that's a good sign for you, isn't it, Merril? The longer they stay out, the more likely it is that they won't convict her."

Reller smiled warmly to her. He had a way of making anyone feel comfortable with that smile. "Never try to anticipate a jury, and you can quote me on that."

"Where are you off to?" she asked.

"I'm going out to the state hospital to see Caril. This must be a very long evening for her."

"Oh, good. Look, if I give you my number, will you call me after you see her and tell me how she is and what she's doing? I can use it on the ten o'clock news."

"Why don't you come with me and see for yourself?"

"But how are you going to get me in?" she asked, taken aback. "Don't they check people at the door? If they let just anybody in, every reporter here would be over there instead."

"We'll think of something," Reller said, and they rode out in his car. She signed in under her married name and Reller told the person at the desk that she was a friend of the family.

When they entered the room, Caril pulled a pile of papers she had been reading to her chest to cover their words. Merril reintroduced Ninette and Caril nodded at her in recognition. Relaxing, she told Ninette that the papers were letters from other people, teenagers mostly, who were telling her they were on her side and felt sorry for her. Ninette asked if she could copy some quotes from some of them and use them in her broadcast. Caril looked first at Reller. He nodded, and she handed them to Ninette. "Aren't they nice?" Caril asked several times as Ninette read them and copied some sentences. Ninette was moved by the earnestness in them. But she was mostly moved by Caril's warmth. This was not the frigid girl with the stern face from the courtroom. Perhaps she should have shown this side earlier, but it was too late now.

Caril asked Merril why the jury was taking so long. "We just won't talk about that," he answered.

After talking cheerfully for about forty minutes, Merril and Ninette left. On their way to the car, Ninette sighed, "You know, Merril, I think that girl believes she's going to be acquitted."

Reller stopped in his tracks and looked seriously at her. "Well, so do I."

Back at the McArthur home, John was not so certain. No one brought up the case. No one wanted to talk about the murders, or the evidence, or the courtroom. No one even talked about Caril. They got their minds off of it while they ate dinner. John watched his shows that night, followed by 'Spiritual Thought', and finally the 'Star Spangled Banner' played over an American flag before the TV turned to static for the night.

*    *    *

The next morning the jury bell rang at 11:09 a.m. Everyone filed in. John was tired, Merril was hopeful. Scheele and his team were all business. If the verdict came out innocent, they still had charges of murder in the first degree of Carol King. He would keep Caril in jail indefinitely, forever if necessary, while he ran down the list of victims and charged her for each one. Caril sat down stern-faced. Merril had insisted she get a full-night's sleep, which she had. But this was not the little girl he had visited with Ninette the night before. That was a private face she only showed to those she trusted.

James had taken the day off of school again to see the verdict, but he had not been allowed in the courtroom. He stood in the hall, which was cleared of the public, but was still filled with deputy sheriffs and police officers.

"Have you reached a verdict?" Judge Spencer asked in the courtroom.

On the first count, murder in the first degree, the jury found her innocent. Caril and John breathed with relief, but didn't let it show. On the second count, murder while in the perpetration of a robbery, they found her guilty. Now their chests were tight. She could be put to death if the jury so chose.

They recommended life in prison.

Caril broke down in tears. For the first time she showed them emotion as she turned to the jury. "If you really thought I was guilty, why didn't you give me the chair?" she asked, and broke down sobbing against Merril Reller's shoulder, whose own look of shock showed not only pain, but shame toward the jury. He held her, trying to comfort her. She then said in a broken voice the words that would be the theme of the remainder of her life: "Some day they're going to find out they made a mistake."

John and Ruby McArthur in their home in 1952.
(McArthur archives.)

John McArthur in the 1980s.
(McArthur archives.)

# Starkweather's 11 Victims in Order
(Photos collected from the Nebraska Historical Society.)

Robert Colvert, 21
Gas station attendant.

Velda Bartlett, 36
Marion Bartlett, 58
Caril's mother &
stepfather.

Betty Jean, 2
Caril's baby
half-sister.

August Meyer, 70
Farmer & friend
of Charlie
Starkweather.

Carol King, 16
High school
student.

Robert Jensen, 17
High school
student.

Clara Ward, 46
Housewife.

C. Lauer Ward, 48
Businessman

Lillian Fencl, 51
Maid

Merle Collison, 37
Salesman

August Meyer's home, where Charlie shot his friend, and where police later thought Charlie was holed up. (Lincoln Public Libraries archives.)

The home of Mr. and Mrs. Ward, prominent members of the city and close friends of the governor. (Lincoln Public Libraries archives.)

National Guardsmen walk the streets of Lincoln, Nebraska during Starkweather's murder spree. (Nebraska Historical Society.)

Charlie and Caril the year before the murders while they were dating. (McArthur archives.)

Charlie Starkweather in chains before going into court. The chains were removed when he was taken in. (Nebraska Historical Society.)

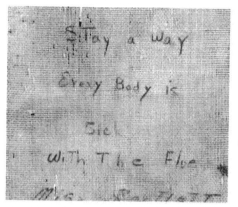

The note Caril left on the front door. It is signed "Miss Bartlett," the name of her 2-year-old step-sister. (McArthur archives.)

Letter from Caril to Charlie begging him to admit to being the only killer before he is executed. (McArthur archives.)

Reporters gathered from around the world to report on the Starkweather/Fugate case. These reporters were recording the interview between Caril Fugate and Ninette Beaver. (Lincoln Public Libraries archives.)

ΗΛΕΚΤΡΙΚΗ ΚΑΡΕΚΛΑ ΔΙΑ ΤΟΝ ΔΟΛΟΦΟΝΟΝ 11 ΑΤΟΜΩΝ

News organizations across the globe followed the story of Starkweather and Fugate. This article appears to be in Russian. (McArthur archives.)

# STARKWEATHER DIES TODAY; WRIT DENIED

## Federal Court Try Fails;
## Van Pelt Refuses Stay

... Mass-Killer's Appointment With Death Unchanged

**By Virgil Falloon**

Mass killer Charles Starkweather was denied a stay of execution by Federal Judge Robert Van Pelt in a ruling Thursday afternoon on the bantam redhead's last-hour plea to be spared death in the electric chair Friday.

The appeal to the federal court was apparently the last opportunity to change the

the court "would not consider the two or three occasions of alleged drunkenness at the penitentiary, even if proved."

"It is not alleged this in any

### Calls About
### Circuit Judge

Guy Starkweather, father

way hampered the preparation of the case and it is not claimed there was such inebriation at or during the trial," the opinion continued.

"It is to be assumed that the state trial took the proper safeguards to protect the defendant's constitutional rights, the judge said. "No violation of his constitutional rights were assigned as error or dis-

Newspaper article reporting Starkweather's death. He had, in fact, been spared at the last minute, and was instead executed a month later. (Lincoln Public Libraries archives.)

Helen and Guy Starkweather with their son Rodney. This photo was taken soon after they received news that Charlie's execution was to be stayed. (Lincoln Public Libraries archives.)

Gertrude & Merle Karnopp escort Caril from the courthouse after Gertrude testified against Caril. Fugate claims Mrs. Karnopp lied on the stand, and later evidence backs up this claim, which explains Caril's demeanor. People who saw this, however, interpreted it as a rebellious nature in Caril. (Lincoln Public Libraries archives.)

Caril with her sister Barbara, their father William, and their stepmother Dorothy. (Lincoln Public Libraries archives.)

Newspaper sketch during Fugate trial.
John McArthur giving his closing
arguments. Merril Reller and Caril
Fugate sit at the desk beyond.
(McArthur archives.)

John McArthur and Caril Fugate
await the decision by the jury.
(Lincoln City Libraries archives.)

Newspaper sketch during Caril
Fugate's preliminary hearing.
From left to right: Elmer Scheele,
Merril Reller, Caril Fugate, Sally
Hays. (McArthur archives.)

Newspaper sketch of Caril Fugate on the witness stand during her trial. Many people believed her cold demeaner meant she was guilty. (McArthur archives.)

Newspaper sketch of Elmer Scheele questioning a witness during Fugate's trial. (McArthur archives.)

Newspaper sketch of Caril comforting Merril Reller by grabbing his arm during her trial. (McArthur archives.)

The McArthur home in the woods on Pioneer Blvd, approximately one mile from the penitentiary. (McArthur archives.)

The Commercial Center - Where John McArthur and Merril Reller had their practice over a hair salon, next to apartments, and down the hall from a meat packing plant. (McArthur archives.)

McArthur Law Offices - Where John and James McArthur practiced law together. It was built during the appeals of the Fugate case as James took over. (McArthur archives.)

James McArthur high school photo, taken around the time of the original trials. (McArthur archives.)

After the screening of 'Badlands' in York, Nebraska at a nearby hotel. From left to right: Terrence Malick, Patsy McArthur, Caril Fugate, Martin Sheen, James McArthur, John McArthur. (McArthur archives.)

Fugate during the press conference before her trial. (Lincoln Public Libraries archives.)

Caril Fugate in the 1970s close to her release. Seen here working as a seamstress in York prison. (McArthur archives.)

# Chapter Nine
## Pro Bono

Caril's sister tried in vain to comfort her, but all that Caril could say was, "I'm not guilty! I'm not guilty!" Her grandmother was most successful, resting her hand on Caril and saying, "Now Caril, listen to me. As long as you got your life you have hope and you have your God... You can't always understand God's ways." She assured her that some day information would be uncovered that would change the situation, "and then you'll be all right... Keep your chin up."

Her father was less gracious. He had attended the entire trial, but when it was over, he wiped his hands of the matter stating to a reporter, "I'll leave things right where they are." He left and never re-entered Caril's life.

With the trial over, John had completed his obligations both to the State and to Caril, and he could have moved on with other, higher paying jobs. The State sent him a check for $6,366.25 for representing Caril. The amount included his payment, as well as expenses, his services over the course of several months, and whatever he wanted to split with his partner Merril. It was half the amount of what *each* of Charlie's two attorneys were paid. It was a blatant slap in the face, and John knew why.

Judge Spencer, who decided on how much each attorney was paid, seemed to have expected him to put up a nominal defense. But John had actually stood up for his client, and for a little bit of time it looked like he might pull it off. He had dragged out what could have been an efficient proceeding and brought international attention to it through his news conference.

John was insulted, but it wasn't because he needed the money. Reller was well off and their office had enough business that both men made a good living. What angered John was that the State would minimize payment if an attorney actually did his job responsibly. Out of protest, John refused to cash the check, and continued to represent Caril pro bono. After some time, Merril convinced him to cash it anyway and use the money for the office. John reluctantly relented, but took no pay from that day forward.

Merril also stood by Caril without pay, but when the two law partners went to York to visit her in prison, the warden, Mrs. Hattie Bowley, a short, hawkish woman with beady eyes, would not allow him to visit, stating that he had not been Caril's official attorney. Only John would be allowed in. Furious, John and Merril began to investigate the reformatory, and within a month discovered a number of violations propagated by Bowley. A former kitchen supervisor testified that a rule of complete silence was strictly enforced creating "a constant condition of tension and despondency, and the inmates generally have a hopeless attitude toward rehabilitation of the inmates, and their mental attitude is generally much worse when they are released than when admitted." Inmates were sometimes even punished for "intending to speak to another inmate."

Women were made to work outdoors in extreme conditions without the proper clothes, causing heat stroke in the summer, and frostbite in the winter. Most of these incidents went unreported, as inmates were punished when they asked for medical aid. One inmate, who had chronic foot problems, was given a job that caused her to stand all day, and was made to wear ill-fitting shoes the entire time, despite her requests to purchase good shoes herself. When she could no longer stand, she was sent to a hospital where she required surgery, and one of her toes had to be removed. Three days after the surgery, she was made to go back to work wearing the same shoes, standing fourteen hours a day. At the end of those work days, she lay on the cement floor because she was not allowed to lie on the bed until sleep hours.

Minor offenses were met with extreme punishment, and often solitary confinement for long periods of time. Caril herself was in constant solitary confinement because her age did not allow her to be with the adult inmates. She was allowed only to sit in a chair and crochet. She was not allowed to lay or even sit on her bed until her stated sleep time.

Some of the reformatory rules were created on the spot as excuses to punish undesirable inmates. Sometimes they were instructed to inform on other inmates, and were threatened with a loss of "good time" if they didn't. Thus, prisoners often made things up about one another, creating internal witch-hunts. Some of the dormitories had no toilet facilities. Convicts who had medical conditions were punished when they asked for treatment. Those who asked for religious ceremonies were threatened with being sent to the mental hospital.

One inmate was punished for sharing her candy with someone. She was also deprived of all privileges for twenty-one days because she said "good morning" to another prisoner. Another prisoner, Shirley Erpelding, was placed in solitary confinement where she was fed only toast and tea for six months because she "smiled at a fellow inmate in the mess hall." During this time, Mrs. Bowley had repeatedly insisted Erpelding sign papers that would allow her six children to be adopted. She taunted Shirley, telling her that her children had been deemed retarded, and continuously harassed her about signing the papers, but Erpelding refused. Another inmate was not allowed to see her one-year-old child because Mrs. Bowley claimed that she "might be used to pass unauthorized notes to people outside the institution."

No one had been standing up for these prisoners because their attorneys typically ended their involvement with their clients once they were sentenced. But once John McArthur saw what was happening, he began to raise Cain. He informed the governor's office, opened a lawsuit against the reformatory, filed for Caril's release based on the inhumane conditions, and he told the news media, who paid little attention to him. Fidel Castro had moved in to Havannah and was turning Cuba into a Communist dictatorship. Caril Fugate was old news. So John turned to Ninette Beaver, who brought the attention to her station, and soon others were echoing their reports.

Hattie Bowley tried to appease John by conceding to his original request, and allowed Merril to enter the reformatory. But it only made matters worse for Bowley. When they went to visit Caril, she told them that the warden had required Caril to write a statement about everything that had happened on the road with Charlie. Furthermore, she had asked her detailed questions about the incidents and forced Caril to answer until Caril broke down crying.

Reller called Mrs. Bowley into Caril's room and yelled at her in front of Caril so loudly the entire reformatory heard him, "If you want to know anything, you ask us! Not the girl!" Mrs. Bowley was unmoved, claiming she was doing her job as directed. Reller insisted she tell him who was directing her, and she would not reply. He then turned to Caril and said, "I direct you not to talk to Mrs. Bowley or anyone else about the happenings concerning the incidents and circumstances that happened the several weeks before the authorities took you into their custody and to talk about nothing about the matters concerning your trial!" Caril only seemed frightened and uncertain what to do, but she trusted Reller like he was family.

Merril then turned to Bowley again and instructed her "not, under any circumstances, to talk to Caril about the reasons why she was in the institution or any of the happenings that led up to her being tried for matters which she was in the institution." He and John were halfway back to Lincoln before Merril finally calmed down enough to speak coherently.

For the first time, Hattie Bowley caved to pressure. She brought Caril to her office and made her watch while she took out the statement and cut it up into small pieces and threw them into the trash. But the warden's difficulties were not over yet. John and Merril were set to file charges directly against her. On February 11, 1959, two days before they could file, Hattie Bowley "retired" after 20 years of service. A letter to the editor of one of the local papers stated how many people felt, and revealed the desire for revenge and punishment over reason, evidence, and rehabilitation:

"I think the lady in charge of the York Reformatory for Women needs a vote of thanks for having a heavy hand in keeping order there. After all, it isn't a sorority, and if those people had been trained when children, perhaps they would not be out there. It's about time we had a few more in charge who have the guts to correct them...

"Why does McArthur insist on further disgracing our beloved city by attacking our institutions and keeping that awful crime story going on and on, when we all feel that justice was more than fair and square in Caril's case?...

"So the quicker we forget the name of Fugate and along with it, McArthur's, the better."

Despite public sentiment against them, John and Merril continued to pour over the records of the case, highlighting every point at which they believed the court had made a mistake and given them cause for an appeal. They started with Judge Spencer's strange conference with Reller where he told him to leave everything to John. This was something Spencer never should have brought up, and was a completely unreasonable demand.

John walked James through the process step by step. By now, James knew that this would be his profession, and he could not get better training, essentially interning on the trial of the century at the age of sixteen.

They received a break that would be even better than an appeal. They might even get a mistrial. It was discovered that one of the jurors had made a bet that Caril would be found guilty. This was an offense so abhorrent that it could nullify the entire trial. As long as any juror had a personal vested interest in a specific outcome, the opinions of all the jurors could be tainted.

John would be filing the request for a mistrial in the morning. He knew that the county attorney's office would be rushing to cover their bases as soon as they found out, so John made a plan to outflank them.

\*       \*       \*

Chief Deputy County Attorney Dale Fahrnbruch and Sheriff Merle Karnopp, both of whom had been instrumental in prosecuting Caril, arrived at H.A. Walenta's shop shortly after 9:00. As soon as the motion for a mistrial and the reason had become known, they had jumped in their car and driven over to talk with the juror who had made the bet. This could ruin everything they had spent months building. They had bent the rules, compromised their ethics, and worked hundreds of hours to put that girl behind bars; they weren't about to let one idiot juror unravel all of that. First, they would have a private conversation with Walenta; then they would decide what to do. They just had to beat the press there.

When they stepped through the door, they were met with a camera in their faces. Ninette Beaver, who was interviewing Walenta, now turned toward the two men. They paused for a moment, getting their bearings; then both realized that John was now one step ahead of them. It was a message; John's dry witted way of telling them that they could no longer perform their back alley tactics without the eyes of the people watching.

"I was kind of expecting you," Walenta told the two men.

*       *       *

John McArthur and Elmer Scheele appeared before Judge Spencer on December 13. John submitted a list of 71 alleged errors in the Fugate trial, but he focused on the bet made by Walenta, a problem that obviously could have affected the outcome. In consideration of all this, he called for a new trial.

"This was a most unfortunate occurrence," Scheele said. "I would have joined Mr. McArthur in a motion for a new trial if the jury had voted the death penalty." And Scheele was telling the truth. According to one of Scheele's former assistants, through it all, the one thing that the county attorney's office did not want was the death penalty for a teen-aged child. They simply could not stomach the notion. It was on the table only because that was the law at the time. The jury had felt the same way. When deliberations began, most jurors would not even discuss the case until the very suggestion of execution was taken off the table.

What the punishment had to do with a betting juror is confusing, however, as is the fact that Scheele was saying he was against Caril getting the death penalty even though he had told the jurors in his final statements that he would leave the punishment to them.  But in the years to come, Scheele would state several times that his office never had the intention of putting Caril Fugate to death, only to put her behind bars for the rest of her life.

After presenting their sides of the case, both parties had to wait a week for Judge Spencer's ruling.  On December 20, they returned to his courtroom for his verdict.  Caril sat on the bench behind her attorneys.  Spencer determined that, though what Walenta did was reprehensible, it did not affect his duties as a juror.  Even though he was set to win money by her conviction, the judge still believed that he could look at the case objectively.  He also dismissed all 70 of McArthur's other complaints about the trial and moved on to sentencing.  He called Caril to approach the bench.

Caril Fugate, barely five feet tall and fifteen years old, wearing her bobby socks and bright blue skirt, stepped up next to John facing the bench.  The judge looked down to her.  "Do you know of any reason why sentence should not be pronounced at this time?"

"Yes," she said softly.  "I'm not guilty."

Judge Spencer paused a moment.  This was not the stone-faced girl who had sat emotionless in his court for the trial.  At last he said, "You are sentenced to imprisonment in the State Reformatory for Women at York for the period of your natural life and are ordered to pay the costs of the prosecution."

John put his arm around her, though it hardly seemed necessary.  She didn't react.  He led her from the court, and she walked to her family to say goodbye.

*     *     *

It was a day in early spring when James came home to find his father smirking about something.  John typically kept his emotions to himself, especially when it came to work, but when something tickled him, he couldn't help but expose it through a little wry smile.  "Well, James," he said, "Do you remember what you told me you saw about that incident?"  He reminded James about the police car he had chased that had Charlie Starkweather in the back seat.  James did remember.  "Well, apparently you really did catch them doing something," John chuckled.  He pulled out an affidavit they had just received and showed it to his son. He had been showing him documents for a while, making comments about their reasons or relevance, sometimes laughing about the absurd incidents.

James had been surprised at how dry legal documents were. He had expected them to have some sort of decorativeness expressing their importance. John had explained to him that sometimes the most important documents were the ones that looked the least impressive; that often the tiniest details in a bland-looking form were more important than the most dramatic eye witness accounts.

The affidavit John was showing him now, though it looked dry, was extremely dramatic. John explained to his son what had happened:

A call had come in to John's office from a former inmate named Otto Glaser. He had just been released from prison and was leaving town, but he had some information that would be useful to them, and if they wanted to talk, they could meet him at the train station. John and Merril met the man at the small platform that abutted the tracks and took him back to their office. Glaser told them that he had been in the hospital ward approximately two weeks before Caril's trial. He was there until December 12. Because there was no death row at the time, Starkweather was in the same hospital ward awaiting execution. Otto's room was next to Charlie's. He saw everyone who came to visit Starkweather, and could hear what they talked about. During his first week there, Charlie was treated like everyone else. He was allowed books from the library, but no newspapers. The TV was at the end of the hall where Charlie couldn't see it except when he was escorted to go take a bath. He wasn't allowed earphones for the radio, but he was given about seven or eight cigarettes a day. Things changed, however, during the second week, the week before Caril's trial began. Men appeared at Starkweather's cell door. Glaser didn't know who they were, and their backs were usually to him, but he could identify them if he saw them again.

One of them was there all the time, but most of the time it was all three. According to Glaser, they talked to Charlie about Caril's trial and told him what they expected him to say. At least once every visit they told him that Caril had said he was crazy, bowlegged, or some other insult to make him angry. And it worked. Starkweather got agitated and started cursing, saying he should have killed her when he had the chance.

The three men told Charlie almost every day that a great deal depended on his testimony and that there were certain things he shouldn't say. It was just as important to leave out the things he was told not to say as it was to testify to the things he was supposed to say. They told him that Scheele was a man of his word and Starkweather wouldn't be executed if he said exactly what he was told to say. Starkweather shouted and insisted that he tell the story his own way, but the men would calm him down and remind him that his life depended on "playing ball" and leaving certain things out. At last Otto heard what it was they wanted him to keep out when Starkweather blurted it loudly. He had almost killed Caril at the Ward house because she tried to get away. He had had to use considerable force to keep her from running and had intended to kill her at the Ward home. Something had stopped him, but he didn't say what.

Glaser continued to explain that Starkweather had threatened to kill Caril if she didn't bring him his gun in Wyoming when he shot his last victim, and that he had intended to turn and shoot her next if the police hadn't arrived. She had served her purpose and he was ready to dispose of her. He told the mysterious threesome that he regretted not having killed her before leaving the Bartlett home, because if he had, he would have escaped. The three men repeatedly and emphatically told Charlie never to mention any of that. They also spent a lot of time coaching him on what exactly he should and should not say regarding the murder of Robert Jensen. The discussions often became loud and profane. Starkweather kept insisting that he wanted to tell the story his own way, but the three men kept saying that his life depended on his "playing ball."

Glaser began to notice that, about the time that Caril's trial began, Starkweather's treatment improved greatly. The Lincoln Star and the Omaha World-Herald were delivered to him. During the entire period of the trial Starkweather was taken out of his cell from 9 am to noon, then from 2 pm to 4:30, the time when James saw Charlie in the back of an officer's car. Otto asked Starkweather where he was going and Charlie told him that he was being taken to a consultation room so he could be in constant contact with the prosecution. Everyone in the ward believed that there was an open phone line from the county attorney's office directly to the penitentiary so Starkweather could keep in constant contact.

Otto also spoke directly with Charlie many times. Starkweather told him that he realized at the Meyer house, and was convinced by the time they arrived at the Wards' house, that Caril would escape, tip off the police, or get them captured somehow. Charlie believed his big mistake was not killing her when he had the chance. He repeated to Otto what he told the police, that he should have killed Caril at the Bartlett home along with the rest of her family. Now, however, he intended to show in her trial what he could do. His one last wish was for Caril to be executed so he could finally accomplish what he was unable to do on the road. He often said "When I go to the electric chair, I want Caril sitting right there on my lap." He began to believe that he would not be electrocuted if he did as his visitors said. Instead, he began to believe that she would be killed, and he would be spared. She would be his twelfth victim, and he liked that.

John began to understand why Charlie had been so at ease during Caril's trial. If what Glaser was telling them was true, Starkweather believed he was getting a reprieve for his testimony against Caril. It also explained why he was so dodgy in his statements when John questioned him, and why he stayed so close to the "self-defense" statements.

Glaser continued by explaining that ffter Charlie's first day of testimony, he had returned to his cell with a carton of cigarettes and a case of candy. He was given a second carton of cigarettes that evening. The three men came to see Starkweather again that night and informed him that he'd be questioned by Fugate's attorney the next day and he must be careful to say only what he had been told to say. After each question he should think carefully before answering, and, if necessary, simply refuse to answer.

After Starkweather's second day in court, he returned to the cell with more candy and cigarettes. He was given earphones and allowed to listen to the radio whenever he wanted. The television was moved so that it now faced Charlie's room. When he felt like having a cup of coffee, an attendant would bring it to him, day or night. When it was announced that a verdict had been reached in the Fugate case, Charlie put on his new earphones and listened intently for half an hour, often remarking how anxious he was to have her found guilty and get the chair. When the verdict was announced, he shouted and laughed and said that his only disappointment was that she didn't get the chair.

There was silence in the office for some time after Otto finished telling the story, save for the clacking of the typewriter from the secretary typing the last of the story. When she was done, Otto Glaser read through it, made sure the affidavit was accurate, then signed the bottom. After he left, Merril turned to John. "I don't think we'll say anything about this just yet. Especially not to Caril."

"Are you going out to York today?" John asked.

Merril nodded. "She gets pretty lonely out there."

*     *     *

Merril saw Caril much like the daughter he never had. He visited Caril every Saturday, even though it was an hour drive to and from York, and there was not much to talk about regarding the case. He spoke with her about his own life and background, and optimistically talked with her about what she would do when she would be released, which he continued to believe would be soon. He even drew up official adoption papers for himself and his wife to be her legal guardians when she was released from prison. (John was, at present, her legal guardian, being her appointed attorney.)

Caril had lost most of her hope the day they had fingerprinted her and taken her mugshot. That day she thought, 'This is it. You're going to stay here.' There were entire days that would go by when she would just cry out of loneliness for another human being. Some days she sat by the window, which looked out over the front gate, and watch. She kept believing that someone would come for her and take her away from all of this. Whenever a car pulled into the reformatory, her heart would skip, thinking maybe they had come for her. Of course it had not, and her heart would sink deeper every time.

But Merril's decision to adopt her gave Caril hope that she would have something to look forward to. Things were not going well for her in prison. She was still in solitary confinement and wouldn't be allowed to mingle with the other inmates until she was 16-years-old, which was several months away.

Mrs. Bowley, though retiring, was still in charge for the next ten months. She was more erratic than ever, and she allowed her extreme mood swings to affect her treatment of the prisoners. Bowley was sharp with Caril, sometimes mocking. Once she gave Caril a large meal and watched as she cut the steak. When Caril put the knife down, Mrs. Bowley leaped at her, grasped the knife threateningly, then laid it down saying, "This is how you put down a knife!"

On Christmas Eve she came in dressed as Santa, smiling and wishing Caril a happy holiday, but the next day, Christmas, she forced Caril to write the statement about Charlie. After that incident, Merril began his weekly visits. He became a celebrity among the other inmates, as his attempts to get better treatment for Caril improved matters for all of them.

Meanwhile, John got confirmation of Otto Glaser's story. Another former inmate and a former guard both signed affidavits stating that Charlie had been given special treatment in exchange for testimony against Caril. The other inmate confirmed that the three men had indeed told Charlie to leave out information about his threats to Caril.

Elmer Scheele impatiently met the press's inquiries about this matter with a statement that he was looking into it. Though Caril was widely believed to be guilty, the public outrage over the county attorney's office collaborating with Charlie Starkweather would be even more egregious, and Caril became hopeful that she would get a new trial. Merril wasn't certain whether to encourage her hopefulness or not. He was realistic, but this was the first ray of hope they had had for a long time.

The information was submitted to Judge Spencer in contrast to a series of eight affidavits submitted by Elmer Scheele stating that no one had encouraged Charlie to testify in any way but the truth. Though Scheele's affidavits doubled theirs, his were all signed by people who either currently worked at the facility, or by those whom

McArthur and Reller were suggesting broke the rules in the first place, including Scheele himself, who had included his own affidavit asserting that he had no communication with Charlie other than that in court.

When the motion came before Judge Spencer, Scheele called Sheriff Karnopp to the stand who testified that he had asked Caril to write a note to Charlie stating that she didn't want to see him again. She had written:

*Chuck*
*Chuck*
*Chuck*
*Chuck*
*Chuck*
*Chuck*
*I don't want to see you.*
*I don't want to see you.*
*I don't want to see you.*
*I don't want to see you.*
*Because I mint do something I mint*
*Be soory for latter on.*
*Becse I mint do something I mint be*
*Sorry for latter on.*
*Caril Fugate*
*Caril Fugate*
*Caril Fugate*
*Caril Fugate*

On cross-examination, John was able to use this opportunity to show another devious side to the sheriff's department's motivation. "Mr. Karnopp, were you anxious to curry favor of Charles Starkweather?" he asked.

"Not particularly. No, sir."

"What was your reason for going to so much trouble at his request?"

"Well, you know, I kind of believe in treating them the way I like to be treated even though they are criminals."

"Well, Charles had asked repeatedly to see Caril Ann, had he not?"

"He had."

"And you brought him a note from Caril Ann saying that she didn't want to see him, didn't you?"

"That's right."

"You knew, of course, that the effect of that would be to turn Charles Starkweather against her, did you not?"

"I never gave that any thought, no, sir. I don't know that it did."

"As I understand it... Mr. Starkweather signed his statement after you had shown him the note, Exhibit Sixteen?"

"Yes, it was after that."

"Then, upon reading the note from Caril Fugate that she didn't want to see him, he signed this statement which incriminated her. Is that the way it worked?"

"Well, he signed the statement."

"Did he refuse to sign such a statement until you proved to him that Caril Ann didn't want to have anything to do with him?"

"That wasn't mentioned at all, no, sir."

"How did it happen that he read the note first and signed the statement afterward?"

"Because I had the note and I wanted him to see it so he wouldn't think that I had lied to him about her wanting to see him."

"Why hadn't he signed the statement before you showed him the note, do you know that?"

"I don't believe it was ready."

Scheele went forward and had Karnopp explain that showing Charlie the note and having him give a new statement right after were entirely coincidental. "Upon receiving the completed written-typewritten statement, unsigned, then is when you and I returned to the penitentiary and that's when you delivered this note to Starkweather?" Scheele asked.

"That's right," Karnopp responded.

"And then, we commenced with the reading of the statement, he making corrections and signing each volume as it was read?"

"That's correct."

"And the obtaining of this note had no connection whatsoever with the obtaining of the statement?"

"Not any whatsoever."

"And that's common in the handling of prisoners, to grant any reasonable request that they make?"

"I have always made it my practice."

"As a matter of fact, you checked with me before making the visit to the state hospital?"

"I did, yes, sir."

"And it was done with my knowledge and my consent?"

"It was."

"That's all," Scheele said.

John now approached the witness. "You say that you talked to Mr. Scheele before going to see Caril Ann about this note?"

"I did, sir."

"Did you contact Caril Ann's attorney before doing that?"

"No, sir."

"You did not?"

"No, sir."

"Did you give Caril Ann a copy of that note?"

"A copy of it?"

"Yes."

"No," said sheriff Karnopp. "I didn't. There was no copy, just the original."

Judge Spencer chimed in at this time, "Did Caril Ann have an attorney at that time?"

"No," Scheele answered.

Karnopp answered further, "I don't believe she had an attorney at that time. That was the day after she was brought back from Wyoming."

John asked him, "Wasn't that after the time that Bill Blue had been out there a couple of times and interviewed her at the state hospital?"

"No," Karnopp answered. "I don't believe that he had at that time. I think Mr. Blue came into the picture on Monday."

"On the Monday following?"

"That's right."

"And have you made other trips and done other favors for Mr. Starkweather besides getting this letter from Caril?" John knew the answer to this all too well. His own son had caught them doing him the favor of driving him around town.

Scheele knew what McArthur was getting at, and he objected.

"Overruled," Judge Spencer said. "You may answer."

"That's the only request he's ever made of me," Karnopp said.

"And is this the only thing of this type you have done for him?"

"Yes, sir."

John suddenly became very direct, and snapped, "And in reality, wasn't that done for the use of the State in the prosecution of Caril Fugate?"

"I told you what I did it for," Karnopp answered, "and it's in the record."

"Very well," McArthur said, calming. He wouldn't be able to prove what his son had seen, but they knew that he was on to them.

Merril and John were hopeful that Judge Spencer would see through all of this and allow a trial without the tainted and unreliable testimony of Charles Starkweather. But they would have to wait for his answer.

Though their client was unpopular, Reller and McArthur became well known around town as attorneys who really fought for their client. The number of calls increased. They were finally able to move out of their tiny offices and into a pair of normal sized offices north of town.

It was a flat, rectangular brick building Reller had had built, renting out all the offices and saving one for he and McArthur in the top corner. Other rooms were filled with a mixture of apartments and businesses, so when they moved in, a steady rumble of televisions, voices, and transactions played throughout the day. Their office was directly over a beauty salon, something Reller had not considered before moving in, because all day they could smell the pungent odors drifting up through the floorboards.

They dealt with the noises and the smells, and moved into their offices, John hanging his high school diploma, and Reller hanging the heads of animals he had shot on safaris around the world.

Neither attorney reduced his time on Caril's case. They continued to work on it as hard as they ever had, and without pay.

Then they got the bombshell. Judge Spencer denied their request for a new trial. James couldn't believe it. He had an innately strong sense of justice, and had come to believe firmly in the rightness of the legal system. A juror had bet on the case, and now the county attorney's office had gotten away with blatantly manipulating a witness. His youthful idealism couldn't understand how this could have happened. John now explained to him that, like life, the law is not always fair, which is why the system created checks and balances in the form of appeals.

And now, he explained, they were actually in a better spot than it seemed, because now they could prepare a writ of certiorari and file it with the United States Supreme Court. The purpose of this writ was to state a complaint to a higher court that a person did not obtain justice in a local court because it was impossible to obtain an impartial trial in that area. "There is no way to avoid the inertia of public opinion against her here," John told him several times. If successful, the appeal would move the case outside the state where John believed Caril would receive a fair trial. While he certainly would have liked to have a new trial in Nebraska where Caril's name could be cleared, his ultimate plan all along was to get enough reasons to have it moved out of state to a higher court. Judge Spencer's denials had helped these efforts.

"Well," James said, "you shouldn't have too much trouble getting it, Dad."

"Why not?" John asked. He always wanted James to figure it out rather than simply to tell him.

"Because there was a gross violation of Caril's constitutional rights. She obviously didn't have a fair trial with a betting juror and a perjured witness. And the Bill of Rights guarantees a fair trial for every citizen of the United States."

John shook his head. "The Constitution and the Bill of Rights don't guarantee anything to the average citizen, son. They are applied in federal courts, but if you talk about constitutional rights in a state court, you're whistling in the dark. If you're defending a client, you'd better concentrate on something that might have some relevance to his innocence or guilt."

James was, and always remained, an optimist. He had a hard time believing that the US Supreme Court would not see the injustice here and step in. But when John's petition was denied, he learned his first harsh lesson in the realities of the legal system.

"In a big case like this," John later told his son, "justice simply breaks down."

*     *     *

Caril was running low on options. She would spend the rest of her life in prison if something was not done.

Before his execution, Caril wrote to Charlie, begging him to confess what had really happened. She hoped that in his last days, perhaps when speaking with a priest or minister he would have a change of heart.

In one of the letters, she wrote:

*After I have been denied a new tril today, I am asking you to do somthing not much you to do but you know it will mean a lot to me.*

*After All Barbara and I have suffered Because of the loss of are family, I beg of you to at least confess to a minister that I am innocent so that I won't be the only one that knows I am innocent.*

*You know that you are the only one who know the truth beside God.*

*This is all I ask of you to do for me. Please.*
*Caril Fugate*

Charlie never responded to any of her letters.

John contacted the governor, asking that a stay of execution be granted to Charlie so they could have more time for him to admit the truth. He helped Caril draft a letter which was sent to the governor which read:

*After thinking it over carefully I would like very much to have it arranged so that I could see Charles Starkweather before his execution and have a talk with him.*

*I believe there is a chance he may tell the truth about things that happened especially about the death of my family and the other things that happened.*

*I would be willing to have this meeting in front of a ministerial that would be agreeable to you.*

The visit was denied.

Merril could not stand to see her living so hopelessly. He had to do something, so he helped her put together a telegram to President Eisenhower. It was a desperate move, but anything was better than just waiting around.

I AM NOW FIFTEEN YEARS OLD STOP ABOUT A YEAR AND ONE HALF AGO ON A DAY WHEN I WAS IN PUBLIC SCHOOL NINETEEN YEAR OLD STARKWEATHER WHOM I HAD TOLD SEVERAL DAYS BEFORE IN FRONT OF MY MOTHER NEVER TO SEE ME AGAIN WENT INTO MY HOME AND KILLED MY TWO YEAR OLD BABY SISTER, MOTHER AND STEPFATHER. STOP STARKWEATHER FIRST CONFESSED I HAD NOTHING TO DO WITH HIS MURDERS WHICH IS TRUE STOP LATER HE CHANGED HIS STORY AND SAID I HELPED HIM DO HIS MURDERS WHICH IS NOT TRUE STOP HE FORCED ME TO GO WITH HIM WHEN I GOT HOME FROM SCHOOL AGAINST MY WILL. STARKWEATHER WILL BE EXECUTED TOMORROW. STOP I HAVE BEEN DENIED BY GOVERNOR BROOKS A REQUEST TO SEE HIM AND SEE IF HE WILL TELL THE TRUTH IN FRONT OF A MINISTER OR SOME ONE ELSE WHO WOULD BE FAIR BEFORE HE IS EXECUTED. STOP I KNOW OF NO ONE ELSE TO TURN TO BECAUSE ALL OF MY FAMILY I WAS LIVING WITH HE KILLED. STOP I KNOW YOU ARE VERY BUSY BUT PLEASE HELP ME IN ANY WAY YOU CAN. THANK YOU

CARIL ANN FUGATE

The response came back: "The Starkweather case is entirely a state matter. The President has no jurisdiction or authority in any way to comply with your request."

*     *     *

Charlie's execution was delayed twice while higher courts reviewed his case. Whatever promises the District Attorney's office made to Charlie were not honored, especially once the story of their dealings became public. The first time he was supposed to be executed was on Good Friday, 1959, but a stay was imposed for several appeals to be completed. The second time was set for May 22. Editors for the Star, Lincoln's morning paper, waited up all night to see if there would be a commutation or a stay of execution. Their deadline passed with no word, and at last they went for printing.

The citizens woke up the next day to read the headline in their morning papers, 'Starkweather Dies Today; Writ Denied'. But he had not been executed. Just 98 minutes before the scheduled electrocution, after the Star had gone to print, US District Judge Richard Robinson of Omaha stayed the execution for two weeks to allow an appeal to the US Circuit Court of Appeals. Charlie had learned only 20 minutes before the execution that his life would be spared a little longer.

But the appeal failed, and the final day was at last scheduled for June 25 at midnight. While awaiting execution, Charlie drew beautiful portraits with western themes. He also wrote an autobiography, which Marjorie Marlette helped him get edited and submitted to Parade Magazine. When they agreed to print it, Marlette helped negotiate the sale. It was titled "A Mass Killer's Handwritten Story of a Life of Rebellion":

*I was lying upon the top bunk and was feeling low and hopeless. It all seems like a fantastic dream... I said to myself, why had everything had to happen to me... I hated the world with all the poison of a granddaddy rattlesnake.*

He described his early childhood as a utopia where he stayed at home playing cowboys and Indians with his brothers. Then everything went sour when he entered school.

*That first day in school I was being made fun at, picked on, laughed at... When people tease, make fun of and laugh at a little youngster in his early childhood, that little youngster is not going to forget it.*

He described the children making fun of his bow legs and his speech impediment. They avoided him and he had to play alone. When he had to speak up in class, his voice got stuck in his throat. The first time he played a team sport, not only was he chosen last, neither team wanted him on their side. When the teacher tried to suggest he sit out as an alternate, Charlie ran into the basement and sat in the darkness, brooding.

*That was one of the first of my black moods. I sat there and said to myself that someday I'd pay them al back. An overwhelming sense of outrage grew in my mind for a revenge upon the world and its human race.*

He described playing in the sandbox alone, in the playhouse alone, looking out at the other children, wishing he fit in. But when others wanted to play where he was, the teacher made him leave instead of making them play with Charlie. Alone, Charlie began painting. He described painting something for his mother.

After school, some of the children followed him home, imitating the way he spoke, mocking the way he walked, pointing and giggling as they called out at him, "The bowlegged, redheaded woodpecker!" One of the children pushed Charlie in front of an oncoming car which almost hit him. Far from feeling sympathy for him, the other children continued to laugh at him. The bully then took the painting Charlie had made for his mother and tore it into pieces.

That night, his father called several school officials complaining loudly. When he got off the phone, he told Charlie, "From now on if anybody starts picking on you, knock the devil out of them. You won't get a licking from us and if that school tries to because you're fighting for your rights, you just tell your mother."

*The next day in school I received my first fight. The teacher did give me the devil but I didn't tell Mom. I just kept on fighting. My rebellion against the world became so strong that I didn't care who I fought with or the reason why.*

He described getting a reputation as a fighter. This attracted other kids in the neighborhood who wanted to beat him down to build their own reputations, and Charlie found himself fighting all the time. To get away from it all, he went hunting. He loved the solitude of hunting in the woods.

*I've done quite a bit of hunting and killed quite a bit of game, but I have deep affection for the animals I have killed... Many a time, I didn't shoot a game animal, instead I sat motionless, watching their tactics of living in the forest.*

He said that he felt remorse for the people he killed, but he referred to them as "the people killed," not the people *he* killed. It was as though he could not bring himself to fully take responsibility for what he had done. And he still referred to it as self defense.

*I pray that God will be forgiving of what has been done. My thoughts at the time of the killings was that it was right to protect yourself and kill in self-defense.*

He could not even take responsibility for going on the murder spree, blaming Caril for keeping it going.

*At the time I figured I had enough and was going to give up, we were driving back to Lincoln from Bennet. Caril then threatened out loud that she wasn't going to give up, and that I, or no one else was going to make her.*

*And with a shotgun laying across her lap with the barrel pointing directly at me, and with her fast talking, she convinced me that we didn't have anything to gain by giving up.*

*My feelings toward Caril now are of great regret for ever knowing her... Today my love for Caril is completely dead.*

He said of the electric chair he had no fear. He admitted that it was the price he was paying for taking the lives of others. He ended by saying he had found God, and that he had one piece of advice for young people:

*I would tell them to go to school, to go to Sunday school, to go to church and receive the Lord Jesus Christ as your own personal Saviour. And I would say to them to obey their parents or guardians, and stay away from bad influences.*

\*     \*     \*

220

On the night of his execution, teenagers lined the streets listening to their radios. News reporters crowded outside the prison. Caril waited inside her cell, hoping and praying that Charlie would have a change of heart at the end. A little after 10:00 p.m. a body was brought out of the prison under a cover and taken away. Confusion murmured through the nearby crowd. Charlie wasn't supposed to be executed for another two hours. Some people went home, thinking it was over. But it wasn't Starkweather who had died. The doctor who was supposed to pronounce Charlie dead had fallen over of a heart attack and died suddenly himself.

Charlie was inside talking with the chaplain. They read the Twenty-third Psalm: "Yea, though I walk through the valley of the shadow of death, I will fear no evil..."

Charlie said nothing of Caril.

Two officers escorted him into the small execution chamber. He barely regarded the witnesses as he voluntarily walked to the wooden chair and sat down, a slight grin on his face. As the officers attached the leather straps to him, Charlie simply said, "They're too loose. Can you make them a little tighter?" They tightened them. Deputy State Penitentiary Warden John Greenholtz asked if he had any last words, and Charlie merely shook his head.

John McArthur was there, as were Charlie's attorneys, Elmer Scheele, Ninette Beaver, and Floyd Kalber. They watched exactly what Clement Gaughan had predicted in his closing arguments when he defended Charlie in court. They watched a young man die.

# Chapter Ten
## Escobedo

Every year in early December the schools of Lincoln, Nebraska held what was called County Government Day which was arranged to help high school students understand how their government worked. Seniors from every school were chosen to follow one elected official. Because of his interest in law, it only made sense that James would shadow the county attorney. That county attorney was still Elmer Scheele and the other senior touring with the county attorney was Dewey Jensen, Robert Jensen's brother.

It was an unusual group, and a potentially uncomfortable situation, especially for James. But he made the best of it, and none of the three brought up the subject of Caril or Charlie. As Elmer showed them around, James and Dewey talked with each other about their hopes and ideas for the future. They both had interests in law, government, and justice, so they spoke of where they aspired to go to college, law school, and what they hoped to accomplish in life. Dewey knew that James' father had defended the girl convicted of having murdered his brother, but, unlike most other people, he didn't hold it against James. When the day was done they parted friends. As for Scheele, he had seemed impressed with James.

In the spring of his senior year, James began working at his father's law office on the north edge of Lincoln. He started by helping him prepare income taxes for farmers and other clients, charging $15 apiece. John taught him the basics, and James learned the rest simply by reading the instructions on the IRS forms. That summer, James was able to dedicate himself full time to the office. Though he could not work in any official capacity, he ran errands for John and Merril, learning where everything was in town, how to fill out forms properly, and making connections.

That fall, James enrolled at Union College, a small Seventh-day Adventist liberal arts school located on the edge of Lincoln. Following his first year at Union, James switched to the University of Nebraska majoring in history with a minor in English and enrolled in the University's "Three and Three" pre-law program which allowed him to enroll at the Law College prior to his having obtained his B.A. Degree. He had witnessed through his father's questionings and speeches in court how useful a good command of language could be. He also learned through assisting in research at the office how useful a knowledge of history was.

During the summers he split his time between assisting his father and working as a brick mason. Though it was hard labor, it helped James appreciate the life of a lawyer and made him all the more anxious to complete his legal studies. Nevertheless, he forever looked back at his brick laying days with pride. For the rest of his life, whenever he drove past a building he had worked on, he would point at it and say, "I helped build that house."

*     *     *

Caril Fugate, on the other hand, was growing up in prison. She spent most of her sixteenth birthday scrubbing floors. She had been moved into the general population that day, and could now associate with other prisoners. Although she had been released from solitary confinement, it hardly seemed like it for quite some time. She went to the dining hall and sat at a table with ten women who just stared at her. The evening meal was the same. Caril didn't know what to say. She was curious about them, and they were curious about her, but no one knew how to begin the conversation.

Afterward they sat in the recreation area watching shows such as 'Lassie', and other tame programming. Shows that even alluded to violence were not allowed. It was all the same to Caril, however. She was more interested in activities, such as knitting and sewing. Suddenly she heard a whisper, "Watch yourself at mealtime." It was a woman sitting across from her, knitting. Her dirty blond hair was turning gray, she was slightly plump, and wore a face that had many prison years written on it. She continued, "The girls at each end of the tables are stool pigeons. Don't tell them anything or they'll turn you in for punishment. Matter of fact, so will almost anybody else."

"Isn't there anyone here you can trust?" Caril asked.

"No, there isn't," the woman said, still looking down at her knitting. "And I'm not about to trust you until you wise up. Just keep your mouth shut and your eyes open and try and learn the ropes. I don't need any more trouble than I've got."

On the way back to their rooms, the woman touched Caril's arm and whispered, "Happy birthday."

Just as she got to her room, the supervisor caught up to the woman. "That'll be three days' lost lobby, Martha. You know better than that."

Caril rose every morning at 5:45 or 6:15, depending on whether she was working outside or inside. She stripped her bed and turned up the mattress to show she wasn't hiding anything. She opened the window to air out the room, then stood in the corridor waiting to go to the bathroom. She brushed her teeth, made her bed, then had to stand in the hall while the supervisor checked the rooms. Four mornings a week they did laundry. There was no radio, and newspapers were clipped by the supervisor to censor anything undesirable.

The women were at first curious about Caril, but once they knew how tidy she was, they assumed she was a snitch. "Scram, kid. We don't need the diaper patrol!" they would say. Martha also avoided her for a time, to stay out of trouble. But occasionally, when no one was looking, she would whisper something to her. "You've got Mrs. Saddoris," she reminded her one day, speaking about Caril's teacher. "You can trust her and you can learn from her."

Once, when Caril found that she had an extra bra, she nearly panicked. Turning to Martha, she asked what she should do. People might assume she had stolen it, and if she reported it, the administration, still run by Mrs. Bowley, would only punish her.

"When's you're period start?" Martha asked.

"Any day now."

"Well, start it early. Then you can wrap the bra in paper like a used Kotex and ditch it."

The only day out of the year when everyone could talk all day was Christmas. Caril stepped up next to Martha, her head bowed. Martha tried to engage her in conversation, taking advantage of this one day of partial freedom, but Caril wouldn't respond. "I'm not going to make it," she told Martha. "I'm never going to get out of here and I'm just not going to make it." Martha knew what Caril was talking about. She had seen when Reller came to tell her the State Supreme Court would not grant her a new trial.

"Nothing's forever," Martha told her. "Is he going to give up the case?"

"No. He said he and Mr. McArthur – he's the other lawyer – he said they'd keep fighting it."

Martha nodded. That's what many said, but none of them stuck around. They probably were going to abandon Caril now, but Caril didn't need to know that. "You have any idea of how long I've been here, Caril?" she asked.

"I hadn't thought about it much. I mean, I've wondered. A long time, I guess."

"Ten years," Martha told her.

"I'll never make ten years. I won't even make it to tomorrow. It's just no use."

"You don't have any choice," Martha said.

"Yes, I have."

"That's dumb. Not that I haven't thought about it myself sometimes. But you'd feel pretty stupid if they decided to spring you and you'd already knocked yourself off."

"Well, what am I going to do?"

"Same as I've done," Martha told her. "Figure out the system and learn to live with it. Everybody gets out sooner or later. You just have to take it one day at a time and hope for the best. Just don't make it any tougher on yourself than it already is. Look at me, for instance. I'm not what I used to be, maybe, but I'm still alive and kicking."

"It's just hopeless," Caril said.

"Nothing's hopeless, and nothing lasts forever." Martha assured her.

That New Year's Eve, Mrs. Bowley assembled the women. She was at last officially retiring. She handed the keys over to the new superintendent, Mrs. Ellenson, a robust, tall woman who looked like she'd been around the block. With that, Mrs. Bowley walked out of the room, and left Caril's life forever.

Under Mrs. Ellenson, the rules loosened. She allowed the women to talk, though that only reminded Caril how little anyone wanted to speak with her. Radios were allowed, and women could smoke at certain times, as long as one of the supervisors lit the cigarette.

Caril had two mentors, Martha Mason and her teacher, Mrs. Saddoris, both instructing her on opposite sides of life. Mrs. Saddoris gave Caril her school lessons, helping her pass her correspondence courses. Caril didn't understand how all this could help her, but Martha encouraged her to keep working at it. "Get your education so you'll have something when you get out," Martha told her. "That's the only important thing to think about around here, getting out." Martha taught her how to get along in prison. "Always try to get on the good side of the people who control your life. Smile, even if you hate it. They're not going to be too hard on you if they know you're not giving them any trouble. Keep the supervisors and the warden happy and they'll stay off your back. If you go the other way and try to fight them, they'll break you."

Merril Reller also stayed in her life, much to the surprise of Martha. Every Saturday, like clockwork, he was there. "Keep doing the best you can," he told Caril. "We'll always keep fighting this as long as you do your part." Caril did her part. She never got in trouble for anything. She followed every rule, every regulation to the letter. Most of the inmates resented her for it, but she didn't lose any friends because they were snubbing her anyway.

She became an accomplished seamstress, read three books a week and worked several jobs. At last she became the "gate girl," the one entrusted with the keys to let visitors in and out. Though she was in prison with a life sentence, the staff had so much faith in her that they knew she would not take advantage of the position.

Then the day came when Martha would be released. The night before, Caril helped her pack. "Look Caril," Martha said. "It's just like I told you from the start. You can't trust anybody around here. I'm leaving and I'm never going to see you again. I'm not going to write to you. It's against the law, and even if it wasn't, you'll be better off forgetting all about me."

"I can't do that," Caril said, slumping down. "God, I'll never get through it now. I just want to get out of here so bad."

"You'll get out of here one of these days," said Martha.

The next day Caril walked to the front gate to open it for her only friend. Martha got out of the car that would drive her to freedom and approached Caril. "You mind if I do that?" she asked, referring to the key. "I've been waiting a long time." Caril took the key chain from around her neck and handed it to Martha, who unlocked the padlock and threw open the gate. She stepped past the perimeter and breathed deeply. Then she turned back around and put the key chain around Caril's neck. They stared at each other, but neither could think of anything to say. Martha turned suddenly and got into the car. Caril watched as it disappeared into the streets of the small town of York; then she closed the gate and locked herself in.

*     *     *

By the time James began law school in the autumn of 1963, he already had as much experience in a law office as someone who had been practicing a year or so. He had started on his law degree early, studying alongside the husband of John's secretary, Donald Hayes. The two worked ahead of others, often at the top of their class. By the end of the first year, James was asked to write an article in *The Law Review*, the primary journal for lawyers across the country.

His father and Merril Reller continued to search for a good opportunity to appeal Caril's case to a higher court. It had been five years since the Fugate trial, and John still believed firmly that if her case could be heard somewhere outside of Nebraska she would be acquitted. But he and Reller had to be careful and do it at the right time. If they tried to appeal to a district court or the Supreme Court immediately, they might be shot down and told that it's a matter for the states, which would end their chances for appeal. Even if the law altered, they would not be allowed to appeal again. They essentially needed to wait for the law to "catch up with them," as James later put it.

One day James got called into the dean's office. Wondering what could be wrong, he made his way into the room and sat down. Edwin Belsheim, the dean of the school, sat across from him. Belsheim had advised Caril early on, before John had been appointed as her attorney. He had tried in vain to get the case moved to juvenile court, and had tried to help John as he continued to attempt to have the case moved to the appropriate venue. He had also written an article that was cited in an important decision called the Escobedo case which had helped the Supreme Court come to its decision.

He confided in James how much he felt that Caril had been railroaded, how unfair he believed the State had been toward her, and how much he admired James' father for standing by Caril. He had been surprised at how the State had ignored the Constitution in its proceedings, and was shocked at the results of the trial. He was even more shocked at their handling of the appeals process, not even granting relief when a juror had made a bet on the trial. James listened, and he learned. Belsheim wanted to hear updates about the case from James, and in return he gave him suggestions and advice to pass on to his father. Belsheim told James during one of their visits that he felt the courts simply ignored the plain language of the law, and was instead influenced by public sentiment.

James' tort professor, Dale Broeder, also took a great interest in the case and often asked him for details. Broeder had been involved in civil rights law for years and had been involved in a study of how jurors decided cases during deliberations. Much of Caril's case involved issues he had dealt with for years, and the courts' decisions on her case would affect his future work.

James, now fully grown to six feet two and thin, at only 150 pounds, was known around campus as someone who had his foot halfway into his practice. Sometimes it worked to his advantage, as with his two mentors; sometimes it worked against him, as when students and professors who felt Caril was guilty snubbed him. The Nebraska Supreme Court later adopted the Certified Senior Student

Rule allowing senior law students who met certain criteria to appear in court under the supervision of a regular practicing attorney to argue cases. It was rumored that the rule was based on James and Donald Hays' experience. The first student to be bestowed this honor was James' cousin, Douglas.

Revolutionary changes were happening in the national legal system. The Warren Court Revolution had begun and The Supreme Court was reviewing many cases typically handled only by state courts. In Gallegos v. Colorado in 1959, the Supreme Court held that juveniles were to be accorded due process rights when prosecuted for a crime. In Mapp v. Ohio in 1961 the Supreme Court decided that the Fourth Amendment, requiring a search warrant prior to any law enforcement search, applied to all state issues, not just federal ones. In the case of Gideon v. Wainwright in 1963 the Supreme Court found that all persons accused of a felony were entitled to counsel. In Escobedo v. Illinois in 1964, the Supreme Court held that the basic right to legal counsel began before the trial. This was soon followed in 1966 with Miranda v. Arizona in which the Supreme Court determined that the right to legal counsel began at the moment of arrest, and not at an arraignment.

James, John, and Merril were following these decisions closely as they all related to Caril's case, and the ways that the police had violated her 4th Amendment rights. Up to that time, the Supreme Court, for the most part, had refused to intervene in state criminal prosecutions even where the violation of Constitutional rights were evident. But now that it had determined that these violations would be overseen on the Federal level, the door was open to an appeal.

The changes to the law were so frequent and revolutionary that it was difficult for any lawyer to keep up to date on them while continuing a practice. James, on the other hand, had the best of both worlds. Still in law school, he was able to keep up to date on the changes as they occurred, and he passed the information on to his father and Reller, who in turn gave him valuable experience working at their law firm, and James was able to see how the things he was learning in school applied to the real world.

The law was moving in the direction they wanted it to. Since the Federal courts were getting more involved in state cases, they would likely be able to move Caril's case out of state. It was all a matter of time and patience. As long as Caril kept her nose clean in prison, they might have a chance once the legal precedents were set.

Reller continued to visit Caril to make sure she did just that, and so far, she was a model prisoner. Now in her twenties, Caril had made it through her teen years as anything but rebellious. She was heeding the words of her friend, "Always try to get on the good side of the people who control your life." She continued to have few friends among the prisoners, who were jealous of her ongoing perfect record, but the staff respected her. They gave her privileges and a great deal of trust. Most people in Nebraska would have been horrified that this woman they so greatly feared had the keys to her own release, yet she did not take advantage of the opportunity or try to escape.

Of all the recent changes to law, the Escobedo Decision proved to be the break for which McArthur and Reller had been waiting. Danny Escobedo had been arrested and questioned, and made a statement before he was formally charged. He had asked to see his attorney, but the police had denied his request until after the questioning. Professor Broeder had written in his article that he believed the Supreme Court would find in favor of Escobedo, and that this would open up a whole litany of other cases where people had given statements without their attorneys being present, including Caril's. Such a ruling would profoundly affect the significance of the 4th and 5th Amendments to the Constitution as they applied to state criminal prosecutions.

"This is it," Broeder told James excitedly. "Tell your father to file the habeas corpus petition." James rushed to the office to tell his father and Merril Reller. John had already used the decision to help him with another case where the police had threatened to arrest a man's wife, who had nothing to do with the case, if he did not confess to a crime he had not committed.

"This is going to mean a lot of work and a lot of research," John told his elated son. "Are you willing to help?"

"Let's get started," James exclaimed, smiling ear to ear.

The petition for a right to habeas corpus went out within a month to the Federal District Court of Nebraska. If the petition was passed, Caril's imprisonment would be deemed illegal, and she would either be released, or granted a new trial. Though she wanted to be released, Caril preferred a new trial because it was important to her that she be proven innocent of the crimes. Caril turned 21 the same month, and she began to hope for the first time since she had been imprisoned.

What made the appeal tricky was that the Escobedo decision would have to be applied retroactively to 1958 in order for the petition to pass. James, also 21, helped prepare the petition. It was the most important document of the case, and John wanted his son to know and understand the pressure.

James, who had an interest in flying and had obtained a pilot's license, flew them to St. Louis for the appeal in his small, single prop airplane. As they flew in they spotted a new monument that was being built, a giant, silver arch that would symbolize the gateway to the Midwest. But James barely noticed the scenery. He had just gotten his wisdom teeth removed and was in terrible pain. When they arrived, John and Merrill went out to eat on a riverboat while James rested. It was supposed to be a crowning moment for him, the filing of an important petition that he had helped with, but he remained quiet for most of the trip, observing his father and Reller, going to a baseball game with them, then flying them back through the high altitude and suffering through the pressure on his mouth.

They got an answer within a couple months. Van Pelt, the district judge, ruled that the Escobedo decision did apply to Caril's case, and that it applied retroactively. It was their first victory. James and Caril could barely contain themselves. Merril told her she'd probably be out within a couple weeks, but John cautioned them against too much optimism. The State could appeal the decision, and it did, to the United States Circuit Court of Appeals for the Eighth Circuit. It was a minor setback, but any court would have to respect the Escobedo decision, and with one judge already deciding in their favor, especially a judge as highly respected as Van Pelt, they were sure his ruling would be upheld.

However, while the appeal was still pending, the Nebraska state legislature, led by the attorney general, took action. They passed Bill 836, the Post-Conviction Act, which John and Merril called the "Keep-Caril-In-Prison Act." It had no useful application for any case in the state other than Caril's, and the judge who wrote the decision, Edwin Carter, specifically admitted in his brief that the act was to keep "a certain case" out of federal court. The act stated that a petitioner "must exhaust all remedies in the lower courts before appealing to a federal court." In other words, they would have to spend months, or even years, going through the motions of appealing to courts they already knew would turn them down before they could move the case out of state.

John and Merril applied to have the case heard in District Court anyway, claiming that Bill 836 was passed after their initial filing, but this time Van Pelt found against them as a matter of "comity," meaning that the Nebraska courts should have a chance to remedy their own problems. The McArthurs and Reller would have to return to Nebraska and go through the legal system that they knew would not find in their favor until they appealed their way back up to the district court. And thus began the long, slow climb up the legal ladder.

# Chapter Eleven
## The Legal Ladder

Patsy Ponder was the school nurse at Union College, the local Seventh-day Adventist college where James had started as an undergraduate student. She had come from Texas where her family lived on and off the army base where her father had been a master sergeant. She was smart, opinionated, driven, and she stood out from the standard mold of a woman of the 50s and 60s. She had gone to college at Loma Linda University in California, and had moved to work temporarily as the Union College nurse. She had a small apartment that she expected to live in during her short time in town. The landlady, who lived on the opposite side of the house, spent most of her day sitting at a window figuring out what the neighbors were doing and gossiping about them. When Patsy began working at night, the woman scrutinized her comings and goings with suspicion.

Patsy was dating the brother of James' sister-in-law when James suggested they go on a double date. He was flying single prop airplanes, so he suggested that he rent the University plane, which he often flew on Saturdays. Though both were already dating someone, James' true purpose was to get to know Patsy better, so he was disappointed when she had to cancel.

But he didn't let that stop him. He called Patsy on the phone a few days later. "I've noticed you in church the last few weeks," he said. "I've wanted to get acquainted, but every time I've tried, it just didn't work out. So I'd like to take you out some afternoon." He took her up flying on their first date where she could look out over the whole city. After the flight they sat and chatted for a long time. He spoke mostly about the law, how excited he was to be starting this profession, and he told her all about the Fugate case.

Patsy was taken by his passion about the law, and in particular how deeply he believed in Caril's innocence. She had barely heard the story before. From her boarding school in Keene, Texas, Patsy had heard the shocking news about the murders, but it was a distant thing, almost unreal to her. But in Lincoln it was very real. Everyone had an opinion, mostly negative, and Patsy was impressed that James could stand up for his beliefs against such a tide, and so she began dating James exclusively just before Thanksgiving.

She soon learned first-hand just how negatively most people felt about the case. Any time she told someone she was dating a McArthur, she was met with an icy stare, or verbal abuse. People told her without hesitation that Caril was guilty and got what she deserved, or that she should have "been sitting on Charlie's lap when he got the electric chair." Most had no idea they were quoting Charlie's own line. Some people stopped talking to her when they found out who she was seeing. Patsy lost friends, and she sacrificed any hope of popularity among her peers. It didn't bother her very much, but she was surprised and amazed that people would feel so strongly after such a long time. Even her landlady made verbal jabs at her when she saw Patsy pass, telling her how evil the McArthurs were, and saying that Caril had stuffed her baby sister down the outhouse.

But Patsy stood by James. A woman of strong convictions and a deep sense of justice, she admired his tenacity more than she cared about their judgment, which she quickly began to learn was based on gossip and old fears. James shared facts of the case with her and told her how the new laws were affecting it by guaranteeing people the right to legal counsel. Though she knew she was looking at the story through a biased point of view, Patsy could see plainly that James, John, and Merril were working with evidence, while the other people who spoke about the case were talking about rumors, most of which had their basis on things Charlie Starkweather had said.

She met the family for the first time that year at Christmas. Impressed by the size of the family on their large acreage, she was surprised by the understated nature of John, the bold attorney about whom she had heard so much. Most people painted him as a demon defending the devil. James had described him as a great orator. She expected someone like Perry Mason. But the reserved man she met was more like a shy monk who barely spoke. It was hard to imagine this man in front of any courtroom, let alone orating at the center of the trial of the century. She found it odd when, while the rest of the family gathered in one room, John went into another and paced around, flipping a coin and talking to himself. James explained to her that he did this when he got a thought about one of his cases. Soon he returned to the room and continued graciously, yet sparingly, speaking with his children and their significant others.

She was particularly surprised when he put on the Nebraska football game on a Saturday, something most Seventh-day Adventists didn't do, and became very animated and passionate about the choices the Huskers were making; cheering when they succeeded, calling out to them when they didn't, and grumbling when he felt the referees made a bad call.

When they visited, James and John typically went into one room while Patsy and Ruby sat in another. She had a lot in common with James' mother. Also a nurse, Ruby worked closely with the Red Cross and had become an organizer at various national disasters, so Patsy enjoyed listening to her many stories. Patsy could hear the two men chattering about cases and legal theory. She saw their hands twirling their eye glasses through the open fireplace between the rooms. As their discussions got more heated, their glasses twirled faster and faster until it looked to Patsy like they would fly out of their hands and shatter against a wall.

Patsy witnessed John's dry witted way of dealing with a difficult client one day when she was at their house and she answered the phone. He was in the next room reading a book, and Patsy leaned in and told him the phone was for him.

"Okay, okay," he said, and he went back to reading the book.

Patsy, a little taken aback, returned to the kitchen. She knew that the woman on the phone was waiting, so she walked back into the room where John was reading his book and reminded him. He acknowledged her, and kept on reading. Back in the kitchen, Patsy heard the woman begin to make noises on the phone. She reminded John again, and again, he acknowledged her, but continued to read his book. This time, Patsy heard the woman call out through the phone, whistle, and make every kind of noise to get his attention. Patsy reminded him again, and without explanation, John simply said he'd get it, but kept reading the book.

Finally, she re-entered the room and said, "The person on the phone is whistling, trying to get your attention."

John grinned and said, "Well, I'm deliberately not going in there. I talked to her today. I told her what to do, and she ignored my advice, so I'm going to let her sweat a little bit."

At last understanding, Patsy went back to what she was doing and let the woman make her whistling and shouting noises. After a little while, John went to the phone and picked it up.

James was not wealthy. What money he had went into renting the airplane and flying. Next to law, it was his greatest passion, competing only with his love for movies. When James and Patsy went out, they usually took her car, as his own, which he called the "Butterscotch Special", was so ugly that he didn't wash it because the dirt hid how ugly it really was. The only thing that James owned that was worth any money was his portable electric typewriter that his father had purchased for him for law school. He was enormously proud of the thing, and showed it off the way other college students showed off their cars. For him, what he could accomplish with words on a typewriter was more exciting than the material possessions that teenagers usually valued.

Patsy admired the fact that James knew exactly what he wanted, exactly what he believed in, and he went after both. She had known a lot of people who talked about the changes coming to the country, but she didn't find many who could tell her why they believed what they did. She felt that the growing counter cultural movement was more about excuses to skip school or work and get high than it was about anything specific. Unlike James, they had little understanding of the causes for which they "struggled." For these reasons, Patsy accepted James' proposal for marriage set the following year. Things would not be easy, however, as James would be continuing law school, and if Patsy continued working as a nurse at

Union College, her pay would be docked from $360 a month to significantly less because she would no longer be considered the head of the household. She switched jobs and began working at the Red Cross, which did not have such rules.

They set the date for August, which was none too soon for James. The war in Vietnam was growing, and James would only remain ineligible for the draft while he was in law school. He had considered getting a teaching job when he graduated, which would keep him exempt, but getting married did the same thing, and he would be able to go into work with his father full-time. A few minutes before they were to be married, John stepped up to his son and told him, "Well, James, you know, as of midnight tonight, the president says that exemption is no longer going to apply. So you're just barely getting in under the wire."

James thought he was joking until he saw the news that night. As of midnight on August 26th, 1965, President Johnson issued an executive order which struck down the exemption for a newly married man to be drafted. James had avoided the draft by only a few hours.

They lived in a tiny attic apartment that James rented from his brother Frank. James continued law school while helping with the appeals, getting increasingly involved. It was a bureaucratic circus as the State delayed as long as they could while John and Merril filed motion after motion. No matter what they said in their briefs, the State came back with excuses as to why they could not hear Caril's case, always taking as much time as the law would allow them. It became a matter of formality for John and Merril, going through the motions so they could prove they had done it and move on to the federal courts.

By the time James graduated from law school in 1966, they had made it almost all the way through the Nebraska legal system and were filing an action in the District Court of Lancaster County, the last hurdle they would need to jump before finally getting to take the case out of state. Though the legislature had succeeded in delaying the hearing for several years, McArthur and Reller had gone through their bureaucratic processes, and now the State Supreme Court was obliged to have an evidentiary hearing. It was still just a formality, but John, Merril, and now James prepared for it as thoroughly as they had prepared anything. The hearing was scheduled for February, 1967.

James and Caril, both still young, were nevertheless optimistic. They were 24, and though they had seen a dark side to the world, they both believed in the basic fairness of people.

Caril was driven to the Lincoln courthouse by Mrs. Ellenson, the superintendent of the reformatory. Caril was thin, wearing a dress she had made for herself. It was her first appearance in the Lincoln courtroom since her sentencing in 1959. She was nervous, anxious, and hopeful. Merril had told her that everything depended on the "voluntariness" of her statements in 1958, but what did that really mean? And who remembered every detail of something that happened almost a decade earlier? But she had to. Everything depended on it.

The courtroom looked different. When she had been there during her trial, the crowds filled the room. Now there was only a handful of reporters, her lawyers, the new county attorney, and the judge. The only thing that was larger was the number of people on her side of the table. John now sat at the front, followed by Reller, behind him was James, and Caril, the smallest, sat at the back of the table.

The hearing lasted three and a half days. On the first day, Caril broke down while describing her time at the mental hospital. She described the shock treatments she saw given to patients, and she was threatened with the same if she did not cooperate. On cross-examination she could not recall exactly what day she saw the shock treatments administered. She had to admit that she had never been overtly threatened, but she felt that she would have trouble if she did not do as they told her. Most importantly, she did not know that they were going to press charges against her. Every statement she gave was to help them prosecute Charlie, and she thought she would simply be a witness at his trial.

"I was under the impression I could leave if I cooperated," Caril testified.

"Who left you with that impression?" County Attorney Paul Douglas asked her.

"It was just an impression," she answered.

The State called a number of witnesses, Dale Fahrnbruch, the deputy county attorney who had taken Caril's statements, Audrey Wheeler, the court reporter who had been present, Judge Harry

Spencer, who had presided over her trial, and Elmer Scheele, who now had the judgeship he had sought.

The result was exactly as John believed it would be; she was denied relief. The next day John filed a motion to vacate the judgment and order a new trial. The court hesitated as long as it could, then overruled the motion. The day after that, John filed notice of his intention to appeal to the State Supreme Court. It was 1967, and John had now climbed back to the point where he had been three years earlier.

*　　*　　*

Caril waited in prison and kept her nose clean. She didn't want anything to ruin her chances. This made her almost completely friendless. She was the only one in York's history to go that long without a single disciplinary incident. Other inmates, evidently jealous of her perfect record, competed with each other to try to get her to break by bullying and intimidating Caril. Some tried to frame her, and others tried to manipulate her into violating the rules, but it never worked.

When James went to visit Caril, Patsy came along with their son, Trevor. She was impressed with Caril. Short and frail, she nevertheless held her head up high. She was proud, but very friendly. They didn't talk much about the case, but when it did come up, she was quick and determined. Far from being the sort of hardened jailbird or rough killer many thought she was, she still had much of her childhood charm, though her life had made her wise beyond her years.

James was meanwhile continuing to take many of his own cases. Ironically, his first trial with a jury was before Judge Elmer Scheele. James disconnected himself from the emotion of Caril's struggles and represented his client in the moment. He hoped his history with Scheele would not affect the current trial. Scheele was fair, and even friendly with James, asking him questions about his own practice, and what he thought of the profession. They parted on friendly terms, and saw each other often in the courthouse, always with a high level of respect for one another.

James' new young wife Patsy sometimes had a hard time understanding how James and the other attorneys could avoid showing their anger and resentment. "You don't last long in this profession if you hold grudges," James said, essentially repeating his father. He knew Scheele believed in Caril's guilt, and James disagreed with some of the methods the State employed to get the conviction, but if he allowed that anger to show, he would only do harm to his clients. And he still respected Scheele despite all of that. While never accepting how he had obtained Caril's conviction, he also saw many positive things Scheele did for the state as a county attorney; the many real criminals, Charlie included, he brought to justice. James believed many of the criticisms he had of the methods utilized by the State were the character of the law at that time, particularly its lack of respect for observing constitutional guarantees at the state level – the very problems which were now being addressed by the United States Supreme Court in its recent rulings. For these reasons Scheele and James maintained both a professional, and a personal respect for one another during their entire careers.

In December, as John had predicted, the State Supreme Court denied Caril a new trial. Although this seemed like a terrible setback, it was what they had hoped for all along. At last, having exhausted the remedies available in the state courts, they could finally seek relief in the federal courts by filing a habeas corpus action outside of Nebraska in the United States District Court where they believed she would receive a fair trial. Once again John filed for a writ of habeas corpus with the United States District Court for the District of Nebraska. This time, there was no state law that could stop them, and it would only be a matter of time before they could get a hearing.

James, now primarily in charge of the appeals process because the new laws were fresh in his memory, flew out alone to St. Louis to file for the petition. This time he took a commercial airplane. The Nebraska attorney general's office flew out one of their assistants, and the two men argued their cases.

On the flight home, James was seated next to the assistant attorney general who chided James the entire way back about how guilty Caril was, and how much she deserved to be in jail.

James expected that the man would be disappointed since the same judge who found in their favor three years earlier was still on the bench, Van Pelt. James had even once overheard Van Pelt talking about the case in disgust, fuming, "She needed a lawyer and they gave her an educator!" The decision would have to wait, however. Van Pelt recused himself, citing a conflict of interest. Though no one understood at the time why he had done this, James later noted that Judge Van Pelt's secretary was Merril Reller's sister, Hellen Reller.

While waiting for a new judge to be appointed, Merril took John on one of his around-the-world safaris. They started in Ireland, continued to London for a few days, and then went on to Germany. They then worked their way down through Africa to Johannesburg, up through India, then southeast to Australia before returning home.

Caril did her best to wait patiently while she continued her schooling every day. In August of 1968, at the age of 24, she received her high school equivalency diploma. Excited, she couldn't wait for Merril Reller to return from his trip so she could show him her achievement.

They had gotten as far as Botswana where John shot a gnu that he gave the paradoxical name "Old Gnu." Merril shot a giraffe, which he had agreed to obtain for the natural history museum at the University of Nebraska. During the hunt, Merril started to feel ill, and when they got to Perth, the symptoms seemed to become serious. While walking along the street, he turned to his partner and said rather calmly, "John, I think I'm having a stroke."

They went immediately to the hospital, expecting it to be a simple problem. Perhaps he had picked up a local disease, or had acquired food poisoning. Then, unexpectedly, he fell over. When they got him to a room, the doctors declared it was a brain aneurysm, and there was nothing they could do for him. Merril lay in a coma for two weeks while John waited for him helplessly. At last, he slipped away, and John returned with the body of his long-time friend and law partner.

Caril heard the news on the radio. She was devastated. Merril gave her hope. Sometimes it was the only thing keeping her going. John did the majority of the legal maneuvering to get her out of prison, but Merril gave her the courage to endure long enough to make it out.

He helped her look forward to a possible future out of jail. Reller had even taken what little money Caril had when she entered prison and invested it for her. It was a way to boost Caril's morale and give her something to look forward to.

After he died, Merril's wife, Virginia, whom he had always called "Honey Bunch," took all of his money and assets and refused to give any of it out to the people Merril had appointed in his will. She even refused to give up the small amount of money that he had invested for Caril. His estate was worth three million dollars, and he had left most of it to her, but she believed she was entitled to all of it.

John encouraged Caril to file suit against Mrs. Reller. He even held a deposition of Mrs. Reller in a room down the hall from their offices; an empty, unrented room over a meat cutting space where the putrid smells wafted up and hung in her sensitive nose while the roar of the meat saw buzzed in her ears.

Caril put a stop to it all when she dropped the lawsuit. She didn't want to go through with it. She simply let it go, as she was having to let a lot of things in her life go.

It was her tenth year in prison, and she endured another two long years while waiting for a new judge to be appointed to hear her appeal. Two years without Merril, without Martha, even without her family, whose visits had become fewer and farther between until at last they stopped visiting altogether. James and Patsy visited several times. It was a mixed blessing for Caril, who enjoyed their company, but they also reminded her of the world she was missing. James was her age, and as she watched him build a family and a career, Caril was constantly reminded of the life she was unable to live.

James, meanwhile, was growing to admire Caril a great deal. In December of 1968, Caril became eligible to apply for a commutation of her sentence, which, if accepted, would likely set her free. But to do so meant she had to show remorse for the crimes, thus admitting she had been involved. Caril maintained her innocence, and the worst thing she could imagine was admitting guilt, even if it set her free.

John and James moved into their new office building which they named McArthur Park, after a popular song of the time. It was across the roadway from the rectangular brick building where John and

Merril had practiced. James did his best to fill Merril Reller's shoes, though they were big shoes to fill. John drew up most of the legal motions while James did most of the research.

They were a good team. John usually got to the office early in the morning, James usually arriving about eight. They began their day by talking about cases. John would pass on his experience to James, and James filled John in on changes to the law. A few other attorneys they knew moved into the offices with them, including James' cousin Doug, and they supported one another on cases and sharing of discoveries.

At last, in January of 1970, Judge Elmo Hunter was assigned to listen to their appeal for a new trial in their habeas corpus petition. First, he would have to hold another evidentiary hearing to determine if a new trial was warranted, so Caril was driven to Lincoln again.

This time, Sister Joyce Stechkin drove Caril there. Sister Stechkin was the assistant to the new superintendent. Mrs. Ellenson had retired due to bad health, and a woman named Madolyn Gaffney took her place. She was less strict with the inmates, and allowed them to wear jewelry and makeup, smoke, have televisions and radios in their rooms, and gave them power over decisions in their own lives. Caril was brought to tears when Mrs. Gaffney allowed her to choose from a list of jewelry to wear. It had been a long time since anyone let her have a choice. Gaffney made it a point to talk with Caril every day. Caril knew the place better than anyone, and she could give her the best advice on the feelings of the prisoners. Caril criticized Mrs. Gaffney only once, when an inmate appeared with a black eye. Caril told her that she was allowing too many freedoms, and some of the prisoners were paying the price.

Caril testified at the hearing the same way she had three years earlier. Everything was pretty much as it had been, but this time they were all more hopeful, knowing that, for the first time, someone from out of state was hearing their case. Next in the witness chair was John, an unusual move for an attorney, but he needed to impart certain information on which a portion of the appeal was based. James asked him about Reller not being allowed to represent Caril at the trial when Judge Spencer inexplicably took him into his chambers and told him to leave the case up to John. John described the confusion, and how it started the defense off balance. He also pointed out that Starkweather had been appointed two attorneys, while Caril was only allowed one.

"Do you know if both of those attorneys participated?" James asked.

"Yes, sir, I attended that trial," John answered.

"What was the purpose for attending that trial?"

"Because of the close similarity, it involved the same homicide, same circumstances, and for the most part the same witnesses, and it was a part of my preparation for the Fugate case."

"What was the verdict in that case?"

"Charles Starkweather was convicted of murder in the first degree."

"And what penalty did he receive?"

"He was executed."

"Do you have an opinion as to whether or not – or do you have a judgment as to whether or not the limitation that was imposed by the Trial Judge in any respect affected the defense of the case?"

Melvin Kammerlohr, the assistant attorney general representing the State, objected as "irrelevant, immaterial, self-serving, incompetent."

"I will receive his answer subject to the objection," the judge responded.

Kammerlohr continued his objection, "Not having been exhausted in the State Court, also."

"Same ruling. You may answer."

"I do."

"And what is your judgment?" James asked his father on the witness stand.

"And I repeat the same objection," Kammerlohr interjected.

"Same ruling, gentlemen. You may answer."

"I considered it very damaging to the defense of the Fugate case."

"And for what reasons?"

"Same objection, Your Honor."

"Same ruling. You may answer."

"Merril Reller was a lawyer of very great ability. He had done a great deal of work on that case. He had a lot of energy, extremely capable. More so than myself, I am sure." He described his late friend, his decades of work and dedication to the law.

Kammerlohr then asked John about his own experience as an attorney, pointing out his qualities. Judge Hunter then had his own things to say. "You rather tend to deprecate your own services," he told John. "I am sure you carry the feeling today that you did everything you reasonably could at that time. Hindsight, of course, is always better than foresight, but I am talking about at the time. Do you know of anything that you didn't do that you wanted to simply because Mr. Reller wasn't sitting in the front chair, so to speak?"

"That is a very difficult question to answer, your honor," John said. "Looking back, at that time there were no specific items that I was prevented from doing, and as to the things that I have thought of afterward, that should have been done, which there are a great many, I can not say if Mr. Reller had been allowed to participate any of them would have been done."

After the hearing was over, James walked up to Sister Joyce. "I understand you're allowing the women to wear jewelry now. Is that right?"

"Well, nothing fancy," Sister Joyce informed him. James understood that. In Seventh-day Adventism, which he still practiced, women were not allowed to wear anything more extravagant than a watch. Even wedding rings were forbidden, (married couples changed the wrist that they wore their watch on to signify their union.)

But he knew this would be important to Caril. He pulled a ring out of his pocket and handed it to her. "We've been saving this for you," he told Caril. "We thought you might like to have it."

Breathless, Caril took the ring and slipped it onto a finger on her left hand. It fit perfectly.

"It's very pretty," said Sister Joyce since Caril had been silent.

"Yes," Caril finally said. "It's my mother's wedding ring."

*　　*　　*

The judgment came back in May. The judge had refused their writ of habeas corpus. Their request for a new trial would not be granted. John and James were stunned, and Caril was heartbroken. They had all been so certain. For a decade this had been their greatest hope, to get it out of the state and into a more objective court. And now those ten years of struggle were diminished by a single order.

But they were not completely in vain. John and James now appealed to the U.S. Circuit Court of Appeals for the Eighth Circuit, a three-judge panel who would determine whether or not to overrule the District Court's ruling. It took them more than a year to decide, and in a 2 to 1 decision, they also ruled against Caril. The dissenting opinion, Judge Haney, wrote a blistering account of the other judges, stating that their opinions had no true legal merit.

The McArthurs were devastated. Caril's and James' youthful optimism were wearing thin. But John pointed out the one ray of light in it. The one dissenting judge had been very favorable to Caril. They might be able to make a case out of his ruling for a rehearing en banc, which was a hearing by the entire nine judge panel of the District Court.

Back at the offices, John and James focused on the motion for a new hearing. They cited rulings by the courts over the past several decades that had been in their favor, and described in detail the irregularities of the Nebraska courts which were in opposition to the recent Supreme Court rulings. Again they were denied by an equally divided court, (one had recused himself, and they needed the majority.) Those who had voted in Caril's favor were strongly of the opinion that Caril had never received a fair trial, and was due one all these years later. James and John knew they were getting close, but they were running out of options.

They had, in fact, only one option left, the Supreme Court of the United States. John gave the job of appearing before the country's highest court to James. James would be one of the youngest attorneys ever to appear before them in the history of the country. On the one hand, this was a great honor for him, but on the other hand, the pressure was as great as it could be. Caril's future depended on him convincing the top judges of the country that a great injustice had been done to a girl that many believed was responsible for one of the most heinous crime sprees in the nation's history.

James was to fill out the petition for a writ of certiorari, which would bring the case before the Supreme Court. But before he could submit it, he would have to be admitted to practice before the Supreme Court, something his father had never even done. In order to be admitted, he would have to be nominated by someone who was already a part of it. The only person James knew who was in this very exclusive club was an assistant attorney general who was part of the team trying to keep Caril in prison. But James' uncle, Albert McArthur, also an attorney for many years, had nominated this same assistant attorney general to the Supreme Court Bar Association. He owed his own membership to the McArthur family. And so, even though it was for James to do something he disagreed with, the assistant attorney general nominated him to the Supreme Court Bar Association.

Soon after he was accepted, James got to work on the petition. He spent weeks working on it, citing the cases he had researched in law school and shown to his father throughout the two decades of the appeals. He had to not only show that injustice had been done, but why it was relevant to the country as a whole. He focused primarily on the wager placed by the juror, an act that would surely concern all courtrooms. The Nebraska courts had dismissed the claim, stating that even though a juror had a bet on the outcome of the trial, it did not affect his decision making process. James quoted several relevant cases where jurors made bets, all of which were either overturned or retried. In one of the cases, the bet had even been nothing more than a cigar. The amount was never in question, simply the act of a juror making a bet on someone's guilt made them disqualified by reason of self-interest.

It would be their final hope. The Supreme Court accepted fewer than two percent of the appeals sent to them. If they did not win a new trial here, there was nowhere else to appeal.

# Chapter Twelve
## Growing Up in Prison

"You're crazy," the woman said. "You're really crazy. You're sitting in here when you could be out." The woman was a short-term prisoner who had recently learned that Caril could apply to be released on parole if she just confessed and showed remorse. She didn't have to mean any of it, just show that she was sorry for what she was accused of doing and she could likely be released.

"You don't understand," Caril told her, as she told others who brought up this topic. "I'm not like you. I'm not fighting time. I'm fighting for a principle."

"You're also a little bitch," the woman said.

"Come on. Didn't you ever get blamed for something you didn't do?"

"Yeah. Once, when I was a little kid, my mother said I took some money out of her purse and I didn't do it."

"How did you feel?"

"I was mad. But I couldn't convince her, no way."

"Well, there you go. That's the same way I am, see?"

"Yeah, but when I couldn't get her to believe me, I just left it alone and forgot about it."

"Well, I'm not that way," Caril explained. "I'm going to sit here until they believe me. And if they don't, no one will ever be able to say that I didn't try."

"That's what I mean," the woman said. "You're crazy."

Caril was now 27 years old and she had spent 12 of those years in prison. She had been there longer than any of the inmates, and any of the employees. A tree which had been planted in her early years near the front gate had now grown much taller than her.

Two years earlier she had finally finished the eighth grade after going to school for 45 minutes each day for ten years. She was well behaved and never had a single disciplinary action, a fact that often stunned new employees who had been told in the outside world that Caril was a ruthless killer. She continued to let people in and out of prison as the gate girl. She even let James and John in when they came to visit her.

Outside, the world had altered in dramatic ways. The 1960s had brought revolutionary changes. Every country was embroiled in a bitter cold war, man had landed on the moon, riots clashed with police, assassinations brought down America's dynasty, the Civil Rights movement had changed the face of the country, and music became something completely different than it had been in any decade. Caril saw only part of this through censored newspapers and by the changing class of inmates coming in, who got younger every year.

She also saw James' life change. In February of 1971, he had his second child, me. James had seldom taken Patsy to visit Caril for the first several years of their marriage, but now he brought her quite often, and Patsy often let Caril care for the children and play with them on what was called "the campus," an open area with picnic tables and benches where later the management put up playground equipment. Caril missed seeing children. She feared she might never have any of her own, and she missed her baby sister. She never showed James or Patsy a sign of jealousy or bitterness, something they appreciated, though they knew she must have been having a prism of emotions.

Ninette Beaver also visited a lot. She was fascinated with Caril. This was not your usual prisoner, and not the open and shut case many people believed it had been. She admired the fact that Caril refused to apply for release on the grounds that she wanted to prove her innocence.

During the same year that James' second son was born, Ninette visited Caril with a camera crew. Caril was teaching a sewing class. "It gives me a sense that I'm needed," Caril told her.

She had become a Catholic the year before, and had taken on as her patron saint St. Therese of Liseieux. "She was the type of person that was misunderstood," she told Ninette. "She went into a Carmelite convent at the age of fourteen to become a nun and she suffered the unjust criticism she received from the other nuns, but with her life she showed us such extraordinary companionship with God." Ninette asked her if she had been religious before. "No," Caril answered. "I was never much interested in religion. But I learned a long time ago that, if you're going to make it, you've got to have something. And it can't be people."

From this, Ninette got the idea to do an entire documentary about Caril called 'Growing Up in Prison'. They had more than enough historic footage back at KMTV. She pitched it to Eliot Frankel, a former associate of hers who now worked at NBC in New York. He liked the idea, and began the process of getting it financed through their news department.

\*       \*       \*

The reformatory, meanwhile, went through two more changes in management. Jacqueline Crawford, who took over in the middle of 1971, took a special interest in Caril. At 36, she was the youngest warden in the United States. Jackie had worked as an assistant at the reformatory for many years, and was well aware of Caril's integrity. One day while she was still an assistant she pulled Caril into her office and made her look in the mirror. "Take a look at yourself in that mirror, Caril. You look just awful. What in the world is the matter with you? Your hair's a mess and your clothes are absolutely awful!"

Caril looked at herself, then broke down crying. "Oh, Mrs. Crawford, I'm just not going to make it. I'm not. I just can't go on another day."

"Nuts," Mrs. Crawford said. "Stop feeling sorry for yourself. Don't you have any makeup?"

Caril nodded. Mrs. Crawford told her to put it on and put up her hair.

"What difference does it make?" Caril said. "Why don't you just throw me in the hole and forget about me."

"I don't intend to forget about you, Caril," Mrs. Crawford told her. She demanded Caril go fix herself up and asked if Caril had any money. She did. Mrs. Crawford told her to bring it with her.

Caril went to her room, fixed herself up, then returned a half hour later.

"That's more like it," Mrs. Crawford said. "Feel better, don't you?"

"Yes, I really do."

"Okay. You're coming with me."

"Where are we going?"

"Into town," Jackie told her. "You're going to buy some new clothes and a wig."

Caril stared at her flabbergasted. She had not been out of the reformatory except to go to court in almost 13 years.

"Will you please hurry up?" insisted Jackie. "We've got to get you something decent to wear and then get back here so I can get you started on your new job."

The new job was to work as a tour guide. A number of people were interested in seeing the reformatory where one of the most famous criminals in the world had been placed. They stared into windows, hoping to catch a glimpse of the ruthless girl with the hardened face they had seen sketched in their newspapers. Little did they know that she was the small, light-voiced woman who was giving them the tour.

When the visitors asked which inmate was Caril Fugate, she'd tell them, "I don't see her right now. Actually, the rest of us aren't much interested in each other's pasts, you know. We're more interested in making something of our futures." When the visitors asked her for her name she replied Therese.

The State created a program where inmates would be taken to various small towns to speak with clubs, such as the Rotary, the Kiwanis, and the Sertoma, Mrs. Crawford selected Caril. She went by her pseudonym at these events, and when people asked what she was in for, Mrs. Crawford told them it was because she wrote bad checks. Every person who met her liked "Therese." People who had wished the girl named Fugate had been put in the electric chair now praised the amiable and well spoken girl before them.

When Mrs. Crawford became the chief superintendent, she opened up more privileges, giving the inmates something to look forward to, a reason to stay in line. If they were good, they were allowed to go into town to the movie theater, go shopping, or visit with someone outside the prison. If they got into trouble, they lost these privileges and were often put into smaller rooms. Despair left, and hope for a better future grew.

Mrs. Crawford's most important proposition was a work release program where inmates could get jobs in the local area. Many local residents were apprehensive at first, but when they found how disciplined and reliable the inmates were, more businesses opened up to the program. Caril was not allowed to participate since her sentence was for life. But she was allowed to volunteer for her church. Reverend William Shipman suggested she take care of the children in the nursery. She had shown so much affection to James' children when they visited that it was evident how much she longed to take care of kids.

"No one needs to know who you are," Reverend Shipman said to Caril when she showed some hesitation.

"That wouldn't be right," she replied. "They deserve to know who is taking care of their children."

When Reverend Shipman made the suggestion before his congregation, he was met with apprehension. One of the women told him how she remembered bolting the door and fearing for her family's life when the bodies of the Wards had been found. The Reverend told her to go home and think about it. She returned the following week with her baby in her arms. Caril was in the nursery nervously smoothing out the cribs for the third time. The woman approached her, looked at her, then handed her baby to Caril. "This is my little boy Johnny," she said. "He's just one month shy of being a year old. You take him, now. I hope he doesn't give you any trouble."

Caril took him appreciatively. "Oh, what a big boy," she said, rocking him softly.

"I see you thought about it," Reverend Shipman said to the woman outside of the room.

She answered, "You know, I went home last Sunday and thought about it and discussed it with my husband and I just thought we all need a chance to prove ourselves. I just put myself in her place and thought, well, my life would really be over if no one would trust me again."

"Amen," Reverend Shipman answered.

*  *  *

Caril was still waiting for the Supreme Court to rule on her case. The law always went achingly slow.

But not the news. Ninette arrived with her NBC crew and began filming the institution. They started with Caril's regular tour of the facility. They saw her room, met the warden, saw the kinds of things they did. The camera man was very disappointed. He had flown up from Texas to see a hardened criminal in a harsh environment controlled by a strict warden. Great, dramatic television. No one acted like they were supposed to. Caril, especially, was not what he expected. She struck him as an ordinary, middle class woman nearing her 30s. You could line her up with other women from the suburbs and never pick her out. She was neither violent, nor bitter, nor tough. Just a sweet natured, short woman.

They followed Caril on several of the outings, including some recreational, and some work release programs. They filmed her taking care of the children at the church, and her interaction with those in the community. When Jackie went to the State Chamber of Commerce, she took Caril as the chief speaker to explain the benefits of their program, and the cameras captured the speech Caril gave: "Our philosophy is to deal with the total woman. Our program does not deal with why she is there, but what she does while she is there. When she comes into the institution she has nothing. She hates herself, she hates society, and she wishes she was anywhere but in an institution. Step by step she progresses through the institution. The more privileges she can assume, the more responsibility she assumes with it. If, for any reason, a woman cannot handle any of the privileges given her, they can be taken away, and she must then begin again to earn them back. In order for total rehabilitation to be successful, the community as a society in general must become involved. It is from the community that the inmate comes, and it is back to the community the inmate returns. There is no way the two can be separated, and expect a total, complete rehabilitation of the offender. It is not my intention to convince anyone that every prisoner can be corrected in the community. I don't believe that. There is a small percentage of the prisoners in every penal institution, who are dangerous. Officials estimate say about 15 percent. They are dangerous to themselves, and to everyone around them, inside or outside, and would function best in a mental institution rather than in a penitentiary. If penologists believe, and they say they do, that 85% of the prisoners are receptive to corrective treatment, then I wonder why salvageable men and women are kept behind bars. Are they kept there to be taught to live in prison?"

Everyone listened intensely, including the camera crew, which was surprised by what they had seen.

After filming, the camera man ordered a stiff drink. He had been shaken by what he saw; at how "normal" it all was. Ninette explained to him that it was this very thing that she wanted to capture. It was the normalcy of it all that made it fascinating.

*       *       *

The documentary begins with a shot of the electric chair in which Charlie had been executed. Floyd Kalber explains that Charlie's execution marked the last time the chair had been used, describing the scene as he had witnessed it. "It was not a pleasant experience witnessing Starkweather's execution," he says, "but it was brief and decisive."

He then says that this left the matter of Caril Fugate. He explains that she had been with Starkweather when the murders were committed, and that her mother, step-father, and half-sister were among the victims. He tells about Caril's explanation that she had been Starkweather's hostage, but that the jury didn't believe her, and that she was sentenced to life in prison.

It then cuts to the prison gate and the barbed wire at York Reformatory, Caril's 29-year-old voice speaking over the image saying, "I've always looked to next year, or maybe next year... But I've never stood in the mirror and said and looked and said 'My goodness girl, life.'  Because I think probably, personally, if I had really said in my mind, this is it, you are forever and ever and ever doomed to a penitentiary, I don't think I would have made it."

The title appears, and Floyd Kalber then describes the murders, beginning with those in Bennet as a camera pans across the town. Inside the Bennet home, photographs of Robert and his girlfriend Carol King still sit upright on the shelf.

"It doesn't seem like it has been one day rather than 14 years," Robert's mother says.  "And of course it has made our way of life different…  I'm rather a recluse.  I hate being out among crowds. People are wanting to talk to me about it and be kind will come to me and say, 'I hate to bring up the subject, but…'  Well I know very well what they're going to say so I'll say the subject is never off of my mind, and you're not bringing up anything."

It cuts to Robert Jensen's father as he tends the general store, one of the center-points of the town.  Speaking very matter-of-factly, yet reflective, he talks about how so many stories that you read about are just statistics, and until it happens in a small community or within one's family, it's just another news story.

"But it isn't, I gather," Kalber says.

"No, not when it comes home, it isn't," Robert Jensen Sr. says.

The documentary cuts to Caril saying that it's something that she will always carry with her.  "It lives in the back of my mind.  It's behind a little door.  And right now, the past is over with.  There's nothing I can do.  I can't change it.  And I have to make now, today, tomorrow, and my future.  There's no way to go back.  And if there was any way humanly possible that I could go back, and I could change what happened.  If I could in any way bring back those people, give them back their life that he took, if there was anything I could do, I would.  But there's just nothing I can bring back those people, give them back their life that he took, if there was anything I could do, I would."

Kalber then describes the murders, showing news footage gathered during the murder spree.  He ends by explaining that Starkweather first told police Caril had nothing to do with the murders, but later changed his story and implicated her in at least two of the killings.

It cuts to Caril explaining that she went with Charlie because she did not know her family was already dead, and that Charlie was threatening to have them killed if she didn't do exactly as he said. "As God is my witness, I did not know that my family had already been killed," she says. "People don't really realize it, that I lost my family, too."

The documentary continues to show footage and give background information on what happened. When it goes into the interview Caril gave to Ninette, Mrs. Jensen says, "The thing that struck me most about her then and still was her very, very cold eyes. Unfeeling look that she would have."

The interview is replayed, followed by Robert Jensen Sr. repeating in essence what his wife said. Caril then explains that she was in a sort of daze throughout the trial.

The subject soon turns to HA Walenta, the juror who had bet on the trial. He explains that before the trial began, he had admitted that he had already formed an opinion about the case. He claims that during jury selection he had said, "I thought she'd ought to sit in Charlie's lap and save the expense." Soon after, he explains the thought process of the jury when convicting Caril: "We realized that a person that young could be misled, easily misled, and I think that probably had a lot to do in our thinking of the verdict that we gave her. I know I've got some grandchildren that are about that same age now. And I'd hate to think what would happen to them if somebody, an older person could get them doing some of the darndest things, too."

"But you still had to bring in a conviction," Kalber says.

"Well, that's true," Walenta says. "That's right. She was guilty. They didn't ask us why."

The documentary describes her conviction, sentencing, then early days in prison.

"It's been very lonely," she says. "It's hard to grow up without a mother. It's hard to grow up without a father. And it's really hard to even try to keep contact with a family relationship. It's terribly hard for my sister to come and visit me... When you see girls with their family comes to visit them, their mother and their father, and you think, gee, I wished I had a family to visit me. And you're happy for them. And a lot of times when girls have problems with their family and things like this, I think how lucky they are. Maybe they do have a fight. Maybe they do have family problems, but at least they have a family. And it makes a difference. It makes a difference when you know you have people who love you, and who care about you."

She then switches subjects quite quickly, tears welling up, then falling down her cheeks as she says, "I really wish that there was something I could do. I wish there was some magic word I could say, or a magic phrase or something that would, that could bring these people back. I'm sorry. I'm deeply sorry it happened. And I swear to all mighty God I never killed any of them. And I only went because I had no choice."

"For a long time I went through a period of wishing that I was someone else," Caril says. "I was great at beating myself. I was great at being down on myself more than anyone was down on me. I used to think that I didn't have the right to do a lot of things, or even to feel a lot of things. And through counseling, and it was with a minister, I found out two things. One, that I am Caril Fugate. And it doesn't leave a bitter taste in my mouth. For years it used to. I would get real upset if people said my last name, because it was like someone throwing mud, and it hurt."

Filmed footage of the reformatory shows her at work with others, and her taking lessons to graduate from school. An interview with her teacher tells about her schooling, and says quite frankly that she's surprised that Caril has been there as long as she has.

An interview with John McArthur shows him leaning forward in his chair before a plant in his office as he says of her time in the reformatory, "She had to maintain a very precarious balance. She had to walk a tight rope. She could not identify with the inmates over much or she would become an inmate in spirit and feeling and personality, in outlook. She had to be aloof from the management, or she would incur the enmity of the inmates. So her position did become unique."

The scandal regarding the prison's warden is described in detail, as well as the reforms that made life better in the reformatory. Jackie Crawford explains her policies, reminding the viewer that inmates are just like everyone else, just people who made bigger mistakes than the rest of us.

It describes the program that introduces inmates into the community, allowing them to work in local businesses, and earning the privilege to go bowling and swimming. Caril talks about how much she admires the York community, and the people who have been good to her.

The locals, in turn, speak highly of her. In one interview, a member of the church she attended says, "Now she's pretty near 30 and it's time to give her a chance to prove herself. She can't prove herself in there. She'll always do just like she is here. She's got to go out in society and be back among society people before she can really prove to people that she is what she professes to be."

Several people, including Governor JJ Exon and Director of Prisons Victor Walker, state that the time for Caril's release seems to have arrived, but Mrs. Jensen is not convinced, as she says, "I don't think she's paid for what she did, I don't think she can ever pay for what she did."

Her husband primarily agrees, saying "Well, in the first place, I don't think there is any doubt about her guilt, and I don't think there is any doubt about her ability to realize right and wrong. In fact, I think probably she was the instigator of most of this. But she's had a trial, and a fair trial, I think, and as far as she paying, or anyone paying for taking another person's life, I don't think they can do that, but we have laws, and that's what they're for, to be applied to things like this. And if she's coming up for parole, I'm sure we have qualified people to pass on that. It's hard to not say things that you, but I know that you can be destroyed by hate and bitterness just as hate and love can be your salvation." He fidgets as the camera zooms in on his reticent face. He looks as though he isn't sure how much of his true feelings he should be revealing. "I don't know how much influence a so called pressure will have at the parole board, but I don't think it should have any. They should be qualified people, and they should look at it in that way."

"In other words, you would not do anything yourself to prevent her release, if they think she's ready to come out," Kalber says.

"No, I wouldn't," Jensen says. "Another year, another five years, another ten years, she still couldn't pay for that. But if the purpose for that is rehabilitation, well, half of her life time ought to be enough to rehabilitate her."

"I don't know how a father can arrive at this point," Kalber says.

"Well, I tell you what, if they... why I'd..." Jensen cuts himself short. He had been adjusting himself uncomfortably throughout the interview, looking away, as if trying to find the right words. Now he looks as though admitting something he'd held secret for a long time. "That's what my son would have said. Forgive them, they didn't know what they were doing. He would have, too." He's silent for a long time after that, looking down at his hands, as though hearing his son's voice, or just reflecting on something he'd had difficulty coming to terms with. "And that's what I've thought for some time now."

"That just about says it all, doesn't it," Kalber says.

"It does, as far as I'm concerned," Jensen agrees.

*　　*　　*

After watching the documentary, Dick Trembath, who had run the camera on much of the footage more than a decade earlier, now watched from the comfort of his home in Cleveland, Ohio. After it was done, he sat in his chair and stared at the carpet for a while, thinking hard about it. He told his wife that he had second thoughts about the whole thing, about what had happened, or rather, what they observed and assumed happened.

"It bothers me," he said after a long silence. "I don't know how the others feel, but I think it tells me that we've got to be awful careful in this business. We projected a searing image, an image of a fourteen-year-old girl who didn't act like a fourteen-year-old girl... But was she a tough little kid or was she someone who just blindly followed orders? Out of fear, or shock, or whatever? We never tried to find out who Caril Fugate was... We never questioned some of the assumptions we made about her. We photographed her and wrote our copy to go with what we thought we saw. There were conclusions drawn, and, tonight, I'm not so sure that they weren't based on a very shallow thing - the physical appearance of a fourteen-year-old girl who looked and acted like she could be guilty."

His wife was shocked. She and Dick had always assumed Caril was guilty and got what she deserved; possibly less than she deserved, even. She tried to comfort him by reminding Dick that he wasn't on the jury that put her away. He stood and looked out the window into the darkness.

"You know, when you take a picture you change lives, and it's interesting what remains – the image of a nasty little girl with a dirty little smile and very good posture. But when you look at that picture, I think you have to ask yourself something. Is this a defiant killer or is this a fourteen-year-old girl in shock?"

"What do you think?" his wife asked.

"We'll never know," he replied. "But I've got a very big doubt in my mind about who she really is and what makes her tick. Good middle-class attitudes she probably picked up from the kind of people who staff the reformatory. And she handled herself real well with the camera on her. I'll bet she didn't give the crew one bit of trouble. She did everything just right. And I think that's what really bothers me."

His wife suggested that perhaps Caril was just a natural actress.

"Maybe," he responded. "But just suppose that she happened to be one of those people who do exactly what they are told to do."

"Even by Charlie Starkweather?" she asked.

"Especially Charlie."

"Oh, my god," she said.

* * *

Caril received more than three thousand letters after the show aired. Five of them were proposals of marriage, while three were hate-filled. The rest were very kind well-wishers, most of whom felt she was innocent, even though the documentary had not taken a side either way. Nebraska's Governor Exon received five hundred letters asking for Caril's release. He responded by saying he could do nothing without the approval of the Parole Board. The Parole Board, meanwhile, could do nothing until Caril applied for Parole. But Caril still wanted to prove her innocence, and the very act of applying for parole was an admission of guilt. Caril wanted to at least wait out the decision of the Supreme Court.

At last James received the denial. Only one judge, William O. Douglas, who was one of the most liberal judges in US history, had found in their favor. It had been partly expected, but it still came as a great disappointment. This was the last hope to get a new trial, and it had failed. It was over.

Caril was invited into the superintendent's office. The assistant superintendent told her with tears in her eyes. Caril reached out and hugged her. She didn't allow herself to cry. Instead, she comforted one of her captors. She then asked for permission to speak with James, and she was left alone to make the call. They did not talk for long. It was factual and to the point. James told her they would now move toward getting a commutation of her sentence so there would be a definite amount of time, and then she could apply for parole. It was a pretty good chance they could get it since she had exhibited such good behavior in prison, but she would never be able to prove her innocence. Caril could hear the pain in James' voice. He was such an optimist, and had fought so hard for her. She felt worse for him than she did for herself.

After she hung up she thanked the assistant superintendent, walked across the field to her building, and closed herself into her room. For a while she stared at herself in the mirror. She spotted a few gray hairs growing. No one would ever give her a chance to clear her name. It was over. Caril opened the drawer and pulled out the Valium pills she had been saving. No one had noticed she had been hoarding them, keeping them hidden in her desk so no one could take them away. She had held on to them for a last resort, and now she had reached that point.

She swallowed them all, and went to sleep.

# Chapter Thirteen
## Commutation

James got a call from his friend Terry, who told him how sorry he was to hear the news about Caril. James told him that they had been expecting a defeat, and now that they had done everything they could to get her a new trial, they could move on to getting her released on parole, which he was certain they could accomplish.

Caril, meanwhile, was spending another Christmas in prison. The Valium she had swallowed had not been sufficient to end her life, so she would simply have to continue on, as Martha had insisted. Caril hid her feelings under a heavy cloak of cheer. It was too happy, however, and Jackie saw right through it. She confronted Caril with her firm realism.

"No, I'm just fine," Caril insisted.

"Sure, you're just fine," Jackie came back sarcastically.

Caril's lip quivered, and she fell into Jackie's arms sobbing. "Oh my god! It's hopeless! It's absolutely hopeless!" She sobbed for a long time, saying over and over that she would never get out of there. "Nobody believes me, and they're never going to believe me! They hate me and they're going to keep me in here forever!"

Jackie allowed her to cry for a while, then she straightened her up. She told her to pull herself together, but Caril was inconsolable. "Caril," she said sternly, "you'd better start shaping up, you hear me? Now, you get out of here. Go to your room, wash your face, and fix yourself up. Then come back here and we'll start working on your parole. It's about time we got you out of here."

Caril pulled herself together and walked out, a little more hope filling her. Jackie watched her go, and when she was alone, tears filled her eyes as well.

*  *  *

One of Jackie's greatest additions to the reformatory was a nursery and a playground so the staff could have a place for their children to go. It was a double blessing, as visitors had a place for their children to go while they talked with the inmates they had come to see. Patsy and James placed me in the nursery and let Trevor play in the playground while they visited with Caril.

Caril hid her frustrations from them, except when they were relevant to the case. She didn't like the basic concept of parole, based on an assumption that she was guilty, but since there was no other choice, she played along. Whenever she could, she spoke with them about their lives, and what life was like outside the reformatory. She was looking forward to seeing the world again, though it had been so long, she would hardly know it. So much had changed in fifteen years.

The Parole Board visited her on June 6, 1973. Some of them had been on the police force during the murders, others worked in corrections during the time of her confinement. They all knew the case, but they also knew that she had a perfect record. In fifteen years she had never been written up for a single disciplinary infraction. She told them about her work at the church, about graduating high school, about the friendships she had made, and about some people who had offered to allow her to move in with them if she was released. The Board was impressed, and they set a hearing for August 22. It was the first victory in 15 years. When she turned 30 in July, she had officially spent half of her life in prison. It was hard for her to remember what life was like before it.

*  *  *

Caril was once again driven to the penitentiary in Lincoln, just as she had been in 1958; but this time, the only crowds were the reporters who had gathered expecting a protest. They were disappointed to find it was only Caril, dressed in all white and looking much older than before, arriving with Jackie Crawford, then James arriving a few minutes later. The members of the Board of Pardons and Parole arrived, and then thirty-five more people showed up sporadically over the next half hour or so. Five were witnesses asking the Board to keep her in prison. The other thirty were all witnesses to her good character asking that she be released. Some were people who worked at the reformatory, one was a minister, and twenty of them were members of the church where she worked, all of whom had made the hour long trek early in the morning to come and speak on her behalf.

James and Caril saw them through a half closed door as they passed on their way to give their testimonies. They were sitting in the warden's office, a bland, high ceilinged, 19th century room large enough for occasional hearings to be tried inside it. The people who opposed Caril's release from prison passed the door first. Caril noticed Mrs. King, the mother of the slain teenage girl, go by. Caril turned to James and said, "I don't blame her. I don't know what I would do if I was in her shoes." Caril didn't blame any of them. She felt sorry for them, and what they had been through. When she saw Mrs. Jensen pass, she said that she felt so bad that this woman had lost her son, and she knew that Mrs. Jensen would never believe her. "If I was in her shoes," Caril said, "I would probably feel the same way also."

After everyone had assembled in the meeting room, James and Caril were called in. The door opened to a room lined with the people they had seen pass the door, those opposed to her, and those from York who had come to speak on her behalf. In the front were the three members of the Board of Pardons and Parole, and at the center, a large, gruff, intimidating man named John Greenholtz. His imposing presence took up the room of two people, and even sitting, he was taller than Caril was when she stood. His gaze looked down at people with an expression not to cross him, and his eyes dug into them to see if they were lying. He spoke with a directness that shot immediately to the point, with no patience for double talk.

He began the session with his powerful voice in check, explaining courteously to Caril the purpose of the meeting, which was not to decide if she should be set free, but whether the board should recommend that her life sentence be commuted to a finite term of years. As long as the life sentence was in effect, no parole could be possible. It was a necessary first step. However, he said, it could all end here if they did not decide in her favor. "I know this is an important day in your life," Greenholtz said gently to Caril. His expression was much more informal than she had expected. "Just tell us how you feel about the whole situation up to this point. I don't mean to embarrass you."

Caril stood up straight and answered, "It's hard to express how you feel in the situation I am, because I know my whole future depends on this day and the outcome of this day. Actually, I feel-if the purpose of institutions is rehabilitation-I myself feel the institution has done everything possible that they can to this point. I've participated in all the programs." The rest of the board asked her questions about her life in the reformatory, and she told them about her activities in the prison, the community, and the Church of the Nazarene. Most importantly, she told them she would be able to function in society after her release.

Edward Rowley, one of the members of the board, asked her if it was true that she had never had a single disciplinary report in fifteen years. She answered that it was true, to which Rowley commented how unusual that was. Caril explained that, having realized that she would be incarcerated for a long period of time, she had determined to make the best of things and to take advantage of every program that could help her in her development as a responsible human being. It sounded coached, but with Caril, it came naturally. Fifteen years in the penitentiary had not weaned her of much of the youthful optimism she had gone in with.

Another member of the board asked about her future, but she was reluctant to speak about it with reporters around.

"You don't intend to stay in the limelight, so to speak," Greenholtz said. "In other words, you'd more or less like to get lost in society?"

"Right," Caril answered. "As much as possible."

Harold Smith, another member of the board, who had been a part of the original manhunt in 1958, probed Caril about her many attempts to gain a new trial. Caril answered by saying it had been her decision, but her attempts to vindicate herself "until the last door was closed" was over. She explained about the U.S. Supreme Court decision, and thus she was seeking release through parole. "But I did pursue it more or less five years longer than need be, because I was in hopes I would get it."

Edward Rowley spoke up again, "You are aware of the fact that we don't condone the seriousness of your crime." This stung Caril. She still maintained that she had committed no crime. He seemed to detect this as he continued, "Or the seriousness of anyone's crime. We've discussed this before. We've discussed the fact that in your particular case there are many supporters and many persons in opposition."

"Right," Caril answered. "Which they are entitled to."

Rowley went on by saying, "As Mr. Greenholtz has often said since I've been on this board, we should have the wisdom of Solomon and the judgment of Job and the luck of the Irish, or however you want to put it."

"Courage of Daniel," Greenholtz corrected.

"And the courage of Daniel. But we have to some way make a decision and decide where retribution ends and rehabilitation takes over. And it's not easy for you, or us, or society."

At last Greenholtz turned to James and said, "Counselor, do you have anything to add, or ask, to what we've already said here?"

"Yes," said James. "I would like to make a statement on behalf of Caril." Then he stepped forward, stated his name and began his statement. He usually prepared speeches and testimonies with notes and research. But this time he had made little preparation, and spoke from the heart. He told them that he had known Caril for many years, since before the original trial nearly two decades earlier. And the thing that struck him about her was her consistently positive attitude, a quality James admired above all else in people. "It's not merely a lack of disciplinary problems," he declared, "it's really a more affirmative action on her part, that she was actually looking forward, doing something. She was entering the program. She wasn't just 'not being in trouble.' She was helping herself, helping the administration out there because she was helping other inmates. And I'm sure you're all familiar with what she's done in that respect." He continued to praise her initiative and her efforts, despite the hardships and loneliness she suffered. He concluded by saying, "I think her whole life in the institution has really been looking forward to this day. And I think it's evident there was an example of a successful rehabilitative effort... positive attitude and interest on her part. And work on her part. And hope."

"In other words, counselor," said Greenholtz, "you are referring to the contributions she has made to her own self-improvement, in addition to the institution's programs she's been involved in?"

"Yes," James answered.

"We're aware of all that," Greenholtz said.

James had done all he could. He had shared with them everything he had experienced regarding his client and friend with whom he had, in many ways, grown up. He sat down. Now it was all up to Caril.

"Miss Fugate," Greenholtz said, "do you have anything you'd like to say to the board?"

"I want to thank you for hearing my case. I deeply appreciate it. I leave it totally up to you, whatever you decide."

Greenholtz nodded and said, "You may be excused."

"Thank you," Caril said, and she left the room with James.

After the door was closed, Greenholtz said, "Okay, let's see who else has anything to say on behalf of Miss Fugate."

Victor Walker, the director of the Department of Corrections, spoke up, "Gentlemen, I'd like to say something."

Greenholtz knew him well. "Okay. Come on up, Vic. We'll be happy to listen to anything you have to say, sir."

Victor stepped up and said, "First, I'd like to say that I've been involved with women prisoners for about fifteen years. I was responsible for a women's institution in Louisiana that had a hundred and twenty-five women. I've been responsible for this institution here for two years now. I've known Caril for five. The record that Caril has established for herself over the years – you can look anywhere in the United States and you won't find a woman who has made the cooperative effort that this girl has. She came into this institution when we really didn't have much of a program as far as rehabilitation efforts are concerned. But every little opportunity that was given to her, she responded. She not only responded to the program offered her, she sought things to do to keep her hands and her mind occupied. And, of course, it has been brought out that she never had one disciplinary problem. Women, for the most part, have a tendency in prison to sit back and let the world go by, become somewhat embittered. And they just don't have the aggressiveness to do what needs to be done to promote themselves. In this respect, if anyone-by their behavior and by their cooperation-has earned consideration, Caril has."

John Greenholtz stared at the Director of Corrections with his intimidating "be honest" glare. "You are saying that she is just as ready now as she'll ever be? And any further incarceration would be more or less useless?"

"I think so," the man answered. "I realize Caril was convicted of a capital crime and her co-defendant was executed, and had she been executed, this, no doubt, would have been quite all right. But the point is that we didn't see fit to do that. She is in the here-and-now, and this problem has to be dealt with. Our society has changed its attitude towards youngsters nowadays. For example, a fourteen-year-old today would probably be sentenced under the Juvenile Delinquency Act, which would make release possible at the discretion of the institutional people."

Victor Walker then provided a dramatic pause before continuing. He went on to explain further that the laws had grown to understand better that a child should be considered in a different way than an adult, and he cited several cases where the judge had felt that way. He showed that the laws in that day would not have allowed Caril to be convicted as an adult. "The third point I'd like to make," he continued, "is that if a man is devoid of hope for the future, if he can't see somewhere ahead of himself hope for the future, he might as well be dead. Because, actually, this is what it is."

Victor looked at his old friend Greenholtz. They shared a common bond, both men had led people to the death chamber and told the executioner to carry out the sentence. Greenholtz had done this very thing with Charlie. They believed in a proper punishment for those who deserved it. For someone like Victor Walker to stand up for Caril Ann Fugate was a matter of great importance. Walker knew he had made his point to Greenholtz, so he finished by saying, "I just feel like you should really give serious consideration in Caril's case at this time." He peered meaningfully at the other members of the board. They all knew his stature, and they were perfectly aware of the implications of his standing up for Fugate. "This is all I have to say. Thank you for listening," he concluded, and he stepped aside.

Reverend William Shipman of Caril's church appeared next along with his wife to testify on Caril's behalf. They told about Caril's work in the church's nursery, described her classes for kindergarten children, and her positive relations with many of the adult members of the congregation.

"Would you consider her a sensitive person, Reverend?" Greenholtz asked.

"You mean as to feeling?"

"Yes."

"Yes, I think she is. Not extremely so, but she has feelings."

"Her appearance today – this isn't a façade? Is she this way all the time? She relates very well to people and communicates. In your professional experience in dealing with people, you don't feel this is a façade, do you, in order to gain sympathy or something?"

"No, I certainly wouldn't feel that way. I don't know if it's known to you, but she has Sunday dinners at our home and we take her back at four o'clock in the afternoon."

"You see her more often than we three," Greenholtz said. "The only time we see her is when we visit York. On occasions we run into her and speak to her. We have reviewed her record many times. It stands to reason if somebody wants something, they'll put their best foot forward. We recognize this. That's why we want to talk to people who have an interest in her, because we're going to have some people in here who aren't going to be too favorable."

"I would say this isn't a front at all," the minister said.

Rowley asked, "In other words, you feel she displays genuine-you know, week to week, as opposed to every six months when we'd see her. Right?"

"These past two and a half years of close association with her on Sundays and Mondays, I would say it's very genuine. I'm sure there would be times when it would show."

Rowley nodded and said, "It's hard to sustain, I know, after fifteen years, the genuineness."

Rowley asked if he felt comfortable with Caril around his own children. Shipman said emphatically that he did. Then he added, "We have approximately twenty people that drove down here this morning from our congregation that are waiting here to speak also. And she's been in the homes of many of these people, and, as far as trusting her or being fearful of her, there is no problem at all."

Greenholtz stepped in, "We receive all types of mail. Some people don't trust her that far."

"Doesn't even enter our minds," said the reverend.

"They think of dire things," Greenholtz continued. "They don't see Caril like we do. They don't see her at all. They just form opinions." He then turned his attention to Mrs. Shipman. "How do you feel about this, ma'am?"

"I feel like if these people really knew her and were around her, they would realize this, you know, because she's very helpful in our home. She comes in. She just doesn't sit down, you know, and become a burden. She gets busy, helps set the table, things like this. We feel comfortable with her around."

"She shows initiative," Rowley offered.

"Yes," she said. "She's not lazy or anything like this. Which impresses me."

Greenholtz then said, "Over the years, we have reports of all this. They tend to more or less go along with what you're saying. People who know her like her. To know her is to like her. But then you have to realize there are families of the victims, and we have to try to understand their feelings. Some people are very vindictive."

Mrs. Shipman had nothing to add, so she just nodded. Greenholtz turned his attention to the reverend again. "Do you have any more comments to make?"

"I just want to say we hope. Our hopes are really for her. She's thirty years of age now and digging pretty heavily into her young adult life."

Several women then stood before the board and testified that Caril had taken care of their children at the church, and that they trusted her implicitly. They were asked if they would trust Caril in their homes for any length of time, and they all answered that they would. A few children also came forward and told that they liked Caril as a teacher and as a fellow congregation member.

Then Donna Sacher, a former inmate, stepped forward. Greenholtz had known her, but did not recognize her because she had cleaned herself up so much. "Caril helped me quite a bit," she said. "Because when I first went in, there was no way the State of Nebraska – or anybody else – was going to rehabilitate me. And she helped my attitude quite a bit. I was awfully bitter when I went in there – towards people in Omaha, and everything else. And Caril just more or less straightened my head out." She described how Caril had cooled her down when she got into fights and got her out of trouble several times, and said that she was a leader among many of the inmates.

"Was she generally respected by the majority of the girls out there?" Greenholtz asked.

"The majority of them. There were a lot of girls out there who were jealous of Caril."

The next four people who testified did not know Caril, but had come to testify on principle that she should be released. "I have seen a lot of people," said Edward Neil of Omaha, "who have come out of a penal reform system, and, after about so long, a person reaches a saturation point of reform. A person can absorb no more, and the only way you can prove the rehabilitation is by letting one out. And I think this – she's spent more than half of her life in prison, and this is an awful long time for a person to be in a situation such as this."

Others who testified had seen her on the documentary Ninette had done. They all urged her release. Still others who testified had known her from before the events that got her incarcerated. They all testified that she had been a well behaved girl before the murders, just as she was a responsible adult, and so her general personality was one of serenity.

Then the board heard from the five people who had come to ask she not be given a chance for parole. First was Warren King, the brother of Carol King, and his wife Yvonne.

"Have you considered the length of time she's served in the institution?" Greenholtz asked.

"That don't bring Carol King and Bobby Jensen back," said Yvonne.

"No, it doesn't," Greenholtz responded. "Unfortunately there is no way. Nothing anyone can do. That's over and done with and that cannot be changed. Do you feel Caril should be incarcerated for the balance of her natural life as a result of what happened with her association with Starkweather?"

"Yes."

Her husband agreed, saying, "I feel she was old enough at the time. She knew what she was doing, and – no matter what she does now – I don't feel it gives her the right to be able to be out."

His mother testified next. "Fifteen years isn't very long. It isn't long enough for any of us to get over it."

"Would you say that she should remain there for the balance of her natural life, or not?" Rowley asked.

"I feel she was tried by jury and I feel she should stay there for life," Mable King Swale answered.

"Do you understand the fundamentals of parole, ma'am?" Greenholtz asked her.

"No, I suppose I don't," she responded.

"It means a person is released under supervision, certain conditions. If they violate these conditions, they'll be brought back and recommitted."

"I know. But I don't think she should be yet. I think it's too early."

Greenholtz then explained, "Our philosophy is that people are sent to institutions *as* punishment, not *for* punishment. It is punishment. But then you have to realize that punishment should have an end someday in a person's life, otherwise it becomes a slow, expensive, inhumane method of execution. Then, our whole system of corrections becomes useless, pointless. We could fill up our institutions with people who have to serve their maximum terms; then we would have people that would tend to become animalistic. They would lose all sense of hope."

"Well," said Mrs. King Swale, "she didn't give her victims a chance."

The room was getting hot as the next witness, a frail old woman, hobbled into the room. She was not in good health, and walked with great difficulty. After taking an oath, she said to the board in a trembling voice, "This is really hard for me to do." She looked right at John Greenholtz as she sat in the witness chair. "They said I might read what I have."

"Yes," he responded softly. "State your name for the record, please."

"I'm Mrs. Robert E. Jensen from Bennet, Nebraska."

"You are the mother of…"

"Bobby Jensen."

John Greenholtz then told her what he had told the other witnesses; that parole was a means of giving someone a second chance out of prison after they have rehabilitated and become a different person than when they had gone in. He said that many people had spoken on her behalf, and that she seemed to be a very fit person to re-enter society after fifteen years. "Well," Mrs. Jensen said, "when you stop to think about the fifteen years and the ten victims, that isn't very much for each victim." She paused a moment, then said, "Do you want me to read this?"

"Yes," he said. "Go ahead, ma'am."

Mrs. Jensen read from the paper on which she had written: "I definitely oppose a parole for Caril Fugate, not because I don't believe in rehabilitation or parole but because I feel the degree of punishment should fit the crime. And, considering the brutal way Caril Fugate and Charles Starkweather murdered the eleven victims, punishment has been very slight. I feel that people who kill someone in the heat of anger should be treated quite differently than those who go on a murder spree for their thrills. I think, considering the magnitude of these horrible crimes, life imprisonment would be neither cruel or inhumane punishment. She could never pay for the horrible things she has done, but she has surely forfeited any right to be a part of society in general. It seems more compassion is always dealt to the criminal, and the victims and their loved ones aren't really considered. Nor is society in general. I would question whether a person who could watch such crimes – let alone participate in them – could ever be really rehabilitated so they would be safe to be returned to society. Even if this could be accomplished, she was sentenced to serve all of her natural life in prison by a jury trial and a fine judge, now deceased, and I sincerely feel they meant for her sentence to be carried out and upheld as determined by the courts. And life imprisonment should mean just that – life imprisonment." When she was finished, Greenholtz and the others shifted uncomfortably in their seats, and asked to keep a copy of her statement, which she handed to them.

The last person to testify was someone who had no connection to the case, just a concerned citizen named Henry Wald. "I feel that she obviously had a fair trial," he said. "The case has been through every court in the United States and no change has been made, including the U.S. Supreme Court, I believe. There was a jury of twelve men and women, and they found her guilty and prescribed life. Now, I believe that jury meant 'life' when they said 'life.'"

He continued for a little longer stating that he believed Caril should never be given any chance of parole, and Greenholtz replied that everyone had a right to their opinion. He pointed out that a large number of people had written in saying she should be paroled, and he finished by saying, "Some people have more compassion than others."

That concluded the formal testimony. The room was cleared of the witnesses and Caril was called back into the room with her attorney.

John Greenholtz smiled at her and said, "Caril, we haven't reached a decision today. We'll have a decision Friday. We've got to give this some deep study. There were some people here opposed. We have numerous letters. I must say, you've got a lot of friends. You've got more friends than I've got. I think they're real sincere friends, and they certainly appreciate the things you've done since they've known you. You've taken care of the kids and, well, everything in general they like about you. We'll let you know, and the other people concerned, what our decision will be Friday morning."

Caril acknowledged him, then stood to leave with Jacky Crawford.

"Send up a few Hail Marys for us," Greenholtz called to her.

"Okay," Caril said. "I know a woman who knows how."

*   *   *

James and his family spent most Friday nights at his parents' home where he and his father would spin their glasses and review their cases for the week while Patsy and Ruby chatted and the children played with James' brother's children next door. One Friday morning had been an especially good one. The board had decided in Caril's favor by a 2 to 1 decision. Only Harold Smith, who had been curiously quiet during the hearing, had voted against her. He seemed to have made up his mind before she had entered the room, but it hadn't mattered. Greenholtz, no bleeding heart and often very blunt about prisoners, made a statement after the announcement of the decision that was especially heartening: "The board has met in executive session and, by majority vote, recommends Caril Fugate's case be presented to the State Board of Pardons for possible commutation of her life sentence to a definite term of years for future parole purposes. This decision was determined after careful study and evaluation of her record and her excellent response to work, training, and personal development after fifteen years of incarceration. We considered her age at the time of the tragic event that resulted in her confinement and we feel that further punishment in this case should have an end, whether for retribution, deterrence, or rehabilitation. If it simply becomes an alternate, slow, expensive, inhuman method of execution, then our correctional system is pointless. It is our judgment, by majority vote, that society's purpose has been served and Miss Fugate cannot benefit by further imprisonment and is an acceptable risk for parole consideration."

It was now on to the Board of Pardons to set a definite amount of time for her imprisonment. She had been incarcerated for fifteen years, but prison years worked a little differently. Prisoners who exhibited good behavior and did healthy amounts of work were credited with additional time. Due to her efforts and her unblemished record, Caril had racked up more than twenty-six years. If the board decided to set her time at twenty-five years, she could be released before the end of the year. She might even be able to spend Christmas as a free woman. Caril bought two suitcases and slowly began to pack a little more every day. It was the first time in a long time she had allowed herself this much hope.

But in September, the Parole Board, who had seemed favorable to her parole request, was expanded from three members to five. The dissenting member of the board, Harold Smith, resigned, which seemed on the surface to be good news, but there was no way to know if the three new members would be favorable toward her.

On September 25, the Board of Pardon's decided to review the case, and the date was set for October 30. The three new members were Eugene Neal and Timothy Blankenship, professional parole officers who had worked with ex-convicts before, and Marshall Tate, a man from Omaha who had spent many years as a volunteer working with people in the community who had problems with the law.

The final decision would not lie with them. They would make their recommendation to the governor, the attorney general, and the secretary of state, who would ultimately decide Caril's fate; none of whom had made any public statement about how they felt about Caril's release.

Not long before the hearing, several discrepancies were found in Caril's application which, to some, might look like lies. First, she had claimed to have not filled out an application for parole before, but it was found that she had begun to fill one out in 1969. Caril explained that she did not remember filling it out, but she had filled out many forms, and she probably had started that one believing it to be something else. Second, the form included the question: 'Did you use a gun in the commission of your crime?' In 1969 she had said 'yes,' but in the later application, she wrote, 'I personally did not. He did.' Members of the parole board went to the reformatory to speak with her, and Caril explained to them that Charlie had used the gun, and in the first application she was probably intending to tell them that a gun had been used.

Another supposed discrepancy was that in the first application she said that there had been no witnesses against her, but in the second she stated that Starkweather had testified against her, but he was an unfair witness. She explained that he was clearly an insane man and his testimony should never have been regarded in the first place, so in '69 she had not even considered him to be a valid witness. When they reached question twelve, which was a discrepancy because she had completely filled out the one in '73 and not the one in '69, it became clear how petty the problems were, and Greenholtz stepped in, saying that he found no fault with these discrepancies. He claimed their time would further be wasted by continuing on with other marked "discrepancies," such as another one where she had written in one application that Charlie was "executed" and in another where she had written he was "put to death."

Marshall Tate, another member of the board interviewing her, moved on. "Caril," he said, "could we focus our attention one more time to paragraph fifteen? And by my own observation here, I only see one discrepancy... In 1969, on the second part of your statement, you said, 'By the time I had come to my senses I was so deeply involved that there was no way... to escape from the horrible situation.' Then the very first statement that you have on your 1973 paragraph in relation to number fifteen, you say, 'I had attempted to terminate my friendship with Charles Starkweather, which apparently made him very angry.' Now somehow in my own mind, I think that may have been a discrepancy that the Pardon Board probably read and looked at, and to me, maybe that would need clarification by virtue of this meeting."

Caril didn't know what to say. So many of these "discrepancies" were simply the same things written two different ways, or, as in this case, they were two different things that had nothing to do with each other, yet they were being listed as contradictory. James had helped her fill out the second application so her answers would be clearer, but the basic thoughts behind them were the same. After a short pause, Caril said, "What exactly do you want said?"

"Well," Tate tried to answer, "in one you say, 'I came to my senses, but there was no way to escape from this horrible situation.'

And, in other words, it sounds like to me you are saying you were there, you were involved, and you found yourself without any reason – rather, effort – to try to escape. And over here you say you had attempted to terminate the friendship. I'm curious. What do you mean by 'attempted to terminate the friendship?'"

"When I told him that Sunday before all this happened. When I asked him to leave and never come back," she answered.

"This is what you…"

"This is what set him off," Caril said. "I was not dating him when this actually happened."

Tate continued, "So if you could add anything to that particular sentence, it may have read, 'I attempted to terminate my friendship with Charles Starkweather before all of this started, which apparently made him very angry.' And over here you basically are talking about [the time when] all of this developed. You were just there. You were caught up in it."

"I was caught up in it," Caril said patiently to the man who apparently couldn't understand her explanations. "There was no way you…" she began, but he cut her off.

"All right," he said. "See, those are the two details, paragraphs – these are the only things that I see that are real conflicting."

He went on to ask her about her membership in the church, and her beliefs. "For me it involves acknowledging that we are all sinners," she said, "whether it's a small stand, a big stand, whether it's stealing or whatever. Well, this is what I mean. And I'm speaking as a Christian. Whatever happened in the past, once you accept it – accept Christ – then you are free within your soul. No matter if you are behind prison bars, wherever you are, your soul is free. And this is what it means to me. And I still stand – and I know this is not a retrial, but I am still standing that I am not guilty. And if I would have to stay in this institution for the rest of my life, I would stand on these grounds – I am not guilty. I saw what happened, I told what happened, and I stand up on those grounds. And I would not change one word of my statement that I gave at the time this happened."

It was the most forthright she had been in a long time. She had sacrificed years of her life trying to get a new trial because she wanted to prove her innocence and she had been denied it. Ever since parole had become her only hope at freedom, she had switched gears from proving her innocence to showing how good she had been in prison. But it was frustrating to her that she could not argue for her innocence; that parole took an assumption of her guilt.

Then Tate revealed why he had been grilling her so much. "I don't know whether you are knowledgeable that I am a pastor and that's the reason I asked... Too many people use the church as a scapegoat, and I would have had to suggest that, if I in any way felt that you could use the church by virtue of this incident, that my vote would hereafter – would surely – have been one of condemnation."

"I do not use the church," Caril told him.

Greenholtz was ready to bring the interview to a close. He asked her what she thought she had accomplished during her fifteen years in prison.

"I think I've accomplished the art of survival," she told him.

*      *      *

The final hearing in front of the Board of Pardons was held on the same day Greenholtz and Tate had questioned Caril about the discrepancies. Governor J. J. Exon, the chairman of the Board of Pardons, sat behind an impressive, large, curved wooden table below an enormous American flag. The capitol building, designed by the same architect who had designed the Chrysler building, resembles the inside of a magnificent castle. Its marble floors, high ceilings, and crisscrossing catwalks create an echoing effect that turns low-volume conversations into mutters heard around corners and on separate floors. To each side of Governor Exon sat Attorney General Clarence A.H. Meyer and Secretary of State Allen Beerman. They would make the final decision on Caril's fate. Greenholtz and his team would give their recommendation, and Exon, Meyer and Beerman would give the ruling.

In front of the Pardons Board was a crowd of approximately forty people, including Greenholtz's board, who were now convinced that Caril deserved parole, one other man who spoke up for her, and approximately thirty-five people who wanted to keep her in prison. The McArthurs believed they had already done all they could, and

Caril's other friends had spoken up for her at the smaller hearing, so this event was more of an airing of grievances against her. Among the opposition were the five people who had spoken against her at the smaller hearing, who apparently did not feel they had said enough, and found themselves among more allies in the capitol.

Carol King's mother read from a piece of paper on which she had written the same statement: "I believe Caril Ann Fugate should not be paroled, but should be required to definitely serve out her life sentence. I believe that rehabilitation for her should be totally disregarded. The board would be better advised to give careful thought to the victims of her crime spree and their families. This is the reason there are so many increasing crime rates, in the misplaced tenderness that authorities seem to have for these criminals. The fact that she was only fourteen and a half years when the murders were committed should carry no weight. She was old enough to know right from wrong. I think she should stay there for life."

Most statements were about the same. Warren King had gotten petitions from people in the community to keep her in prison. Mrs. Jensen said about her, "Caril Fugate changes her answers as often as asked a question and conveniently forgets and distorts the facts of her murder spree with Charles Starkweather. She was sentenced to serve out her natural life in prison by a jury trial, and I sincerely believe they meant for her sentence to be carried out and upheld as determined by the Court's decision, and life imprisonment should mean just that – life imprisonment."

Governor Exon's response to them was not a good sign for Caril. "It is not our duty to judge innocence or guilt in this or any other matter," he said. "There is no question in my mind of the guilt of Caril Ann Fugate. I felt she had every chance at a fair trial." But, he explained, "the job of the Pardons Board was to decide what action to take on the recommendation of the Parole Board, which had been to release her."

Ninette Beaver, present at the hearings, sought out Edward Rowley before he entered the private room where the hearings would be held. "Are you going to make Caril wait until her regular review date in June to parole her?" she asked. "Some people are saying you might parole her before the Christmas holidays."

Shrugging, Rowley said, "I just hope we get a chance to consider her application in June."

"You've got to be kidding," she exclaimed. "With her record and the recommendations of the corrections officials and your board? What would be the point in delaying parole?"

"We'll just have to wait and see what happens," he said, shaking his head and walking away.

The private meeting lasted a full hour. Greenholtz and his board sat with the governor and the other two members of the Parole Board and discussed the pros and cons of Caril's sentence. Unlike Greenholtz and his team, the governor, secretary of state, and attorney general could all be voted out of office for making an unpopular decision, no matter how much they believed in Caril's rehabilitation. When it was done, they sent their decision over the news wire.

Jackie Crawford got the news before it went live to the public. She had been listening to the radio, waiting for the news, when a reporter called, asking for a comment from Caril. Jackie asked what happened at the hearing, and the reporter told her what the decision was.

"I doubt she'll have any comment," Jackie said, trying to keep her voice from shaking. "You can try calling back later. If she has one, I'll give it to you."

She tapped the line to cut it off and cradled the telephone in her lap. Trembling, she lowered her head into her hands. After a long moment alone, she stood up and breathed in deep. Caril needed to know before she heard it on the radio. Jackie dashed out and ran toward Caril's room.

Caril was still glued to her radio when it was announced. "Nebraska Pardon Board decided just moments ago that Caril Ann Fugate, companion to Charles Starkweather on a killing rampage fifteen years ago, is not yet ready for a return to society. But the stage was set for possible parole three years hence. On a two to one vote, the board commuted Miss Fugate's life term for murder to 30-50 years, making her eligible for parole consideration as early as May 1976 under Nebraska law. No parole had been possible while the life sentence remained. Secretary of State Allen Beerman and Governor J. James Exon supported the commutation, recommended earlier by the separate Nebraska Parole Board. Attorney General Clarence A. H. Meyer, the third board member, moved unsuccessfully to deny commutation at this time."

From down the corridor Jackie could hear sobbing from Caril's room. She rushed in and saw Caril sprawled across the bed beating the mattress with frustration. One of the other inmates was with her, kneeling next to the bed, patting her shoulder. She looked up at Jackie with tear-filled eyes. "I thought..." she stammered, "we all thought she'd get out right away."

"I know," Jackie responded. "We all did."

The woman left Jackie and Caril alone. Jackie sat down on the bed and Caril jerked her head toward the wall. "Don't touch me," she cried in an uncharacteristic fit of anger. "Don't even come near me. I don't want to see you or talk to you or anybody else." Jackie walked to the door and closed it gently, then sat down on a chair by Caril's desk. She said nothing for a long time until a calm silence settled in. Then she moved to the edge of Caril's bed.

"Three more years," Caril sobbed. "Three more years, and who knows how many more after that?"

After a long time, Caril sat up and Jackie handed her a box of Kleenex. Caril dabbed her eyes.

"I know there's nothing I can say, Caril. But we'll help you all that we can."

Caril crossed her legs and sat hunched over on the bed. The tears had stopped, but her eyes were red with pain as she raised her head up and looked Jackie straight in the eyes and said bitterly, "Mrs. Crawford, what could I have done differently these past fifteen years? You just tell me, Mrs. Crawford. What more could I have done?"

Jackie stared back at her. She had no answer. Caril collapsed on her bed, her energy drained, too exhausted even to cry, and just stared at the wall.

It was referred to by many as "the Fugate compromise." It neither gave Caril freedom, nor satisfied the masses who wanted her to spend her entire life in prison. But it allowed the politicians to stay in office, Governor Exon going on to be senator for eighteen years. James and John saw it as a pyrrhic victory. They had hoped she would get parole right away, but they had become realistic enough to know that there would be some sort of concession, and three years was what they were used to in the slow pace of the legal world. Ninette tried for days to get hold of Caril, to talk with her about it. Jackie told her how upset she was, that the minister of the church was spending a lot of time with her, and that it would probably be a while before she would speak with anyone.

Mark Gautier, now the news director at KMTV, asked her about what was happening at the reformatory. Ninette told him the little she had learned.

"Well, I guess that wraps it up for a while," he said. "At least until 1976."

# Chapter Fourteen
## Badlands

In 1971, John got a call from a friend of his, Larry Reger, an attorney who had recently been chosen to be the executive secretary for the National Endowment for the Arts. Larry had known that people would be coming along wanting to make films about the Starkweather/Fugate story, and he hoped it would be someone he trusted, someone he knew would handle it in good taste.

One film had already been made about it in 1963, 'The Sadist', a disaster of a movie both artistically and financially. With terrible over-acting, a script that wasn't worth the paper it was written on, and direction and production value that had no vision whatsoever, the film was forgotten within a year.

But Larry knew someone that, though young, had a lot of vision, and a great deal of talent, and he was interested in the story. He had gotten to know the director through the NEA's connection with a recently created foundation called the American Film Institute, of which the young man was a part.

Terrence Malick was not your typical film director. He was a Rhodes Scholar who had taught philosophy at MIT. He was careful about what films he wanted to make, and typically made his money in other professions so he could pick and choose at his leisure. He was interested in how violence affected, and was affected by culture, which was one of the reasons why the Starkweather story had caught his attention. Terry had pitched several ideas to Larry, and when he mentioned his interest in doing a film inspired by the Starkweather/Fugate case, Larry exclaimed, "Well, I know her attorneys! Why don't I give them a call?"

James had heard about Terrence when he read a four page article in Life Magazine that talked about Terrence's first film called 'Dead Head Miles'. James was immediately excited about the prospect of Malick making a film about the case, and he told his father that they should meet with them. Terrence was in New York at the time, so he stopped into Lincoln on his way back to Los Angeles. He brought with him his friend Wallace Wolf, an attorney who had worked for 20th Century Fox for twenty years. He had represented some of the biggest names in Hollywood, such as Bill Cosby and Hugh Heffner. He had filed the famous suit the Smothers Brothers took against CBS when they had been wrongfully terminated.

They went to dinner at Village Inn where John and Wally swapped legal "war stories" while James and Terry became fast friends. James had always loved film. As a boy he had been enamored with the movie 'Citizen Kane', and was amazed by the emotional power of cinema. There was a part of him that had always thought that if he had not gone into law, he might have been interested in making movies. Terry told him that he didn't want to make a film based on the exact incidents of the story. Rather, he wanted to take elements of the story and create a fictional one that was inspired by the events.

All of a sudden, James got an idea. "Say, would you like to meet Caril?" he asked.

They answered of course, and James called the penitentiary. He told them about Wally Wolf, but not about Terry. He thought it best to not mention the movie aspect yet, but instead to say that they were bringing another attorney. Permission was granted to come visit, and they all piled into James' green Oldsmobile. Terry mused at the passing scenery while James and Wally talked about their experiences. Wally was currently dealing with the difficulties of his client Roman Polanski, whose wife Sharon Tate had just been murdered by another infamous mass murderer, Charlie Manson.

"You sure have had an amazing career," James told him.

"You know," said Wally, "I was just thinking the same thing about your career."

Terry made one thing clear before they reached the penitentiary. If Caril did not want this movie to be made, he wouldn't make it. It didn't matter how much effort they had put into it, or even that the story he was going to do wasn't entirely based on reality, he didn't feel right about taking elements of her story and making a movie about it without her permission.

When they visited with Caril, Terry told her in a very low key manner who he was, what he had done before, and what he hoped to do by making this movie inspired by her story. He did not need her permission, the story had taken on legendary status and could be portrayed by anyone, much the way anyone could make a movie about Bonnie and Clyde without their relatives' permission. But Terry was the kind of man who would not go on such a venture if he did not have her blessing.

Caril was taken by surprise by the news. She wasn't impressed by the idea of a movie being made as there was nothing glamorous about the things she had witnessed and experienced. She would, in fact, rather everyone just forget about the whole thing, and for the subject to just be dropped from any and all conversations. But she knew that could never happen. She looked seriously and deeply into Terry's eyes as she studied him, then she said, "I see the look in your eyes, and I think you're honest, and I trust you." And with that, she gave him permission to make the movie.

As development of the film progressed, Terry stayed in close contact with James, calling approximately every other week and keeping him appraised of every aspect of production. James was thrilled at the prospect of peaking into an industry he had always admired and pined for.

Terrence invited James to visit the set, but he was busy with his own work. James had a full practice at this point, and Caril's parole was nearing. He also felt it was probably in her best interest if he distanced himself from the film, even though he and Terry spoke on the phone on a regular basis.

To avoid the difficulties and controversies they might face in Nebraska, Terry and his team filmed the movie in Colorado.

Determined to distance the film from the actual murder spree, he also had the characters living in South Dakota, and had them travel toward Montana instead of Wyoming. He wanted to capture the disillusionment of youth, and reflected it through Martin Sheen and Sissy Spacek's characters' indifference to the violence around them.

The film first screened at the American Film Festival in New York where it won best picture, then at the Lincoln Center in Washington, D.C. where it was met with rave reviews. Only one critic gave it a negative review, Pauline Kael, who said it was "too good" and there wasn't enough in it for her to criticize.

Warner Brothers bought the picture around the same time that Caril's parole hearings were nearing. Terry didn't want to do anything that might adversely affect her chances, so he left James' and John's names out of the credits, even though he had wanted to have them in the special thanks. He also wanted to make certain Warner Brothers would not use Caril's name in their advertising, so he flew James out to Los Angeles to help watch over the negotiations in the spring of 1974. James stayed with a brother-in-law in Glendale. When Terry called him and invited him to a party for Martin Sheen, James' brother-in-law asked, "Who's Martin Sheen?" Holding his hand over the receiver, James whispered, "I don't know. I think he's the president of Warner Brothers."

Terry picked James up in his Volkswagen Thing, and as they made their way to the studio, James was struck by how much smog there was, even though the freeways were virtually empty due to the recent fuel shortage. When James tried to roll up the window, he noticed it wasn't there. Terry pointed at the pocket in the door and told him to just put it in place.

Terry showed him around town to various film laboratories and studios. Both men were fascinated by the inner workings of Hollywood. They sat down in a screening room at Warner Brothers and watched the movie together. Terry insisted on seeing every print before it was sent out. James watched for the reference Terry said was in the film in lieu of a special thanks, but didn't notice anything until the very end when Sissy Spacek said "I married the son of my lawyer." He chuckled and told Terry he liked the reference. Terry asked him if he had noticed a certain scene that had come out too red. James hadn't, but Terry sent the print back to be redone.

After a second screening with studio executives, they were walking down an outside staircase when a small, ugly, beat up green Datsun pulled up in front of them. A young man with thick, brown hair hopped out and looked up at James. "You must be Jim!" he exclaimed. This was Martin Sheen, who James by now had learned was not the president of Warner Brothers, but the star of the picture. The three headed over to the party, Martin Sheen's Datsun and Terry Malick's Thing squeezed between Roles Royces and stretch limos. As they walked up the stairs to the restaurant above an art gallery, James noticed he was behind one of the biggest stars in television at the time, George Maharis. He thought to himself, "Man, if people back home could see me now, walking behind the star of 'Route 66'!" He was too shy to approach him, however, and spent his time with Terry and Martin.

But after a while, James overheard Maharis pull Martin aside and ask him, "Could you introduce me to Jim McArthur?" James suddenly realized that celebrity is really a person's point of view, and he saw more clearly what the future held in regard to this story.

The most important critic for the film had yet to see it. Terry promised Caril Fugate a screening, and he intended on staying true to his promise. There was still a month before the film would be released to the public, so James made arrangements with the warden to allow Caril to go see a movie. He then called the local theater to try to arrange a private screening. He was trying to keep a low profile, so he couldn't tell the owner what it was for. There was a silence on the line before the woman asked, "Is this a porno?" He assured her it was not, and he made the proper arrangements.

In attendance at the private screening were Terry, his wife Jill, Martin, James, Patsy, John, Caril, the warden, and James' sister Sue and her husband Calvin. Martin sat next to Caril. He was curious how she would react to the film. She was stern the entire time, showing no emotion except for once. When Martin's character, Kit, walked behind a building and started punching the air, Caril swung her purse and hit Martin in the arm with it. When he looked over at her, she offered no explanation, simply continued to watch the film silently and still. He said nothing until the movie was over, at which time he turned to Caril and asked her why she had hit him. "Because at that moment, you were exactly like Charlie," she said.

They went to a nearby restaurant so they could all talk. James was still laughing about the reference to Caril marrying him. Patsy was concerned about James laughing too much about it, as it might hurt Caril's feelings. Caril seemed nonplused by James' comments, but in general, she was not particularly happy with the movie, and she was forthright about her feelings. She told Martin that she thought he was a wonderful actor, but she didn't think much of the film. It was hard for her to look at it objectively. What Terry had created was a lyrical, filmic poem about lost innocence, but Caril had witnessed this sort of "lost innocence" in a much more savage and brutal way. It had not been lyrical or poetic, and it was hard for her to relate to what she had seen on the movie screen. Still, she liked Terry and Martin very much, and they talked for a long time at the dinner table about their various experiences.

Terry's wife Jill had worked on another film James was fond of, 'The Left Handed Gun'. But her primary career was that of an attorney, and she was thus very interested in the legal aspects of Caril's case, which she went over with John and James. They told her that Caril's sentence had been commuted to thirty years, which made her eligible for parole in the upcoming year. That was their primary focus at this point, to show the positive elements of her behavior in prison, and to secure her parole. They had had to wait a few years after the commutation, but soon their long legal battle would come to its final climax. With her record-breaking good behavior, they both expected that she should have no trouble getting parole, but they had been disappointed in the past, so they were taking nothing for granted. The group then moved on to a small hotel where they took a picture out front, then sat and talked inside for a while before Caril had to be returned to the reformatory.

'Badlands' opened to high critical acclaim and moderate box office receipts. It built the careers of Martin Sheen and Sissy Spacek, put Terrence Malick on the map, and is to this day considered a major classic having been listed several times as one of the top 100 films of the 20th century.

The biggest trouble they had during the release was tracking down theaters who broke the rule about promoting its relation to the Fugate/Starkweather story. Terry was adamant, and made sure no one was allowed to exploit it. He pursued every instance that he heard the rule was being broken, and shut down all use of such promotions. James spotted several exhibitors advertising "based on a true story" or "based on the story of Charles Starkweather and Caril Fugate". In every instance, Warner Brothers threatened legal action against the exhibitor unless they took the references down. Despite their efforts, the story still got out that it had been inspired by the events of 1958, and rumors have spread for decades that many of the most false elements of the movie were true.

James and Terry remained friends afterward, continuing to call and visit on a regular basis. Once, when Terry was in Lincoln, he, James and Patsy went to a park not far from York named Pioneer Village where the theme of western settlers was laid out for tourists and visitors to learn about Nebraska history. It was there that Terry got the idea for his second film, 'Days of Heaven'.

Over the next several decades, many more books, films, songs, and other art forms were inspired by the Starkweather murder spree. As a boy, Stephen King heard about it while it was happening, and he was haunted by the fear of Charlie Starkweather in the same way he later scared the rest of the nation with his stories. He grew up with a foreboding that the young killer would enter his room and find him, and he has said that this anxiety is what caused him to become a horror writer. He later wrote about the experience, "I do think that the very first time I saw a picture of him, (Starkweather) I knew I was looking at the future. His eyes were a double zero. There was just nothing there. He was like an outrider of what America might become." King collected newspaper clippings about Starkweather. He created characters with his personality, named people in his books after him, and referred to the murder spree in several stories.

About the same time that Malick was releasing 'Badlands', Ninette Beaver was releasing her own book about Caril Fugate simply named 'Caril'. She used her own experiences and talked many hours with Caril. The book was the most complete document on the murder spree, the trials, and Caril's imprisonment that had ever been done. It was insightful and very informative, but Ninette could not get to the truth of what had happened. No one could. Only Caril knew what had happened out there on the prairie for two weeks.

The important thing Ninette's book did was to reveal the facts in a world that was quickly losing track of truth in favor of myths and misconceptions about the story. Legend was replacing evidence, and people were mixing up reality with fiction, fitting in their own preconceived ideas. It was hard to change anyone's mind from what they wanted to believe, but at least Ninette Beaver and her team left as accurate a record as possible of the events and their aftermath. Some critics in Lincoln decried supposed inaccuracies in Ninette's book, even though it had been based on first-hand accounts. These criticisms rarely cited what parts had supposedly been inaccurate, choosing instead to point fingers without backing up their claims with any actual evidence of their own.

One of these reviews was written by Marjorie Marlette, whose articles had always shown sympathy for Charlie and a bias against Caril. Marlette had often lied in her reporting on both cases, and now let loose a cacophony of aspersions about Ninette's book, releasing all of her bitterness over having been passed up for the chance of interviewing Caril on national television. The article, entitled 'Cruel Distortion of Today's Caril Ann Fugate', begins by saying, "The woman on the dust cover (Caril) looks like she has some 40 years of hating behind her." The picture itself is simply a photograph of Caril looking in the distance. Marlette accuses the book of "unrealistic explanations of why she may have been innocent in the face of rather overwhelming evidence to the contrary." Of course, Marlette never explains what this "overwhelming evidence" is, nor does she explain how she knows that Ninette's personal accounts of her experiences are inaccurate. She does, however, say the dialogue is "so unrealistic as to be professionally embarrassing," citing an example of when a producer says, "It was a good story while it lasted, but it's over." Apparently, Marjorie never met a television producer or she would have known that this is absolutely the way a TV producer talks. Oddly, Marlette, after saying for the entire review that the book was far too kind to Caril, concluded by saying that Caril must have been shocked at the horrible treatment of her in the book.

Earl Dyer, former executive editor of the Lincoln Star, wrote his own book biased against Caril. In it, he cited several other books which had been based on rumor, then mentioned Ninette's book in passing, stating in the preface that it "had opened to a bad review." He had been referring to Marlette's review from his own paper because national reviews had been glowing about the book. Interestingly, he said nothing about the many bad reviews the others had gotten, but he singled out the only book which had shown any sympathy toward Caril. This sort of one-sided treatment was typical of Nebraska reporting on the subject as time went by.

Bruce Springsteen, who was just becoming popular with his 'Born to Run' album, became enamored with Ninette's book. He read 'Caril' several times, then composed a series of songs about the incident and recorded them privately at home in his living room on his own portastudio four track. He had intended them to be demos to record with his E Street Band, but after listening to the songs with his producers, they decided to release them as they were in 1982 on an album they named Nebraska. The title song was the story of the 1958 murder spree as told from Starkweather's point of view.

It was a strange mixture of fact and fiction swirled into a slow-paced and haunting folk song. His first line, "I saw her standing on her front lawn just a-twirlin' her baton," comes straight from 'Badlands' where Sheen's character Kit first meets Spacek's character Holly. Later, Springsteen gets into specific elements of the true story, quoting how many people died, what gun he used, and even where they drove. Speaking so much from Charlie's point of view with lines like "me and her we had us some fun," it sounds like what Charlie wanted to believe, that Caril was complicit in the murders. And at last it gets at what Charlie really wanted, saying chillingly, "Sheriff, when the man pulls that switch… you make sure my pretty baby's sitting right there on my lap," an almost word for word quote from Starkweather in his last days.

Like Malick and Sheen, Springsteen wanted to meet the people involved with the case, so during his Born in the USA tour in 1985, he scheduled a stop in Lincoln, Nebraska. John had never heard of him, and James only knew about him through his children, so neither one got back to him in time when he called their offices. When James casually mentioned one day that he had neglected to get back to some singer named Bruce something on time, his secretary jumped up with amazement, appalled that he had let such an opportunity pass. But the person Springsteen was most anxious to meet was Ninette Beaver, who had written the book of which he was so fond. His assistant called her on the phone. "The boss wants to talk with you," the assistant said to Ninette, referring to Bruce's nickname.

"Whose boss?" Ninette asked, not familiar with the reference.

"*The* boss," the assistant said.

"I'm sorry, I don't have any boss," Ninette said, and hung up the phone.

A few minutes later, the phone rang again. It was Bruce Springsteen. He told her who he was, and that he was a big fan of her book. She told him she wasn't familiar with his work, and he tried explaining some of his songs. She told him that her children probably listened to him, but she was more from the "Glenn Miller generation."

Springsteen sent her his albums. She listened to them patiently, and as expected, he followed them up with a phone call. "What did you think?" he asked, clearly wishing to please.

"Oh, they're nice," she said nonchalantly. In truth, she didn't understand what all the hype was about, but her children and her younger friends and co-workers were ecstatic and couldn't believe she was being so casual about this.

He sent her several tickets and back stage passes, which she passed along to her co-workers. When Bruce found out what she had done, he sent her more tickets and backstage passes, insisting that she come. She did, and he interrupted the show to shine a spotlight on her and tell everyone what an incredible book she had written. After the show, he met her backstage and asked her what she had thought of the show. Again, she told him it was nice, but she was part of the generation of big bands and suits. Springsteen took it in stride nevertheless, and they all seemed to have a pleasant time together.

The murder spree was referenced in a number of other songs, such as Billy Joel's 'We Didn't Start the Fire'. Peter Jackson's movie 'The Frighteners', which led to the 'Lord of the Rings' trilogy, was based on the idea that a young murderer wants to emulate Starkweather, and does so by apparently kidnapping his young girlfriend and taking her with him. A number of books were written on the subject, most of them quoting from newspapers and rumors, painting Caril as the ruthless girlfriend of Starkweather. Most requests for interviews with Caril were turned down, but she sent out statements insisting she was not guilty.

Dr. James Reinhardt's book 'The Murderous Trail of Charles Starkweather' was published in 1960 with the picture of a skeleton stretched over a map of the Midwest. Its ghoulish arms reach out over Nebraska and Wyoming with scaly roots growing out of its hands. The eyes of the skeleton are pinched, and the bones all appear broken. Next to the skeleton reads the caption "Illustrated with <u>actual photographs</u> of Starkweather's drawings and pages from his "life story" <u>written as he awaited execution</u>." The book is partly a study on psychopathic mental illness, and partly sensationalized drama. He concludes Charlie killed both to serve his immediate needs and because it symbolized the overcoming of opposing forces in his mind. Starkweather, he said, wanted to be powerful, yet he had a deep seated sense of inadequacy and failure. Everything from his rebellious mannerisms to his murder spree were his way to shield his feelings of inadequacy. Reinhardt's conclusion about Caril was the same. Though he had not interviewed Caril, he determined from the things Charlie told him that Caril had not only been a willing accomplice, but had likely spurred Charlie on.

James once had the opportunity to go to one of Reinhardt's speaking engagements. Ironically, the doctor spoke about the psychology behind feeling controlled by a more dominant personality. James went to him after it was over and confronted him with the hypocrisy, pointing out that Caril had experienced the same fear of which Reinhardt spoke. But the doctor would not be moved, stubbornly disagreeing without explaining why.

William Allen's book 'Starkweather', published in 1976, was largely based on the beliefs of James Reinhardt and Marjorie Marlette. Because they had been with Starkweather during his latter days, they were able to give good insight into his personality, and his side of the story.

Unfortunately, Allen reported much of that side of the story as pure fact. Though he states a couple times in the book that Charlie's statements are suspect, he does not inform the reader when the story he's telling is one of Charlie's statements. Therefore, his book reports as fact stories such as Charlie murdering Caril's family in front of her while she watches TV, never mentioning that they were murdered during school hours and Caril's attendance was perfect that day. He also recites the murder of Carol King and Robert Jensen the way Charlie reported it, cleaning up the story when it doesn't make sense. He describes Charlie and Caril opening a savings account together, when in truth, Charlie opened a savings account for himself and put Caril's name on it as someone who could also withdraw from it. And Allen further states as fact that Charlie told Caril about murdering the gas station attendant in December and Caril laughing about it without informing the reader that this was Charlie's story, unsubstantiated by any evidence. There are even points in the book when he quotes from Caril, then places a "…" skipping over the point that shows her true meaning, then skipping to another point that makes her look guilty.

The one reference to this case in a book I could never confirm, but have my suspicions about, was in 'To Kill a Mockingbird'. James, my father, always insisted that the lead character Atticus Finch was exactly like John, my grandfather. Harper Lee was writing the novel at the very time of the trials, and her close friend, Truman Capote, was reading Midwestern newspapers of which my grandfather was often on the front page as he researched his book In Cold Blood. Lee escorted Capote to Kansas where they often met resistance from people who were still afraid of Starkweather. So it is entirely possible, in my mind, that the iconic character was at least partially inspired by my grandfather. However, I have no proof of this, and it is merely my own speculation.

I grew up surrounded by the case. My first impression of it was as a pre-teen when I saw an hour long documentary on WOWT. I turned to my father who was sitting nearby and told him I hadn't known it was such a big deal. I knew Caril, and I knew the details of the story better than I knew American history. As a young boy, when I saw photographs of James Dean I thought it was Starkweather, and that Charlie had been an actor before he murdered people. But I had no appreciation for its importance; to me, it was just something Dad and Grandpa were involved in.

I was told that 'Badlands' was a terrific classic of a movie, not only by my family, but from people in the film community, which, having inherited a love of cinema from my father, I was becoming more and more a part. I couldn't see the genius of 'Badlands', though. I couldn't look at it objectively enough to watch it as a movie, let alone determine whether I liked it or not. When I watched it, I did not see a bold statement about lost innocence, or an exploration of violence in America. I saw a shadow of a story filled with gripping horror and extreme emotions. When I saw Sissy Spacek and Martin Sheen's emotionless faces, I could only see the animated fervor in Caril's face whenever she spoke about the case. When they casually brushed off death in the movie, all I could think about was the brutality of Charlie's unrepentant cruelty. I have never been able to appreciate what is on the screen because I am always thinking about what is not there.

In high school, I really began to realize the extreme opinions of this case when the occasional teacher or student would bring it up and mention how they wished "Caril had been on Charlie's lap when he was in the electric chair." They said it with no irony, not realizing that they were quoting the mass murderer himself. The lies and rumors that spread, and got bigger and broader astounded me, and I began to wonder if I had been told a false side of the story, so I went about doing my own research.

I rode my bike many miles to look through articles and old files at the Nebraska Historical Society, where the official legal records were stored. I stayed overnight at my father's office pouring over transcripts, letters, books, everything that was kept about the case. I read articles written at the time, and quickly learned that the only one that seemed to not be trying to sensationalize the story had been Ninette Beaver, who I later spoke with about it.

In the end, I could not understand how anyone who heard and read the truth could possibly have sent her to prison, and I came to believe firmly that the only reason there was so much animosity toward her was because rumors had turned into legend, and the truth became harder to find. Most of what people believed and said against her were simply untrue, but they didn't know it was untrue, because who is going to go over legal records?

It became clear again how powerful the feelings against Caril still were when, in the late 1980s, a local theater in Omaha did a play called 'Starkweather'. The playwright, Doug Marr, approached the story from a fresh angle, and he had come to the conclusion that Caril was not as guilty as everyone made her out to be. Using the official transcripts from the trial as the script, the play literally showed the courtroom as it played out in real life, switching occasionally to one side of the stage where the actor playing Charlie quoted from Starkweather's memoirs, and then to the other where an actress playing Ninette tried to get to the truth of the story. The play was boycotted by many, some long term patrons pulled their memberships, and protestors insisted to the owners of the theater that it should be removed from production. Much to the credit of the Omaha Community Theater, they did not, and it had a successful run.

The History Channel did a documentary in a format that is all too common, exchanging studious research for sensationalized drama. The narration reports Starkweather's story as fact, and, like so many others who have done stories on the rampage, does not inform the public of its source.

The Discovery Channel did a similar piece, naming theirs 'Deadly Women: A Discovery Channel Investigation'. I was in the process of researching this book at the time, and they interviewed my father and I on the same day. We not only told them what we knew, but we also gathered up pages and pages of documents, photographs, coroner reports, and evidence from years of work on the case. I even made a CD that included all the transcripts of both Caril's and Charlie's trials, along with all supplemental evidence, and offered it to them. They had talked to several other people who said she was guilty, and I asked if they had supplied any evidence to their claims. The producer told me they hadn't, just that it was their word against ours. "Don't take our word for it," I said. "Look at the evidence for yourself," and I offered the CD and the oversized file folder filled with information.

They didn't take any of it. Instead, they returned to their studios and made the documentary they wanted to make. They had already named the documentary 'Deadly Women', and they weren't going to allow the truth to get in the way of good television. Their fifteen minute piece portrayed Caril through the reenactment of an actress as a rebellious teen who hated her family and watched the world through stern, baleful eyes. They even had her wearing a necklace which said "Caril" on one side and "Charlie" on the other.

The star of the special was William Allen, who, unbound by anyone who might challenge him to show where he got his facts from, let fly with not only rumors, but outright lies. "People said that she was a little snip and unevenly tempered," he said without explaining who said it. "She didn't practice self control. She did pretty much what she wanted to. She was even, in some ways, more violent than he was."

He went on to tell the story of the killing of Bob Jensen and Carol King, describing one of Charlie's stories as fact without explaining the source of his story, nor that this story had been changed by Charlie many, many times.

Their "specialist," former FBI profiler Candice Delong, without ever having been involved in the case, declared that "there are too many discrepancies in Caril's story that are too unbelievable." Of course, Ms. Delong never explained what those discrepancies were, and it's doubtful that she ever studied the case at length.

The worst thing made about the killings was a low budget film in 2004 that was also called 'Starkweather'. The two teenagers race through the high desert, (yes, desert,) of Nebraska ruthlessly killing people at random while Charlie is urged on by Caril and a demon who taunts him. It was made with the same cynical disillusionment and romanticizing of violence that is so prevalent of independent films today which portray their mortiferous hero on the posters pointing their larger-than-life guns out of the explosive posters. The characters speak and act more like wannabe gangsters of the 21st century than kids of the 1950s. At times it was almost as though they knew the true story, such as the scene when Caril runs to Officer Romer at the end of the murder spree. Accurately, Caril runs to the officer and gets in his car. But then, inexplicably, she jumps out and makes a run for it, making it possible for Romer to pull out his gun and become the hero while Caril stares back at him defiantly. They never answer the question as to why she would run to the officer in the first place if she wanted to escape.

'Natural Born Killers', which purports to be based on the slayings, runs a close second, when it comes to worst projects made on the subject. Directed by Oliver Stone and written by Quentin Tarantino when neither were at the top of their form, the film again romanticizes the murders in a tasteless orgy of violence, centering on the two teenagers who express their love for each other through the suffering of others, which unfortunately has played well to a generation of movie goers who have a disturbing fascination with savagery and sadism.

By the time it was released, I was in film school and I wound up in a small group of twenty students to whom Oliver Stone was speaking. He didn't know my association with the true story, and I never spoke with him individually about it. But I found it interesting that, though he had a primarily friendly audience of students who loved his film, he began making excuses for it before anyone spoke. He got defensive even after people said positive things about the movie and after a while, I started to understand why. According to Stone, his director of photography had turned to him at various times during the making of the film and said, "This is how much I care about you, Oliver, that I would work on a movie as bad as this for you."

In the late 1980s a TV producer named Michael Larkin contacted Caril directly and asked her if she would appear on their television show called 'A Current Affair'. She had wanted to just disappear, and for the story to be forgotten, but there was something in Michael's voice that Caril trusted; something in the way he spoke that caused her to believe he was in earnest, and she agreed to do it. Larkin called the McArthur Law Offices and talked with James about it, and they set up a time for everyone to meet. They recorded the interview in my family's basement where they could control the lights, and the white walls made for a plain backdrop.

Caril talked a little about the murders, a lot about her experiences in prison, and about the various artists who were turning the story into movies and songs. She broke down crying when she came to Springsteen's song. She was deeply offended by it. "How could someone say that?" she sobbed. "'Me and her had us some fun?' How could he say that?" To artists this was merely a fascinating story that they utilized for their own visions. For her it was a traumatic reality.

Caril's sister was also there. Off camera, she got caught up in the emotion of the moment and tearfully admitted something to Caril she had never told her. Barbara had been dating Charlie first. She had recognized the obsessive nature in him, and had grown attracted to Charlie's boss, Robert, whom she later married. She had introduced Charlie to Caril as a way to get Charlie off her own back, so he would have someone else to focus on while she began to date Robert. Charlie had then approached Caril while she was on a date with another boy and told the boy to get lost because he was now going to date Caril.

Barbara sobbed as she admitted all of this to Caril, and described a nervous breakdown she had had as a result of all the guilt she felt. The two sisters wept together, and Caril immediately forgave Barbara.

The episode of 'A Current Affair' was so popular that it ran three times. People were clearly fascinated with the story, and Larkin believed it would make a good TV movie. He spoke with a producer he knew, Michael O'Hara of O'Hara/Horowitz who did TV movies for ABC, and they told him they were interested. He then went to James and Caril about it.

Caril did not want to be involved in the making of the film. It had taken all of her emotional energy just to have the interview for 'A Current Affair', and she wouldn't be able to handle the rigors of a full production. She also wanted people to believe what was being told in the film, and she didn't want it to be viewed as having been manipulated by her. So she left it up to James to go on her behalf as a consultant.

She did, however, meet with James at his office privately during development of the movie. She went over the story of what had happened on the road again, including details that were less relevant in a legal regard, but would be more dramatically relevant, which he could pass on to the producers. It was the first time anyone was interested in doing a truly accurate depiction of the events, and they wanted to get it right. As she went through the story, she broke down crying several times, and James waited patiently as she regained her composure. There were certain areas she had not talked about since the trial more than thirty years earlier. The dozens of hours they spent in the library going over these details were some of the most personal moments they ever spent together in their more than fifty year acquaintance.

James passed the information on to the producers. Mike gathered records and information from the courts and historical society. He bought the legal transcripts and, like the play, much of the script was directly taken from them. The only question Mike had left of James was what actor they should get to play him. James told him very simply, "Why, Denzel Washington, of course."

I took Michael Larkin around Lincoln a few times, introducing him to locals. In almost every case, they spoke against Caril. "I think she should have been sitting right there on Charlie's lap on the electric chair!" my boss at a pizza joint exclaimed. When I apologized to Mike, he smiled and said, "No, it's important for me to see this. It's how people feel about it."

I took time away from film school to go visit the set in Texas with my father. We first saw them shooting the press conference where Ninette Beaver was interviewing Caril, although Ninette's name in the movie was "Jonette Fox." Ninette did not want her real name used, though she came to visit the set as well. We were revealed to the cast and crew when at one point, Brian Denehy, playing my grandfather, was asking where he should stand, and my father simply pointed out where everyone had been when it happened.

It was an unusual sight, seeing everything from this story I had grown up surrounded by brought to vivid life. Tim Roth, who was playing Charlie Starkweather, was so concerned about doing everything correctly that whenever he learned something new about him he declared, "That's the way we're doing it," and he refused to take any direction otherwise from the director or producers. Mike Larkin had to even go to my father and ask him to please only tell him or the other producers about his observations.

The other producers were less concerned with accuracy. When it was revealed that Charlie had been bow legged and spoke with a stutter, one of the producers wouldn't allow Tim to play it that way, saying, "that will make it look like Charlie was crazy." That same producer had a pair of guard towers built inside the courtroom with armed guards on top.

But in the face of all of this, Larkin managed to hold the production together and got the film through with most of the accuracy intact. It was shaping up to be the most factual film ever made on the subject.

They had originally planned to create an entire subplot about my father and his growth into working as a lawyer, but when that storyline got pushed to the back, Mike suggested that I play my father as an extra. They sent me down to the make-up room where I got to know the crew. They sang happy birthday to me as they shaved my goatee and sliced my long hair into a '50s crew cut. "I've just become your best friend," Mike told my father before presenting me. When Brian Denehy saw me he proclaimed loud enough for the entire courtroom to hear, "You look like you're twelve years old!"

Denehy was bombastic and straight forward to the extent that some people thought him rude. But in point of fact, he was simply honest and didn't slow down for pleasantries. If he liked you, he said so. If he didn't, he made it clear. He loved to read, and he had known about my grandfather for a long time. He considered him a hero, and believed Caril had been terribly mistreated, and he felt it a great honor to be playing the role of John McArthur. I had a lot of respect for Denehy, and I appreciated his great efforts to put together what was a very respectful and powerful performance. But he was nothing like the thin, unassuming quiet man that my grandfather was.

I noticed Ninette watching from the sidelines most of the time studying what was happening and I sidled up next to her and watched, swapping remarks about the production with her. We laughed about the ridiculous, such as the guard towers, and admired the better qualities, such as the cinematography and the incredible performances, especially from Tim Roth and Fairusa Baulk, who played Caril. The more I learned about Ninette, the more I admired her, and felt that her story was every bit as important as anyone else's. She had dedicated a chapter in her book to my father, so I determined then and there to return the favor if I ever wrote a book about the case.

I spent most of the time on set sitting in the crowd pretending to be my father. A friend of mine, who I invited to be an extra, sat beside me. Behind us, a local man was using his knowledge of the story to hit on women. His "knowledge" was based on gossip I had heard circulating for years. My friend turned to me and told me I should tell him off. "Nah," I whispered. "Let him have his fun. And if they're stupid enough to buy it, let them." He went on, telling aspects of the story that were wild and untrue, and the women he spoke to ate it up. My friend held in her laughter until she was eventually doubled over holding her breath.

Then he said, "You know, Caril Fugate married the son of her attorney." My friend looked up at me with wide eyes and a gaped, judging mouth which told me I could not let him get away with that. The woman he was talking to was already saying, "Really? I didn't know that!"

I took in a breath and turned around to him. "That's where I'll stop you," I said. "Most of what you've been saying the past couple days is completely untrue."

"Who are you?" he asked snidely.

"I'm the grandson of Caril Fugate's attorney, and Caril is *not* my mother."

"Well, *I'm* a historian," he responded, his head high as though that trumped my family connection.

I stared at him a moment in disbelief. "No, you don't understand," I said, "that guy over there. He's the man you think married Caril Fugate." I made the terrible mistake of pointing out my father, because for the next several days, the guy wouldn't leave him alone, trying to ask him ridiculous and inappropriate questions, like what it looked like to see Starkweather die in the electric chair.

The director almost always took notes from my father and included them in the film. But there was one point that they simply could not accept. After Tim Roth as Starkweather explained his earlier contradictory statements as hogwash and Brian Denehy said "just like everything else you said here," the judge's line was "Now, Mr. McArthur." My father explained that the line was actually, "Now, John." But neither the director nor the producers, who all lived in Los Angeles, could accept that a judge would be so informal as to refer to an attorney by his first name.

They wisely disregarded one piece of my father's advice. When it came to the execution scene, Judy Schultz, the costumer, brought Tim in dressed for the electric chair. "You forgot one thing," my father said fervently.

"What's that?" the costumer asked.

"The light bulb."

She squinted, confused. Standing behind her, Mike Larkin held in a laugh.

"Well," James said, "you're supposed to put a light bulb in his mouth. How else will you know that the electric chair is working?"

His face remained rigidly serious, and she thought he was telling the truth, so she called for a light bulb to be brought in, but Mike cut in before it got too far, and they all had a laugh at her expense.

When it was done, Mike sent a copy to James to review before it went public. He watched it, then sent it on to Caril. They both approved, and the show aired the following autumn of 1993.

I watched in New York sitting next to my roommates and a woman from Iowa who had heard about the case from her parents. Bored through much of it, she perked up when Starkweather was racing away from the police, and she shouted, "Go Charlie!"

James and Ninette traveled to LA to do something called a Satellite Star Tour, a televised version of a press junket. It required both of them to answer the same questions over and over for every station across the country. Caril asked James to tug his ear, like Carol Burnett did, when it came to the station she would be watching. The two old friends sat patiently and answered the same questions each time as though they heard them for the first time. And when Caril's station came on, James tugged his ear.

After 'Murder in the Heartland' aired, quite a few people who had said to James in the years and decades before that they believed Caril was guilty came up to him in restaurants and other public places and told him that they had changed their minds, that perhaps she was not as guilty of the crimes as they had thought. It was not the vindication Caril had hoped for, but it was a step in the right direction. Most of all, James was able to see the profession he had almost entered, which he was so fascinated by, at work. And he was able to see how it could accomplish the one thing he and his father could not. With the law they could possibly get her out of prison, but a well-made movie could help to win over the hearts and minds of people.

Years later I was having dinner with Terrence Malick at Warner Brothers. I was developing a film of my own, and he was finishing his first movie in twenty years, 'The Thin Red Line'. He and Martin Sheen had remained friends of my family ever since they made 'Badlands'. As we walked through the parking lot afterward I told him the story about the "historian" who had believed Terry's movie as fact and was claiming that Caril Fugate was my mother. I began laughing, but Terry got a very serious look on his face.

He was silent for a moment before he finally said, "I wonder if it was a bad idea for me to make that movie." He went on to say that he had sometimes wondered over the years if in making that movie he had done more harm than good. I knew exactly what he was talking about. Most people would be too oblivious to consider the affect their art would have, but not Terry. He is a deeply moral man who considers everything that might result from his actions. And I had wondered myself how many people, knowing the film was inspired by Caril and Charlie's story, had seen it and mistook it for the real thing. I had always been glad for my connection to this classic film, which in many ways had encouraged me to take the path of filmmaking myself. But I believe what Terry was thinking at that moment was the very thing I had thought about many times. Was it worth it? At what cost do we make our movies, our books, our songs, and our plays, and what responsibility do we have to the truth, and to the results of our efforts? Despite the positive impact of 'Murder in the Heartland', a week after it aired there was a copycat murder spree in Canada by two teenagers who were inspired after they had watched the TV movie.

I told Terry as best I could that he shouldn't worry about it; that it had no real negative effect, and he should only be proud of his work. I was being honest... well, mostly, but I knew that I wasn't getting through to him. Not completely. He would continue to worry about it, and that's what makes Terry so special; he not only makes great movies, he considers how they are affecting people long after they're done. That's what sets him apart and makes him unique in Hollywood, because he *does* consider the philosophical and emotional consequences, as he should... As all artists should. We should all worry about the consequences of our work. Far too often we hear the phrase "artistic license" in reference to something that is merely an excuse for a filmmaker, or a singer, or a writer to do what they want based on their own agenda and their own ego with no consideration of its ramifications on another human being.

A person like Caril Fugate does not have the luxury of artistic license. She went through a true nightmare, whatever her involvement. I am privileged to have grown up exposed to such a story, because it has always reminded me of the responsibility artists have to the truth; that "artistic license" is not a license to do as we please, but rather as a means to better express the emotional and/or philosophical truth of what really happened. And if we stray from that, we are not artists, but merely egomaniacs using another person's experiences in search of self-glorification.

# Chapter Fifteen
## Release

York prison had a furlough system where inmates who were having a parole hearing or were expected to be released within a year could spend several weekends in the public. The point of the program was to help assimilate inmates back into society, or even to apply for jobs they would step into upon their release, but most women used it to go party and get drunk, even though the rules forbade drinking or taking drugs. In 1975, Caril used her furlough to spend the weekend of her thirty-second birthday with her lawyers, who would be her monitors and her hosts. They all knew that parole was already going to be a difficult situation since there was so much public sentiment against her, so they tried extra hard to not cause any trouble. Alcohol, especially, was easy to avoid since Seventh-day Adventism forbade alcohol.

James and Patsy picked her up from York on Saturday morning and went straight to John and Ruby's house where they spread blankets out on the wide, front acreage and had a picnic. Various members of their now very large family came to visit and wish Caril a happy birthday and to share in the cake. She returned with James and Patsy to their home and Caril took their baby daughter Mary for a walk in the stroller around the neighborhood as the sun set. Caril still adored spending time with children, and took every advantage she could of Patsy's willingness to let her be around her kids. Later that night, they all got pizza and watched TV together before calling it a night.

The next morning, while James went in to the office to do some work, Patsy and Caril talked over coffee in the kitchen. They had been getting to know one another quite well during Patsy's visits to the penitentiary, but they had never spent time alone outside of the confines of prison. Patsy was fascinated with Caril's unique points of view on various aspects of the world. The police had recently captured a young woman named Patty Hearst, the famous socialite and heiress who had been kidnapped and brainwashed by the Symbionese Liberation Army. The public was baffled. "People don't understand what fear could do to you when you were a hostage," Caril had told Patsy when they heard about the news. She could immediately relate to Hearst. She explained that once someone has a hold on you mentally, they don't need to point a gun at you every moment to have you under their control.

Something in the comfort and solitude of that morning gave them the opportunity to be more open with each other than they had ever been before. Caril told Patsy about her past, that distant memory now when she lived a normal life with her family. She spoke fondly of her mother, whom she had loved and admired greatly. She had been a proud woman. Though always poor, she had been a big believer in holding her head up high. She didn't even like to receive charitable help from the community because it hurt her pride. She described a few times when her mother accepted help because of her children, but Caril remembered the strain on her mother's face after the doors were closed. She never let anyone see her cry, not even her family. To her, emotions were something to deal with privately, never in public. She had instilled this belief in her daughter, and the resulting stoicism had hurt her in the trial where the lack of emotion in her face confirmed people's preconceived beliefs that she was a ruthless murderer. Caril didn't know whether or not she should regret her decision to remain prideful. She believed, as her mother had, that one should not pour their emotions onto the public, yet she was paying the price of her freedom for that belief. For the first time, Patsy really understood Caril.

They went to the supermarket together, Caril pushing Mary's stroller as they meandered through the aisles. Caril was amazed at how large grocery stores had become. Much of the way culture had changed since the fifties was overwhelming to her.

James returned from work at noon, and they all decided to go swimming together. James and several partners had bought an apartment complex the autumn before, and they liked to use the pool at the clubhouse. Caril jumped in and played with the children in the pool. It was a sunny day, one of those pleasant afternoons when it seemed no evil could exist in the world. There was no prison, no Starkweather, no hateful public, just fun with the family. Reality was reserved for that evening when Caril was returned to the reformatory.

Later that week she was called in to the warden's office and asked, "What did you do last weekend to cause such a fuss?" Caril didn't understand. She told them about all the innocent things they did, and that they never broke the rules or caused any trouble. But someone had called in and reported her on the loose. James and Patsy theorized that it was probably one of the tenants at the apartment complex, but they never knew for certain. The prison was afraid this might hurt their furlough program, and they were afraid for Caril that it might adversely affect her parole. As a result, they did not allow her any more visits.

\*     \*     \*

The following year, Caril and James once again found themselves waiting with each other to hear her fate. John was also with them, and so was Patsy, as moral support. This time they were in the waiting room of the administration building of the York Women's Reformatory. It was a sterile institutional room with uncomfortable wooden chairs. In the room was another tough-looking inmate awaiting her own parole hearing. Caril knew her from the reformatory. She whispered to James that the other woman had killed her husband and cut him up into pieces.

James and John were called into the hearing room to talk with the parole board, leaving Patsy alone with Caril. Patsy didn't know exactly what to say to someone whose entire future was being decided.

Caril had been through far more than Patsy could ever imagine, and now it all came down to this. Her husband had been in charge of preparing the parole, and she had personally witnessed how many late nights and early mornings he had been feverishly getting ready for it. James had grown some of the same habits as his father. He often talked to himself, sometimes quite loudly, especially when he was working on a case. He occasionally paced, but, much to the benefit of the ceiling, he did not flip a coin.

"I don't know what to do," Caril at last confided in Patsy. She went on to tell her that she didn't want to gush into an emotional outburst to the parole board; that would be phony. She wanted to be honest. Her mother had raised her to carry herself with dignity, and Caril always believed in this. But it was this dignity that had helped land her in prison for the past seventeen years. Everyone had interpreted her pride as arrogance and rebellion. She said she felt like she was stuck. She didn't want to lie, but she was worried that if she didn't, she might go back to prison for another fifteen years. Patsy told her that she believed everything would be okay, but in truth, she, too, worried about how they might interpret her actions. Soon after, Caril was called in. She stood on her feet, raised her head, and strode inside the room with dignity, but with care not to seem aloof.

*     *     *

After the hearing, Caril paced nervously in the waiting room while John, James and Patsy sat on the stiff, wooden chairs waiting for the decision. Caril knew that they had been careful, that they had gone over every tiny detail, and had presented themselves as best they possibly could. The board had asked her what she planned to do after she got out, and this time she had answered since the press was not present. She had told them she would move out of state and she was interested in helping people, perhaps in a profession such as nursing. Greenholtz had been relieved that she was planning to leave the state. He had asked if she had any plans to return, to which she had emphatically said, "Oh, no." He was again relieved, and said it would be better for everyone if she didn't.

The only other stipulation they gave her was not to give any interviews for five years. This would be on the record as an order given to her by the board, but in truth it had been by her request. She had asked them to impose a restriction of no interviews so she could give that as a reason not to talk to anyone. Caril did not want to be bothered by the media after she left, and she figured that five years should be enough time for them to forget about her. "I simply want to get out and do the best I can," she said. "I do not want any publicity." She told them that she hoped to get married and have a couple of kids and "just be a regular little dumpy old housewife."

She had spent seventeen years keeping her nose clean in prison and had come through with a perfect record. She had to dodge the goading of other inmates who tried to get her into trouble any way they could, and she had succeeded. It had become like a game for them, their goal to get Caril to slip up at least once before her parole hearing. They had failed. Caril had become so afraid of getting into trouble that she had not even allowed anyone into her room for a long time for fear someone might hide something that would cause her problems.

And now it all came down to this. James was calm because he was certain. They had a lot of people on the parole board who were on their side. John Greenholtz had been very verbal about his belief in Caril, though he had told James privately that if she was released, a lot was riding on her good behavior out of prison. "If she goes out and gets in trouble," he said, "it will do a lot of damage to the parole program." Despite James' confidence, Caril still seemed nervous, so he talked with her about what she would do with her future. She had little more planned out than she had told the parole board. They had been disappointed before and she didn't want to get her hopes up too high, but it was hard not to now. They were so close, and Greenholtz seemed so much on her side.

Then Jackie entered the room. The smile on her face said it all. They had decided to grant her parole. She would be free within a couple of weeks. There was no cheering. It was strangely quiet. Instead, there was a great sigh of relief on everyone's part. It had been eighteen years, and when it came at last, they were just ready to have it finally happen. The only drawback for Caril was still that she would never be able to officially clear her name, something that would nag at her for many years to come.

Jackie also told them that Walter Cronkite was apparently on his way to interview Caril. They all waited to meet him, but he never arrived. Perhaps he heard about the restriction for her to not give any interviews; no one knew. But after waiting for a few hours and celebrating with Caril, James and Patsy finally left.

It was the last time any of them would ever see Caril at the Women's Reformatory in York, Nebraska.

*　　*　　*

Caril's release was covered in newspapers all over the nation. People from across Nebraska were appalled. No one had shown up to the reformatory to protest her parole, but now the courts were flooded with angry letters. However, the decision was final, and there was nothing anyone could do.

On a quiet spring night, thirty-two-year-old Caril Fugate was led to the front gate by another gate girl. It was opened wide, and for the first time in eighteen years, Caril was looking out at a road she could go down without impediment.

Two people from Michigan were waiting for her with a car. She had met them when they had seen Ninette's documentary 'Growing Up in Prison' and had written to Caril very sympathetically. Since that time, they had remained friends, and now they greeted her into their car, and drove her away from York, to their home state where she would make a new life.

Caril attended nursing school and began working at a hospital as an aide, helping to save lives every day. She did not officially change her name, but she left her old life behind. She even cut correspondences that she had been carrying on for years. She told Martin Sheen, whom she had been talking with ever since Badlands, that she would be moving and she would be changing her life, so she could no longer correspond. He wrote back that he understood, and he wished her all the best.

Though her parole had informally dictated that she not return to Nebraska, she quietly entered Lincoln on several occasions throughout the nineties. While in town to do the interview for 'A Current Affair', she went to the mall and was stopped by a reporter, who Caril assumed was going to bust her for breaking the agreement. Instead, the un-savvy reporter asked her the same question she had been asking everyone else who came out of the mall, what had she bought while shopping? On another occasion, Caril had forgotten her credit card at the counter, so when an equally un-savvy store clerk announced, "Will Caril Ann Fugate please come to the counter to get your credit card?" Caril lowered her face and left by the nearest exit.

By the time 'Murder in the Heartland' came along, Caril was fully entrenched in her new life, and did not want her old one to come back and haunt her. But the story, having grown to "legendary status" as James often put it, was out of her hands. All she could do was try to distance herself. When the TV movie became popular, phone calls began pouring into her place of employment from curious individuals and news reporters. She almost lost her job as a result, and had to hide for a while. It affected her relationships with people, she worried about getting involved with a man because of how much it might affect his life. She also determined not to have children because she never wanted to curse anyone with the stigma. At last, in the late '90s, she met a man who stood by her, and they were married, but never had any children.

While James was working on the promotions for the TV movie, he spoke on a Lincoln radio show on KLIN. Caril's sister heard the show, and called and told her. Caril called in to the station the same way anyone asking a question would. Steve Barry, the show's host, was thrilled, and had James and Caril begin talking with each other. The interview went so well that he brought her back the next day and had them take phone calls and answer questions. Caril answered most of them, speaking freely and openly about her experiences. James described the legal procedures. The conversation became so interesting that the radio station pre-empted their entire lineup for the next day and had it fully dedicated to James and Caril returning and speaking and answering more questions.

She has always maintained her innocence, and her narrative of what transpired has never altered. Though many continue to insist upon her guilt, no one has been able to punch a hole in her story. She still wants to be proven innocent, and for people to believe her. After the five year ban she gave a number of interviews claiming her innocence and showing evidence, but when many of these shows ignored what she said and played the rumors instead, she gave up. In the early '80s Caril went on the TV show 'Lie Detector', hosted by trial attorney F. Lee Bailey, (who later became famous for representing OJ Simpson.) Though she passed the test with flying colors and the show's host declared everything she said was the truth, it did little to change people's minds. Fewer than half of the people in Nebraska polled after the show believed she was innocent.

Caril heard so many times that she was guilty that she even began to doubt herself. She went to a hypnotist and had the entire session recorded so she could listen to it later. She wondered if perhaps she had repressed some memory, and if she had indeed done things that she was denying to herself. The result of the session was that she stated everything under hypnosis that she had been saying while conscious.

After these last efforts, she finally gave up on people ever believing she was innocent. She has since wished the whole thing would go away, and that people would forget about her, but she knows that will not happen either; so she makes the best of life for herself, and for those around her.

James and Caril did not talk very often after she got out of prison. She wanted her own life, and desired to put as much of what had happened, including the people, into her past. But they did talk with each other every time the case came up in the media. James represented Caril through all of the various news magazines, movies, and other media that came along searching for information about her. But when the business was done, they typically went their separate ways and on with their lives.

One day in the mid '90s, when James was seeing his daughter off to college at the Lincoln airport, James saw Caril across the hall. She was standing with a dog attached to a leash. No one knew who these two people were, or the large part they had played in Nebraska's history. He approached her privately and said hello. Caril was on her way home. The dog wasn't hers; a stranger who had found out what city she was flying to had asked her to take the dog with her and deliver it to a friend at the airport there. Caril told James about it and laughed, "She has no idea who I am. What would she think if she knew who it was that she handed her dog over to? She'd be horrified!" They visited for a short time, then went their separate ways. It was the last time James saw Caril.

Caril's conviction in 1958 got Elmer Scheele the judgeship he had been seeking, just as it also got promotions for many of the officers who had helped him and the judges who had denied her a new trial. Dale Fahrnbruch, who had been the assistant DA, went on eventually to be Chief Justice of the Nebraska Supreme Court.

In 1960, Elmer Scheele became a district court judge. At about the same time, he was stricken with cancer. Soon after that, diabetes claimed his right foot, then his jaw. He continued working with a bandage over his head to keep his jaw in place. He utilized two buttons that lit up a red light and a green light to indicate whether an objection was affirmed or overruled.

It is unclear how much Scheele and his team truly believed in Caril's guilt, and whether the strong-armed and unethical tactics they used to put her behind bars were a result of their personal conviction that she deserved to be in prison. Paul Douglas, one of his assistants, later claimed that no one in his office had ever really cared whether or not Caril was convicted, but that leaves the mystery as to why Scheele compromised so many of his ethical standards to gain that conviction.

He went on to be a fair judge, however, well respected by everyone, including the McArthurs. He never used his back alley tactics again, and was hard on the police who used some of the same methods he had used in the Fugate case. He continued to respect John and James. So much, in fact, that when his own son needed help with legal matters, he told him to go straight to the McArthurs.

James was an attorney in Scheele's final case on the bench. He had throat cancer so badly that it was painfully obvious to everyone in the room. James felt bad for him, knowing how important speech had been to the former DA. Soon after, in 1972, Elmer Scheele succumbed to his illness and passed away.

Ninette Beaver disappeared into blissful, private obscurity after her book was a national success and eventually moved to Arizona with her husband. Her boss, Floyd Kalber, went on to be the news anchor for the Today Show, and became well known on national television.

James and John continued to practice together throughout the '70s in their McArthur Park offices on Cornhusker Highway. They were good partners, working together six days a week, and James always went to his father's house on Friday nights with his family to visit where the two men sat across from one another, spinning their glasses and going over what they had experienced that week.

As technology crept into the profession, John had a hard time adjusting. He even had trouble with a remote control for a television. His wife was the technical one, always reading the manuals as soon as they came in. Whenever he had to use something, he typically called out, "Rube! Will you come in here?" As James updated the office with every new technology, John continued to use his yellow legal pad for which he was so famous.

In 1981, John was trying a case in Nebraska City. Very suddenly, he fainted in the middle of the hearing. James immediately went to his plane and flew out to get him. John had been afflicted with emphysema, a result of smoking too much throughout his whole adult life. It was serious, life threatening even, and he had to cut back on his activities. He continued practicing law at the office for another year, but he stopped appearing at court for fear that he might have another episode while in session. Law was such a major part of John's identity that he simply could not stop. He gave up all other activities before he ceased going to the office; though he went home early every day, low on energy, even low on breath. Although his life depended on not smoking, James occasionally caught him with the lit cigarette when away from Ruby. At last he had to retire. He simply could not handle the pressure and the stress, and he didn't want to let his clients down.

His retirement party was held at the large house of his oldest daughter. Most people who came were family and friends from the office. They wanted him to enjoy his retirement, to spend his later years away from the stress of the courtroom and have fun with his free time. But they all knew this was a futile wish. John enjoyed nothing more than the stimulating challenge of a legal battle, and when that was taken away from him, it was the beginning of the end.

Soon he needed an oxygen mask to breath. He still moved around, taking a portable oxygen tank with him. He kept up with James' efforts, often going to the office and watching over what he was doing. When James first got a computer, John couldn't understand its use in law. James tried to show him all the amazing things one could do with it, the record keeping, the ease of the word processing.

"Why not just get Lorraine to type it up for you?" he asked.

James laughed and said he was probably right.

It was the last time John visited the office. The following week he went into the hospital. The doctors told him they could do some procedures that would give him an extra six months, but John refused, saying there was no point. All of his six children came in to visit him. He had a private talk with each one, telling them that he had no regrets. "I've accomplished most of what I wanted to do," he told them. He gave them each the same advice, "Use your head, follow your conscience, and keep your cool."

As for why he didn't want an extra six months, he told his oldest son Frank, "There comes a time when one generation needs to make room for the next."

He worked out some final legal matters privately with James, passing on his property, and signing over the deed of the house to his wife. He kept fading in and out of consciousness, losing his concentration, then regaining it. James asked if he'd like to continue the next day. "No," John said. "I want to get this done." It took all of his remaining energy to sign the documents. He stopped long enough to talk with James about personal matters, sharing his beliefs. As for dying, he told James he wasn't afraid. "I'm really more curious. I've never been a religious man, but I've always sort of had my own religion."

Ben, the youngest of John's children, was the only family member who had not yet visited. He was flying in from Tennessee, and he got there just as James was leaving for the office to finish up the legal matters he had worked out with their father. He did so on the computer.

Within an hour of visiting with Ben, John's breathing slowed, and at last it stopped. John Jr. later said of that day, "It was the first time in my life I actually felt like I had truly become an adult."

# Chapter Sixteen
# No One Will Ever Really Know

Opinions continue to run high on the question of Caril's guilt. If you ask around Nebraska, many people who still know about the case will tell you she was unquestionably guilty. Caril has maintained her innocence and has never changed her story even the smallest amount, which has caused my father to continue to believe in her to this day. Ninette Beaver, who came at it from a more objective point of view, has always presented a sympathetic view of Caril, but she maintains a journalistic distance, admitting that Caril did indeed go with Charlie, and none of us know for certain what threats Charlie did or did not make along the way.

Although I grew up with a biased point of view, I have tried to look at it from other viewpoints. With so many people against her, I tried to see if my family was hiding something. But the more I looked, the more it became clear to me that she had simply been railroaded by the legal system. I once put together a school report on the subject, and another student wrote the antithesis, and it was at this time I realized where the discrepancy was. My report was based on the actual legal documents, the evidence; the real words that were spoken by witnesses, judges, attorneys, and reporters behind the scenes. The other report was based on gossip the writer had heard from people of the neighborhood, and at best, newspaper reports that were written during the crime spree, when no one knew what exactly was happening and everything was chaos.

Fear certainly drove Caril. Whatever the reasons for her actions or inactions on the road, fear was a major motivating factor. Ninette Beaver described her as "someone who would be afraid of her own shadow." James, my father, has repeatedly pointed out that it makes no sense for someone to go from being a child who loves her mother and takes assiduous care of her baby sister, to a heartless murderer for one week, then go back to being shy and even mousy the rest of her life. Never before nor ever since has she shown any anti-social tendencies, and we have only the word of Charles Starkweather, a deranged psychopath, that she had shown this type of personality on the road. He told people "Caril Fugate was the (most) trigger happy person I ever knew," and the people of Nebraska ate it up. There's something about killers that disturbingly fascinates the public and makes them more likely to listen to them than anyone else. Just as the crowd at the courtroom stopped listening to experts on the witness stand when Charlie came into the room, so, too, are people today more enamored with the celebrity of a felon who has done something extreme. And once a belief entrenches itself in our collective unconscious, it is hard to get rid of it, even in the face of facts.

People across the nation continue to buy into the rumors of the Fugate story, unaware what the true facts of the story are. Reports on Google and across the internet paint a picture of Caril as the mastermind behind the killings, a ruthless killer who murdered half the victims, including her family. Few, if any, report anything about how much she doted on her half-sister before the murders, the clues she left for the police, or how Charlie was caught because she ran to the police. Several documentaries have been produced that quote Charlie's version of the story as fact, and give no consideration to how complicated the story really is.

To be fair, one could know the facts and still believe Caril was in some measure guilty. By her own admission, she held a gun on Carol King. Even though it was jammed and could not be fired, it still caused the girl to go into the storm cellar where she met a gruesome death. And people are right to say that Caril could have gotten away on several occasions. She would have been taking a huge risk and might not have made it, but she certainly could have tried. It's a matter of motivation on Caril's part, and a question of what we consider to be guilt. Is a person who is so controlled by fear that she does whatever she is told guilty? If the answer is yes, then Caril is guilty. But then, so is Clara Ward, who, though murdered by Charlie, was away from him for an hour near open windows and an operating telephone. She could also have easily escaped and/or gone for help. She could have saved her own life, the life of her husband and her maid, and the shoe salesman who was killed later if she had. Should she be considered his accomplice simply because she was too afraid to do any of these things? If the answer is no, then you cannot say different for Fugate.

There can be no question about whether Caril went willingly with Charlie Starkweather. It goes against every bit of logic, human nature, common sense, and every piece of evidence. If she was accompanying him willingly, why did she post a note on the door that read "Miss Bartlett" when clearly the only "Miss Bartlett" was her baby half-sister? Why would she have dropped hints to her sister and grandmother about saving her family if, in the belief of so many people, she really wanted to kill her family, or had even helped kill them herself? Why not instead invite them in to meet the same end? Why would she switch from showing affection for her mother and baby half-sister to suddenly taking the side of her *ex*-boyfriend, whom she had shown nothing but contempt toward for several days, and turn around and kill those family members she had always loved? Most importantly, if she was with Charlie willingly, why did she run to Officer Romer in Wyoming and jump in his car, when she could just as easily have warned Charlie and gotten away before Romer even saw they were there?

The only question left is, "what is guilt?" Just as it is obvious that she was not with him willingly, there can also be no question as to the stupidity of her actions. When Charlie walked up to the boy she was dating and told him to go away because he was dating her now, Caril should have realized immediately what sort of brute he was. On the road, there were several points at which she should have made some sort of attempt to get away. Scheele pointed out that she should have said something to the officer when he came to her door instead of waking Charlie up. Although it was a stupid choice, it is not evidence she intended for people to be killed, or even to cover up any murders.

The question then remains, is stupidity criminal, especially when placed on a fourteen-year-old child who is prone to doing what she's told to do? It is a personal choice that everyone must make, and the laws are then governed by what we believe as a whole. But one should make these decisions based on facts, not on gossip and lies, which this story has been ripe with for more than five decades.

The public became more aware of this issue when Patty Hearst was kidnapped and brainwashed in 1974. While she began as their prisoner, she seemed to become a willing member of the Symbionese Liberation Army, proudly fighting alongside them rather than being a kidnapped victim. Though she went to jail, it quickly became evident to the public at large that Hearst had been a victim of brainwashing rather than a willing accomplice. The issue got all the way to the president, and Carter commuted her sentence to twenty-two months. James and John cited this incident while preparing for the final parole hearings. Though denied for years, cases such as Fugate's and Hearst's point to the fact that mind control is an issue in some cases where certain types of abuse are employed upon impressionable minds. The obvious difference between her and Caril, of course, is that Patty came from a wealthy, high profile family, and Caril came from the wrong side of the tracks.

Additionally, according to Caril, Charlie told her that her family was being held by his friends, and would be killed if she didn't do exactly as he said. This is a claim that cannot be substantiated through evidence, and depends on how much one believes Caril. If it is true, one does not even need to consider the elements of the foolishness of youth or mind control. Anyone would have to understand a young girl who thinks her family is in danger doing anything to save their lives. It is believed by many that Caril was at the home when her family was murdered, and some even believe she helped to kill them, but this was disproven by the fact that they were murdered while she was in school, and even if one doesn't believe Caril, her attendance records were perfect, and she even walked home with a friend that day. She was in the house for the next week, but their bodies were hidden in the chicken coop out back.

The biggest issue is the newspaper photographs found in Caril's pocket which Scheele focused on during the trial found in

Caril's pocket. Though the photographs themselves did not reveal her family was dead, they had been attached to articles that would have told all about their murders. So the question became, who cut those articles out, and what did they see? In all the years Caril has gone over this story, this is the only part of the story on which she was ever inconsistent. When describing the day at the Ward home to Scheele and his team in Wyoming, the interview went like this:

> *Scheele: And did you cut out any of the pictures?*
> *Fugate: Well, he cut part of them out and I cut the rest of them out.*
> *Scheele: What pictures did you cut out?*
> *Fugate: The pictures of him and I.*
> *Scheele: You cut that one out?*
> *Fugate: I helped cut that one out. He cut part way and I cut the rest.*
> *Scheele: In any event, either you or he cut them out, is that right?*
> *Fugate: I think he cut them out.*
> *Scheele: Were they in there when you cut out the picture of you and Chuck?*
> *Fugate: I don't know. I didn't get to see the paper. He wouldn't let me see it.*
> *Scheele: You cut out the other picture, didn't you?*
> *Fugate: Yes.*
> *Scheele: Were those, the pictures of your mother and dad and little sister in the paper when you cut out the big picture?*
> *Fugate: No, they weren't in the paper. I didn't see them.*
> *Scheele: Either you or he cut them out?*
> *Fugate: Yes.*
> *Scheele: Do you know which one?*
> *Fugate: I think he cut them out, or I think I cut them out.*

Added to this is the fact that both Charlie and Caril described a moment on the way to Wyoming when a newscaster on the radio began to describe the murder of her parents and Charlie turned it off.

It seems likely that Caril would have heard enough of that broadcast to know what it was talking about.

It's possible Caril did cut those articles out and did hear and understand that broadcast; and by extension, she knew her family was dead. Thus she was ostensibly traveling with Charlie willingly. After all, she was claiming that she didn't run away from him because she was trying to save the lives of her parents, and if she knew they were already dead, why didn't she run?

The truth is, she did. In fact, I tend to believe that she perhaps indeed saw those articles because it explains why she ran away when she did. When one looks at the chronology, the lonely two lane highway in Wyoming was Caril's first opportunity to run after they received those newspapers. After the pictures were cut out at the Ward house, Charlie and Caril got into the car and headed west. The next time they were stopped in public, Caril jumped out of the car and ran to the police.

Everything up to that point matches the story. She warned her grandmother and sister that "Mom could get really hurt if you don't leave." She woke Charlie when an officer was coming to the door, yet wrote a note with a glaring clue on it for the police to see. She went along with everything he said, from pointing a gun at Carol King to telling Charlie when Mr. Ward was coming home; all to save her family that she thought was still alive.

If she indeed saw the articles revealing that her family was dead, it would be a crushing blow for her to learn that all of her sacrifices had been in vain; that she had altered her very being to save the lives of a family that had been dead all along. It furthermore explains why Charlie decided to leave the Ward home so quickly and so suddenly; and why he drove all the way to Wyoming with very few stops. If Caril did look at those articles, Charlie had lost his greatest hold on her. By both accounts, the entire trip west was very quiet, and it would make all the more sense if she had received such traumatic news. After that, Caril's first opportunity to make a run for it was on that lonely stretch of road between Douglas and Casper, which she did.

What proves this theory in my mind is the statement Charlie's cell neighbor, Otto Glaser, gave when he told about the two mysterious men who came in to visit Charlie each day during Caril's trial. He said that Charlie blurted out that he had almost killed Caril at the Ward house because she tried to get away. Charlie said that he had had to use considerable force to keep her from running. He said that he "intended to kill her at the Ward home, but something stopped him." He did not say what. But he did continue on to say that he threatened to kill Caril if she didn't bring him his gun in Wyoming, and was about to turn and shoot her, too, but she had already run to the police car. This all implies that something had changed in Caril, something that made her bolder than before. That something had happened when she was at the Ward house. The two men were quick to tell Charlie not to repeat this in court.

The only question becomes, why did she ask for her parents when she was with the police, and why did she claim to have never seen any articles about her parents? To me, if this theory is correct and she did see the articles, I would imagine she would be in so much shock that it would be hard to believe that what she saw was true. After going through as much as she had, anyone would be searching for reassurance that what they saw was wrong, especially a child. It may be that fear was still affecting her decisions, and she could have been afraid that people would have assumed that, if she saw an article once, even if it was at the end of the murder spree, they would not believe her motivations for everything before that time. And she was right. Even without being certain that she saw those articles, Scheele used her alleged knowledge of them as evidence against her motivations for actions that occurred long before she supposedly saw that newspaper.

This is, of course, all speculation, as are most theories about this case. Most of what happened on the road will never be known by anyone. All we know is that a small girl who always showed love to her mother and half-sister disappeared for a week with a man she had ended her relationship with a few days earlier, that ten people died in their wake, and that after that week she was again the quiet girl she had been before. As my father put it, "Why would anyone change so completely for only one week, then go back to being exactly the way they were before without explanation?"

But ultimately, everything that we can say is pure speculation. We should do so with the cool objectiveness of facts, not the subjectivity of rumors, and perhaps we will have some sense of what happened. And it is worth looking over because it asks several legal questions in the same vein of how both James and John saw the law, "the practical application of philosophy." Those questions are: To what extent can you go to save the lives of friends and relatives? How much can we tolerate, and how much should we expect from children? How much leeway should the police be given to bring justice? To what extent does mind control play a part, especially upon the youth? How much does fear play a part in a person's decisions, and to what extent should we tolerate it?

As for what happened to Caril on the road, ultimately, I think Ninette Beaver put it best when she said to me, "No one knows what really happened except for her, and I don't know if she really even knows anymore... No one will ever really know."

# Author's Notes
# & Acknowledgements

The majority of this book is taken directly from files kept at the McArthur Law Offices regarding the Fugate case. They include pages from the trials, transcripts of conversations, affidavits of people involved, interviews and statements of witnesses, judgments, applications, personal letters that relate to the case, police records, letters both to and from the attorneys and judges involved, as well as other interested parties, and also other letters acquired as evidence. There are also newspaper clippings, photos, notes, and other paraphernalia from the many years of the original case and appeals.

The transcripts of the trial, photographs, and written evidence of the trial are from the microfilm department at the Nebraska Historical Society. I have posted a pdf of the transcripts at:
www.probonobook.com

My father was able to fill in a great deal of information that fell between the moments recorded in documents thanks to his incredibly photographic memory. One might believe this is biased, but I took advantage of every opportunity I had to check his facts, and in every instance he was backed up by objective evidence.

My mother, meanwhile, was able to provide a huge amount of personal information about the family, particularly during the years when she joined the family and first started learning about the case.

The other McArthur family members, Frank, John Jr, Linda, and Ben all provided vast amounts of information about life at the McArthur household before and after the trials, as well as during them, and gave several anecdotes. Ben was also helpful in ironing out some of the writing of the book in general.

Unfortunately, I was too young while my grandfather was alive to fully appreciate who he was, so I did not interview him, nor gather any information about this story from him. However, he did fill out a book that asks various questions about a person's life, which Marilynn, Frank's wife, held onto. This book gave valuable insights into who he was, his early life with his wife, and what was important to him as a person.

A special thanks is due to Jamie Ball and Heather Lundine for helping to edit this book.

Equally important to this book was Ninette Beaver. Through her permission, I utilized a great deal of information from her book Caril, co-written by B.K. Ripley and Patrick Trese and published by J.B. Lippincott in 1974. Almost every instance of the media's coverage of the murders and the trials come from this book, as well as the specifics of life in prison for Caril. I am forever indebted to her for having the integrity to stand up for the truth both with me, and through her years of incredible journalism. Information about Ninette's life comes from an interview I had with her on the phone in 2009, and pieces of information she told me while on the set of 'Murder in the Heartland' in 1993.

Ninette Beaver's documentary 'Growing Up in Prison', produced in 1972 by NBC, was also an invaluable resource, and extensively used throughout this book.

Other information about the media came from the KMTV archives, articles from the Lincoln Journal and Lincoln Star newspapers, primarily obtained through the Lincoln City Libraries records, and from the book Headline: Starkweather, written by Earl Dyer in 1993, published by Cornhusker Press.

I also referenced articles written by other individuals, such as Marjorie Marlette, which I credited in the course of the book.

'Murderer's Own Story', written by Charlie Starkweather and edited by Marjorie Marlette, was an article in Parade Magazine in 1959, which I made reference to and from which I used some quotes.

Several people gave me basic information over the years about the story, whom I should thank here. Margerie Kennedy told me about what Caril was like as a girl in school before the murders, and how other kids reacted during and after the murder spree. Winnie McArthur told me about my grandfather when he was a child. John Ward told me a bit about Robert Culvert, Starkweather's first victim. A lot of the information in chapter three about Caril's personality before the murders, and her opinions on guns and hunting came from letters from former friends of Charlie's who wrote to my grandfather during the trials.

Martin Sheen and Terrence Malick told me about the making of 'Badlands', and the screening in York, as well as the stories about the release of the film. Michael Larkin gave me some of the information about shooting 'A Current Affair' and 'Murder in the Heartland'. Stephen King and Peter Jackson both talked about their interest in the case on various interviews, though I was never able to reach them for comment. Nor was I able to reach Bruce Springsteen, but information about his career and his recording the album 'Nebraska' is widely available. Doug Marr wrote the stage play version of 'Starkweather', and was able to tell me some information about the release of the show and its reaction.

Starkweather, by William Allen and published by Houghton Mifflin Company in 1976, was used sparingly to put together some of the pieces of Charlie's youth. Most of the rest of the book is untrustworthy, as Mr. Allen chose to state much of Charlie's version of the story as fact without citing the source. (Interestingly, he tells the reader near the beginning that Charlie's stories are to be regarded with suspicion, but then doesn't tell them when he's quoting from one of Charlie's stories throughout the book.)

Dr. James M. Reinhardt's book The Murderous Trail of Charles Starkweather, published by Thomas Books in 1960, also provided some useful information about Charlie's youth, and the workings of his mind; though his book also often quotes Charlie's version of events without always revealing the source.

Some of the legal information came from other court records, the Nebraska Law Review, and various reports from national court cases, such as Escobedo.

Caril's chronicles of the time during the murder spree, and her own statements of that time period, are used very sparingly, and are always referenced to make it clear it is her version of what happened. I understand why people might not believe what Caril has said on faith alone, and so I have always done my best to give the facts as the public knows them. That is why I narrated the story of the time during the murders from the point of view of the public and the media.

However, one section of the murder spree, just before she escaped, when she ran to Sheriff Romer, comes directly from Caril's point of view. Based on the fact that there were several witnesses who confirmed her story, including the drivers of the other cars present, and Joseph Sprinkle, who had been wrestling with Charlie in the middle of the road and confirmed everything Caril said about that part of the story, it seems credible enough to report as fact.

I did not interview Caril Fugate for this book as she has expressed a desire for privacy, and I chose to give that to her… and I would encourage all others to do the same.

Made in the USA
Lexington, KY
12 September 2012